Other books by Dr. Schlesinger

Stop Drinking and Start Living
  (with John J. Gillick, Ph.D.)

Cognitive-Behavioral Approaches to Family Therapy
  (edited with Norman Epstein and Windy Dryden)

Taking Charge

How Families Can Climb Out of the Chaos of Addiction . . . and Flourish

STEPHEN E. SCHLESINGER, Ph.D.
LAWRENCE K. HORBERG, Ph.D.

A FIRESIDE BOOK
Published by Simon & Schuster Inc.
New York London Toronto Sydney Tokyo

*The information in this book is not intended to replace
the services of a qualified health professional.*

10 9 8 7 6 5 4 3 2 1
Library of Congress Cataloging in Publication Data
Schlesinger, Stephen E.
    Taking charge: how families can climb out of the chaos of addiction—and
flourish/Stephen E. Schlesinger, Lawrence K. Horberg.
      p.   cm.
    "A Fireside book."
    Bibliography: p.
    1. Substance abuse—Patients—Rehabilitation.   2. Substance abuse—
Patients—Family relationships.   3. Compulsive behavior—Patients—Re-
habilitation.   4. Self-care, Health.   I. Horberg, Lawrence K.   II. Title.
RC564.S324 1988
616.86—dc19   87-28643
ISBN 0-671-64261-8   CIP

We are grateful for permission to reprint excerpts from the following:
    Tennessee Williams, *Cat on a Hot Tin Roof.* Copyright © 1954, 1971, 1975 by Tennessee
Williams. Reprinted by permission of New Directions Publishing Corporation.
    Bob Woodward, *Wired.* Copyright © 1984 by Robert Woodward. Reprinted by permis-
sion of Simon & Schuster Inc.
    Gary Crosby and Ross Firestone, *Going My Own Way.* Copyright © 1983 by Gary
Crosby and Ross Firestone. Reprinted by permission of Doubleday, a division of Bantam,
Doubleday, Dell Publishing Group, Inc.
    Thomas H. Holmes, Ph.D., "The Social Readjustment Rating Scale." Reprinted with
permission from *Journal of Psychosomatic Research,* 1967 vol. II., pp. 213–18. Copyright ©
1967, Pergamon Journals, Ltd.
    Lauren Bacall, *Lauren Bacall by Myself.* Copyright © 1978 by Caprigo, Inc. Reprinted by
permission of Alfred A. Knopf, Inc.

This book was the product of two authors. The order and the use of their names is
random and does not reflect any differences in the authors' levels of contribution.

To
Marilyn, Nora and Aaron Schlesinger
and
Nicole, Mia, Sam and Marilyn Horberg

Contents

Preface   9

Part I   Getting Started   15
   Chapter 1   Introduction   17
   Chapter 2   Defining the Problem   41

Part II   Strengthening the Family   53
   Chapter 3   Increasing Self-care Activities   58
   Chapter 4   Living a Full Life   80
   Chapter 5   Developing Support   88

Part III   Confronting the Addiction   101
   Chapter 6   Using the Benefits of Family Membership
              to Support Family Health   103
   Chapter 7   Intervening: Withholding Support for the Addiction   115

Part IV   Thriving as a Family   143
   Chapter 8   Moving Forward and Getting Better   145
   Chapter 9   Flourishing   166
   Chapter 10 How to Get Treatment   188
   Chapter 11 Self-help Groups   210

Epilogue   233

Appendices   235
   Appendix 1   Drugs of Abuse   237
   Appendix 2   Useful Organizations   257

Appendix 3   State Programs   263
Appendix 4   Recognizing and Increasing the
              Self-care Skills of the Family   268
Appendix 5   Improving Stress Management   271
Appendix 6   Living a Full Life: Clarifying Wants,
              Standards, Strengths and Feelings   273
Appendix 7   Living a Full Life: Examples   275
Appendix 8   Developing Support   277
Appendix 9   Developing Support: Examples   279

Preface

We have written this book for three audiences: loved ones of addicts, individuals who have been addicted and who wish to recover, and clinicians who hope to assist families in their recovery from the effects of addiction. By "recovery" we mean the process of repairing the damage done by addiction and creating more satisfying lives. We will be very specific when we propose ways to approach recovery, and throughout the book we will discuss families who have used our approach.

Living with an addiction is often a hellish experience, fraught with desperate choices. Without learning how to gain understanding and support, coping with a loved one's addiction is impossible. Vital decisions are made arbitrarily. Yet, millions of families have learned to take charge. They have succeeded in coping. Many have gone beyond coping to the point of flourishing.

TO THE LOVED ONES OF ADDICTS

We have written this book directly to you and for you. Its contents have effectively helped families take charge of their lives. We want to help you understand your recovery in new ways so you can figure out what to do next. The book is free of confusing technical terms and differs from other books because it emphasizes recovery rather than horror stories about the devastating effects of addiction.

TO THE RECOVERING ADDICT

The ideas we discuss with your family are equally applicable to your own recovery. You, too, are a member of an ailing family. You, too, need to learn how to flourish. The approach taken in this book has been as useful for recovering addicts as it has been for their families. Throughout the book we describe addictive disorders bluntly, without pulling any punches. We encourage family members to take an inventory of the effects of addiction on family life. Yet we avoid scapegoating the addict, turning him into the "villain" responsible for all of the family's problems. We believe that everyone is better off if each family member learns to take responsibility for his own happiness rather than to blame others for his distress.

TO CLINICIANS AND STUDENTS

We have designed this book to present concepts in a frank, down-to-earth manner, free of jargon. Students of psychotherapy will recognize the contributions of many schools of thought woven into the material, unlabeled. Although we do not present this as a text on psychotherapy, the material will be useful to you as you assess, treat and educate families affected by addiction.

TO ALL OUR READERS

We made two basic decisions about the language in the book in an effort not to obscure our ideas by being overly wordy. First, we refer to one addict and one drug. Second, we use one gender.

One Addict, One Drug

Some families have one addict in their midsts. Others have more than one. Some addicts use one type of drug. Others use many. You will find the contents of the book relevant regardless of the number of addicts in the family and regardless of the drug(s) of choice. However, we must emphasize that we have made no attempt to tailor the material to fit every type of situation. At times, it may appear that we are referring solely to single addicts using one drug each. This is for clarity's sake, and it is not intended to minimize the problems families experience when they have more than one addicted relative or one relative using several drugs in their midsts. Periodically, we will address the problems of widespread addiction within a family, and we will discuss the effects of addicts who use several drugs (typically referred to as "polydrug abusers"). If you find a difference between the situations we discuss and some of the problems you encounter, please remember that this book is not a cookbook for recovery. It is a resource designed to help you think about your family.

One Gender

As you read through this book, you will notice that we have referred to addicts, loved ones and therapists as "he" and "him." This reference to one gender is for simplicity's sake, and it is not meant to imply that only males are involved in addictions or that our treatment is male-oriented. Our approach is as unbiased as the addictive problems we treat.

Confidentiality and the Use of Case Studies

The examples we use to illustrate points in the book have been drawn from actual cases. We have changed names, places and events to respect people's privacy, but the cases retain their illustrative value.

THE SCOPE OF THIS BOOK

This book truly was a joint effort, a result of a healthy partnership. In it we are presenting the fruits of our clinical experience and the struggles and successes of our patients. We have provided exercises throughout the book, and also in the appendices, to bring our concepts to life for you and your family. The objectives of the exercises are to help you flesh out your understanding of yourself and your family, to identify possible targets for change and to stimulate the kind of thinking that will help you conceive a different course of action. The exercises are not standardized psychological tests and as such cannot be scored meaningfully. They will, however, help you understand your family differently.

Although we can describe our experiences and stimulate the thoughts of our readers, we cannot offer this book as a self-treatment manual. The ideas, procedures, illustrations and suggestions included in this book are intended to complement, but not to replace, psychological treatment or participation in self-help groups. All matters regarding your and your family's recovery require the attention of a psychologist or other qualified professional.

SPECIAL NOTE TO CLINICIANS

The book's content was shaped by our experiences helping families, training clinicians, designing and directing treatment programs and consulting with other addictions specialists. The voice is that of two clinicians educating loved ones of addicts. Being addressed directly as a loved one of an addict may sound foreign; however, we believe that there are many advantages in presenting therapeutic concepts to clinicians in the same manner in which they are presented to patients.

First, as a reader, you gain the opportunity to identify with the role of the patient. Let the words work on you, and learn from your own reactions. You will be more empathetic.

Second, this format provides you with one concrete method of presenting therapeutic concepts, a sample to work from. We do not speak abstractly about what might be said to a patient. Instead, we invite you to observe us speaking—albeit in print—to a large group of people working to overcome the target problem. Armed with fresh examples, you may feel better equipped to modify and integrate our concepts with your own approach.

Third, this book is based on our developmental model of recovery. We present a comprehensive approach that should equip a skilled clinician to chart the course of treatment, including detailed objectives and methods for achieving them. The language should be helpful in setting goals and in structuring treatment and education for the loved ones of addicts.

We have shown this material to students and colleagues. It has been gratifying to find our concepts and ideas popping up in their process notes and tapes. We were encouraged to note that other clinicians have been getting the same results we have with the interventions we suggest. The material here is a good supplement to your other efforts in this complex area.

A project like this is enhanced by the assistance and support of many people. This book took shape thanks to the love, support, understanding and patience of our families, Marilyn, Nora and Aaron Schlesinger and Nicole, Mia, Sam and Marilyn Horberg. We are indebted to Dr. Ina Schlesinger for her repeated readings of our manuscript drafts and, for their helpful comments, to Marilyn Horberg, Joanne Rosenberg, Greg Kolden, Toby Perlman, Mary Devitt, Helen Anthony, Ariel O'Hara, Deborah Weinfield and Doctors Barbara Hunter, Dan Goeckner, Marty Zelenietz, James May, S. Vincent Miranti, Alexander Eschbach, Sidney Schnoll, Lee Gladstone, Edward Sheridan, John Gillick, Tim McGinnis and Laura Yorke. We are grateful for Bonnie Lee's literary research and to Linda Kyle-Rimkis for her inspiring appreciation of the needs of the whole family. Last, and most important, comes our gratitude to our patients, who shared ideas with us in their recovery. From them, we learned how it is best done. Each contributed to our understanding of the recovery process and helped us refine our ideas and treatment techniques. Without them, this book could not be.

PART I

Getting Started

A mountain climber's version of the journey
—through the regions of Exasperation, Effort and Empowerment.

Chapter 1

Introduction

Associating with addicted loved ones has a high price. Social circles shrink, economic and emotional security are threatened, psychological growth is stymied and relationships among family members are strained. The longer the problems persist, the greater the damage. This book helps acquaint you and your family with the process of repairing the damage and creating more satisfying lives.

THE PREMISE OF THE BOOK

Our basic premise is: *Families can recover from the effects of an addict's drug use or drinking and from the family's chaotic entanglement with an addict.* The family's despair results both from exposure to the addict's destructive behavior and from the uncomfortable roles family members assume in relation to the addict and to each other. You are probably uncomfortable with your own behavior and may be neglecting many of your own needs. Some of the family's actions may permit the addict to continue drug use without meeting the full consequences of his behavior. As a result, family suffering continues. The problem many families have is that they assume too much responsibility for addicts, despite the addict's behavior, and too little responsibility for their own welfare. It is important to remember that *no one causes another person's addiction.*

THE GOAL OF THE BOOK

We wrote this book with one overriding goal: *to help struggling families learn to flourish.* To this end, we will help you find realistic bases for the hope that your life will change, formulate an understanding of the nature of your difficulties and set a direction for resolving your problems. Hope and understanding make it possible to develop a new vision of the future. Vision and enthusiasm may lead you to move in new directions.

To succeed, you will need to take five main steps throughout the recovery process. First, you will need to know that you and your family can flourish and to *imagine what flourishing would be like for you.* This will involve developing realistic expectations for recovery and an overview of the recovery process. Second, you will need to *identify some immediate actions to take* and to imagine subsequent actions to boost you toward your goal. Third, you will need to *take credit for steps you take* in the direction of your goal. We will encourage you to identify gains toward your ultimate destination when you make them and to recognize them as progress, even if they are small. It would be unrealistic—and very discouraging—if you looked for the "big splash," that moment when all your problems become clear and their solutions spring to mind. It is more realistic to give yourself encouragement along the way. And you can do that only if you know where you are going and can acknowledge your progress step by step. Fourth, you will need to *join with others for support* when that will be helpful. Fifth, you will need to learn to *take care of yourself.* For these steps we will suggest approaches in the form of discussions, exercises and tasks. How you take these steps may vary at different points in your recovery, but the need for all five continues throughout the life cycle.

Although you will not learn all the answers to your family's problems, by reading this book you can learn to ask better questions about your family's difficulties, to identify problem areas with more confidence, and to stimulate your thinking about possible solutions. We have designed the book so that it will be helpful to families at all stages of recovery.

WHAT WE MEAN BY "FAMILY"

We interpret the term *family* in its broadest sense, to include any person or group of people with a strong bond of affection or attachment to an addicted person. This definition encompasses some obvious relationships: with children, spouses, parents and siblings of addicts. But it also can include extended family members (such as grandparents, aunts, uncles and cousins), friends and lovers. It also may include employers if they feel close to the addict and experience many of the same reactions as relatives and close friends. The quality of the relationship with the addict, rather than genetics, will determine who is included in your family.

With this definition in mind, we want to stress that our aim is to help you end the pain you have felt as a result of your loved one's addiction. Often, including the addict in every state of the process of moving toward family health can help in this; if the addict is willing to contribute positively to the process, strive for his inclusion. In this way, you and your family members work with each other rather than against each other. There are no "bad guys." However, if the addict chooses not to join your family in health, then we believe nonaddicted family members serve themselves best by reconstructing and preserving family life without him. If he undermines the effort, proceed without him, reserving the option of inviting him to join in the effort at a later stage. Although the decision to abandon your hopes of including the addict may itself be painful, you and members of your family need to establish health as your goal and then choose the best path to reach it. A reluctant addict who keeps other family members in chaotic relationships merely perpetuates chaos. Moving beyond pain is the courageous course many families have charted with us.

WHAT WE MEAN BY "ADDICT"

For the sake of brevity and clarity, we use the term "addict" throughout the book, a term that unfortunately carries many negative connotations. By "addict," we mean a person who engages in certain behaviors (e.g., drug use, drinking, gambling, eating, sex, shopping) in a compulsive manner despite the harm he causes himself and/or people who are close to him. We don't mean to endorse any stereotypes or to imply that people who are addicted should be rejected or demeaned.

RECOVERY IS A JOURNEY

The process by which the family arrests the damage done in its association with the addict and moves on to develop a richer family life is called *recovery*. Our patients have described family life before recovery as chaos, in the midst of which peace occasionally breaks out. Yet millions of loved ones of addicts have found ways to overcome chaos and feelings of hopelessness to create and maintain happier lifestyles.

Sometimes, addicts lead the way for their families. They may be in treatment or be members of self-help groups. But often their sober loved ones initiate the process of restoring sanity to family life.

Getting Started

Recovery is not an event. Rather, it is a series of steps and tasks that lead the family away from its despair and chaos. Think of recovery as a journey. As with any journey, successful travel starts with deciding on a destination and includes careful preparation and anticipation of problems along the way. And so it is with a family's journey through recovery.

This book is a travel guide for that journey. We will suggest ways to think about destinations, ways to determine which destinations are absolutely unacceptable and ways to choose the best destination for your family. Since families have different experiences, needs and goals, this is not going to be a package tour; there is no single specified route that every family takes. You will likely need a tour guide to help you along the way, and these guides are available in the form of therapists and self-help group sponsors. Meeting fellow travelers at various points to compare notes may be indispensable, and they can be found at self-help group meetings.

Getting started on the road to recovery involves a simple principle: Actively doing something—almost anything—is better than doing nothing. The emphasis is on doing. Becoming active is the first step in getting started. Movement toward your goals will depend first on summoning the energy to start doing things in new ways.

The Route of the Journey

We want you to imagine a mythological world in which there are three different regions. As you read through the rest of the chapter, you will have an opportunity to undertand each region in some detail. Your creative task will be to build a picture of the regions for yourself, based on our descriptions as they relate to your own experiences. Ultimately, the picture you construct will help you make the remaining chapters of the book work for you. We have named the regions the Three E's.

I. *Exasperation:* Chaos, shame, hopelessness
II. *Effort* in a grey world without clear reward: unrelenting effort to avoid slipping back into the world of chaos and with the dim hope of achieving some as-yet-vague reward.
III. *Empowerment:* Living with meaning, sense of purpose, vitality, energy

In Region I, Exasperation, chaos is a fact of everyday life. For example, a typical day for the Perelli family started when Mrs. Perelli was unable to awaken her husband for work after his night of bar-hopping. She called his boss to explain that he had the flu, trying to keep the fear, rage and shame out of her voice. Later that morning, Mr. Perelli was awakened by a call from his son's school principal telling him his son had been caught with marijuana on the playground. When the son arrived home, Mr. Perelli flew into a rage in front of the neighbors. Later that evening over dinner, Mr. and Mrs. Perelli argued viciously about the state of the family finances. On reflection, Mrs. Perelli described this as an average day in her family. Exasperated, she contacted a psychologist to arrange for family therapy.

In Region II, Effort, members begin to do things that are different and more socially accceptable, but without a clear idea of where they will lead. At this stage of family development, for example, Mr. Perelli had stopped drinking and was going to work regularly. As he walked into the office each morning, he wondered whether he was the target of jokes and whether he had a future with the firm. He set about the task of straightening out the mess left from his drinking days. He had begun caring for the children. Mrs. Perelli had started going to self-help group meetings and was working. Mr. and Mrs. Perelli both met with school counselors to set a course for their son. They continued attending family therapy sessions, despite difficult feelings stirred up between them. They joined a health club and began exercising regularly. They also began accepting invitations to family gatherings, enduring the shame of family scrutiny. In a comment to their psychologist, Mr. and Mrs. Perelli noted, "All this work is no fun, and we don't know where it will all lead." They often felt weary, vulnerable and joyless.

In Region III, Empowerment, family members develop a sense of purpose and become meaningfully involved in many aspects of life. They feel new energy and become aware of deep feelings because they no longer are consumed by the addiction. Mr. and Mrs. Perelli renewed initmate relations, both physically and emotionally. Their son became more involved with his friends and performed in school at the level of his potential. With their renewed energy, Mr. and Mrs. Perelli pursued their careers with fresh vision and purpose. They felt the love and respect of relatives and friends. Life was not without pain, however. Mr. and Mrs. Perelli had to endure their share of losses and disappointments, but they did so without losing their sense of purpose and direction. When the firm that employed Mr. Perelli went bankrupt, he suffered, but he organized a job search quickly and found a better job.

Now that you have a general understanding of the regions, we invite you to use your imagination to develop a more elaborate picture of the journey. Imagine that each region is a self-contained world. A person may live for a long time entirely within one region without becoming aware of the others. Imagine further that Region I exists deep below the surface of the earth, that Region II exists above Region I just beneath the ground and that Region III exists on the surface of the earth under the open sky. Hidden passageways lead from Region I to Region II and from Region II to Region III. Camouflaged pits in the surface of Regions II and III make it possible to fall, without warning, from higher levels to lower ones.

When we explain this metaphor to our clients, several have compared the physical layout of this three-layered world to the literary visions in Jules Verne's *Journey to the Center of the Earth* and *The Time Machine* and in Harlan Ellison's *A Boy and His Dog*. Others have compared its content to religious visions of hell, purgatory and heaven, or Egypt, the desert and the Promised Land. Having a concrete vision of these three regions will help you chart your course and imagine what it could be like to flourish.

Moving from *exasperation* through *effort* to *empowerment* is a process of growing up, developing emotionally. Direction in this journey will come from your answers to four basic questions. You will need to ask yourself these questions over and over again in each region every time you need to take action or make a decision. Answers to the four questions lead you to the passageways to higher regions. They also alert you to the pits through which you can drop to a lower level of functioning. The four questions are:

1. What kind of experiences do I want right now?
2. What choices or actions would I admire in myself in this situation?
3. What strengths do I have that would be valuable in this situation?
4. What do I feel right now?

Without clear answers to any one of the four questions, it is difficult to enter Region III, Empowerment, in which you pursue what you want, take action and make decisions you admire, relying on strengths you have, and trusting your feelings. The passageway to this region is hidden. Correspondingly, to avoid falling back into a lower region, you need to know what experiences you do *not* want to have, what you do *not* admire in yourself and what weaknesses you have. For example, one client constructed a list of the pits that led him into, and had kept him in, Region I, exasperation:

1. Overeating
2. Overspending
3. Letting others take control of his plans
4. Procrastinating on an important assignment at work
5. Trying to seduce a woman in a bar, on a bus or in any other anonymous setting
6. Visiting with his emotionally abusive father

To understand the three regions better, it will help to understand how the four questions are generally answered in each. The table "Themes of Answers to the Four Questions in Each Region" presents a summary.

Themes of Answers to the Four Questions in Each Region

Characteristics of the Regions	Question 1 *What kind of experiences do I want right now?*	Question 2 *What choices or actions would I admire in myself in this situation?*	Question 3 *What strengths do I have that would be valuable in this situation?*	Question 4 *What do I feel right now?*
III. EMPOWERMENT Purpose and meaning Alive! and lively risk taking Commitment Involvement with others Responsibility clearly defined	*Fulfilling dreams.* A person can dream, plan to fulfill the dream and enjoy it when it comes together. Dreams are based on true understanding of needs. His sense of entitlement and sense of responsibility are realistic.	*Taking responsibility.* A person lives out his own values, takes credit for his successes, and defines ways of improving further.	*Believing in strengths.* A person feels loveable, likable and effective. He can define his strengths and count on them when taking on challenges.	*Experiencing at a deep level.* Full range of positive and negative feelings and passions. Sense of personal competence leads to a feeling of serenity.

II. EFFORT

Relentless effort in a grey world, without certain reward

Going through the motions

Surviving

→ *Safe pleasures.* Blandness and socially acceptable pleasures are all that one looks forward to. Fulfilling deep needs seems impossible.

→ *Pleasing others.* A person gets vague satisfaction from choosing socially acceptable alternatives.

→ *Groping for strengths.* A person is able to win recognition from others but feels hollow, as if merely going through the motions or as if he is an imposter.

→ *Tentatively opening up to feelings.* Deeper feelings are emerging but are difficult to define. "Is that all there is?"

I. EXASPERATION

Chaos, shame, helplessness

Vulnerability

→ *Conflict interferes with pleasures.* Needs are not understood; rarely gratified out in the open.

→ *Little is admired.* A person holds many conflicting standards, but only at a shallow level. He violates his most basic standards. Life is chaotic, and he perceives others as looking down on him.

→ *Few strengths are evident.* A person's opinion of himself swings from inferiority to superiority.

→ *Denying and discounting feelings.* Feelings are superficial and mainly in reaction to chaos and confusion.

Genevieve's Readiness for a Weekend Alone with Jim
Recovery reflected in the four questions

Region	What do I want?	What would I admire?	What strengths do I have?	What do I feel?
Region III. Empowerment	I want to be away for a while so that I can visit my friend Joan, work out and go to church. But I also want to see a play with Jim and have a sexual/romantic date with him.	Telling Jim what I want. Looking attractive and fit. Listening to my friend. Praying with sincerity at church.	I can plan a great evening, push myself in a workout, listen to and support my friend, look attractive, show affection to my husband and understand a good sermon.	I am excited about my plans for the weekend. I am a little annoyed that my friend Joan still holds a grudge against Jim. I am tired and need a nap before we go out.
Region II. Effort in a Grey World	I don't know. Maybe we will try something new. There's probably nothing we would both enjoy, and it's all too expensive. The plays are probably weird. I'll see what Jim wants to do.	Jim will want me to wash the floors and take care of the mound of bills and mail on our dresser. I suppose I should go to church.	I guess people think I'm nice. Jim thinks I'm loyal and dependable. I don't know.	I'm not looking forward to anything. It seems so much work! I wish the weekend were over.
Region I. Exasperation	To binge on Häagen-Dazs, to run away, to have an affair with my boss, to join a convent and to kill Jim. It's all his fault.	Nothing! What do people want from me? I'm dumb for staying with Jim. But I'm disloyal for wanting to leave. There's no way to win.	I'm a lousy doormat! Maybe I'm a saint, who knows?	Like garbage. I'm scared and I feel sick. I'm completely lost.

To illustrate the ways in which the four questions are answered concretely at different stages of the journey, let us examine a specific situation. Genevieve is a thirty-four-year-old advertising executive, married to Jim, a forty-two-year-old stockbroker who was once addicted to cocaine. In the table called "Genevieve's Readiness for a Weekend Alone with Jim" are Genevieve's reactions to the prospect of spending a weekend with Jim, discussed at three different points in her recovery. Jim was drug- and alcohol-free throughout Genevieve's recovery.

We will now introduce you to the details of the journey. Our introduction will begin with an overview describing the course of the journey, from region to region. Succeeding chapters will describe the step-by-step tasks involved in successful travel to family health. The overview will help you organize those individual tasks and understand them in the context of the overall journey.

REGION I: EXASPERATION

When you are trapped in Region I, there is an abundance of shame, hopelessness, panic, despair and vulnerability. You feel that your survival (psychological and perhaps even physical) is at risk. Tennessee Williams's plays are often about characters trapped in the exasperation of Region I. The following excerpt, from *Cat on a Hot Tin Roof,* succinctly illustrates what Region I is like.

> **Margaret:** . . . But now, since you've taken to liquor—you know what?—I guess it's bad, but now I'm stronger than you and I can love you more truly!
>> Don't move that pillow. I'll move it right back if you do!
>> —Brick?
> *[She turns out all the lamps but a single rose-silk-shaded one by the bed.]*
>> I really have been to a doctor and I know what to do and—Brick?—this is my time by the calendar to conceive!
> **Brick:** Yes, I understand, Maggie. But how are you going to conceive a child by a man in love with his liquor?
> **Margaret:** By locking his liquor up and making him satisfy my desire before I unlock it!
> **Brick:** Is that what you've done, Maggie?
> **Margaret:** Look and see. That cabinet's mighty empty compared to before!

Brick: Well, I'll be a son of a—
[He reaches for his crutch but she beats him to it and rushes out on the gallery, hurls the crutch over the rail and comes back in, panting.]

In Region I, *life is chaotic.* You feel that your life—even your own behavior—is out of control. Promises you make to yourself are easily broken (e.g., "no more one-night stands," "no more food binges," "no more credit card purchases," "no more concessions to my addicted wife," "I'll do my taxes," "I'll fix the furnace," "I'll take my child to the doctor"). There are phone calls in the middle of the night. "The other shoe" drops, and drops often. Consequences of self-neglect terrorize you and your family.

In Region I, *you feel isolated.* Even in a crowd, you feel desperately lonely. You do not feel lovable or likable. When others respond to you with warmth, you wonder whether they would like you if they really knew you. You fear that they want something from you or that you would have to cater to them, please them or win their approval. So you *must* keep distant in order to survive as a person.

In Region I, *you are in a state of emotional pain.* Life traumatizes you so that you must either distract yourself or face extreme levels of discomfort.

In Region I, *you are afraid of change.* Because you are convinced that life will work out badly for you, the prospect of change is very frightening.

In this state of exasperation, how does an individual typically respond to the four questions?

Exasperation. Question 1: What Kind of Experiences Do I Want Right Now?

Typically, the individual often feels that he:

a. Does not know what would satisfy him
b. Could not get it if he knew what it was
c. Would not be entitled to it if he did manage to get it
d. Would lose it if he had it
e. Would be rejected by others if he admitted that he enjoyed it

Pleasures are hidden, secret, taken on the sly.
Sources of pleasure usually bring about pain, because the individual

has not learned to gratify his deeper needs safely and responsibly. He suffers shame, rejection and loss because of the way he goes about meeting his needs. Recall Tennessee Williams's Margaret and her bizarre attempt to force Brick to impregnate her. Like many in Region I, Margaret had so little insight into her needs and the reactions of others that she pursued her fantasy in a destructive way. Her awareness of her needs was limited to just one or two elements of the situation (e.g., baby, marriage to Brick). She was not aware of other critical elements such as the type of attitude she might hope her baby's father would have, the importance of the father's consent and motivation and the importance of the voluntary aspect of love.

Ambivalent feelings confuse preferences and obscure the value of most experiences. Consider, for example, how the wife of an alcoholic might feel when her husband comes home late bearing flowers for the first time in ten years but has alcohol on his breath.

Exasperation. Question 2: What Choices or Actions Would I Admire in Myself in This Situation?

The individual typically feels ashamed and worthless, even when he receives praise from others. On a daily basis, he feels ashamed of his own shortcomings, particularly when they appear to be noticed by others. Unable to look at himself in an honest way, he is blocked from coming to grips with feelings of inferiority. He is not pleasing anybody, particularly himself. To soothe himself, he does one or more of the following:

a. Latches on to empty, grandiose gestures or phrases (e.g., "I'm tops in my field," "I saved someone's life")
b. Forces others to behave in ways that may be unnatural for them (e.g., Margaret forcing Brick to impregnate her)
c. Becomes pious and self-righteous to defend himself from feelings of worthlessness and of being unlovable

Values come to mind in the form of external criticisms rather than plans or principles that shape action. Anger at oneself is projected onto others so that the individual believes that others look down on him. For example, one client habitually came late to meetings, felt ashamed, expected everyone to feel contempt for him and felt angry at them. He often resolved—for that moment—to be on time for the next meeting, but he quickly forgot his resolve. Instead of thinking, "It's important to me to be prompt, to show respect for my colleagues' time and to be a team player," he let himself feel victimized by others.

Exasperation. Question 3: What Strengths Do I Have That Would Be Valuable in This Situation?

Typically, the individual is unable to:

a. Pinpoint strengths and skills
b. Describe them accurately and consistently
c. Believe in his ability to succeed in challenging situations
d. Commit himself to take on a challenge and follow through on the commitment

He often feels anxious, helpless and inadequate; he feels panic and lacks confidence, despite his actual level of objective success. Victories are understood in grandiose terms that feel empty when examined. No practical understanding of strengths is available to the individual at times of stress. For example, Jonathan was a successful and nationally recognized trial attorney. Despite his record, he could not understand what made him so successful. As a result, he could not be assured that he could perform well in a new trial. Consequently, before every courtroom appearance, Jonathan spent fifteen panic-filled minutes vomiting in his hotel room bathroom. Following each successful verdict, he felt empty and ascribed the outcome to fate.

Exasperation. Question 4: What Do I Feel Right Now?

Typically, the individual has trouble:

a. Recognizing different feelings
b. Putting feelings into words
c. Accepting his feelings ("I shouldn't feel this way")
d. Telling other people about his feelings
e. Feeling secure after telling others about personal feelings

The individual is emotionally isolated. He feels overwhelmed and mystified by mood changes. Sometimes he feels a sense of panic; sometimes he feels numb. Mostly, he merely reacts to the chaos and confusion and feels helpless to stop it. A sense of shame develops, and he frequently gets depressed. When he experiences the trauma of a loss (loss of a hoped-for experience or loss of face), he may feel bad but often he loses awareness of the connection between feelings and events. He may explain the feelings as:

a. Confirming his status as a victim
b. A sign of physical illness
c. Hunger for food, drugs, sex, shopping or other compulsive behaviors

In a state of exasperation, the individual often feels conscious of the need to escape.

REGION II: EFFORT IN A GREY WORLD

When you feel intense determination to separate yourself from the patterns that harmed you in Region I, you will be ready to break into Region II. Soon after freeing yourself of chaos and shame, you are likely to feel relief. But after functioning in Region II for a brief period, it is not uncommon to feel regret at having made the hard-won changes that seemed so necessary at the time.

One twenty-eight-year-old man—we will call him Shel—sought help in separating from his chaotic alcoholic father. Shel described his movement into Region II as follows:

When I got to his house, I knew I couldn't cater to him anymore. The police car, parked out front with its blue lights flashing, gave me the same sick, humiliated, terrified feeling I had had all my life. What did he do this time? Only, now I knew what the feeling was. When I was a kid, I had no idea. Now I could see that my father's illness was killing him and that it may have crippled me. On this occasion, the police were responding to a complaint made by someone who became frightened when my father staggered outside without his pants. As I walked up the path to talk with the policeman, I knew that this was an experience I was *determined* not to repeat. Instead of hiring a

31

lawyer to seek an acquittal, I hired a lawyer who helped arrange court-mandated treatment.

It was then that I began to see myself a little more clearly. I was going nowhere fast. I had gotten into the habit of smoking marijuana every night after work. I was drifting on my job. My apartment was a mess. I hadn't filed income tax returns in two years. I had a lot of physical aches and pains that worried me. I hadn't had a girlfriend in ten years. The women I went out with were very strange, and I needed to be high in order to get in the mood to be physical. I thought of myself as an imposter in my job. The only problem I worked on regularly was rescuing my father. He filled all of the empty spaces in my life. I had given him all my energy.

I came to treatment two weeks after the last incident with the police. Shortly thereafter, I intervened with my father to give him the opportunity to get into treatment. I stopped using marijuana, started going to school, worked hard to succeed at my job, stopped seeing my scuzzy girlfriends and —in short—was a good boy. For three months, I felt relieved by my success. Then, the empty and lonely feelings started building. No one needed me. I was alone. I *hated* being alone. My life stank.

I started noticing all the couples walking around. Single guys started looking weird to me. "What's wrong with them?" I'd ask. I hate to admit this, but I actually caught myself feeling nostalgic about the good old days with my father. I wanted the phone to ring, even if it were my father calling for help. When was *my* life going to start?

Feeling lonely, desperate and bored, I started trying some new things. I joined a ski club, took acting lessons and started going to church. In those early days, I had some nice experiences but nothing really hit the spot. Real pleasure, real confidence seemed beyond my reach.

In Region II, *you feel committed to do what it takes to ensure your survival*. Whereas in Region I survival was often in jeopardy, in Region II you learn to take action to block a slide into chaos. You become sensitive to conditions that put you at risk and learn to make better choices to steer clear of danger. For example, if your addicted spouse has been on the wagon and has a slip (comes home drunk), you learn to resist the desire to take reponsibility for his cure; you choose not to rescue him or browbeat him. Instead of taking the bait, you learn new ways of responding that help you steer clear of the chaos. You gain confidence in your ability to survive and a strong will to do so.

In Region II, *you explore and experiment as you learn ways to enrich your life*. Freed of the chaos of Region I, you now can attend to your own needs more consistently; you add to your understanding of yourself and the world by trying new things. To the extent that you have withdrawn from outside challenges and personal standards, you will need to expend effort to re-engage in life. The more you experience, the more insight, information, resources and confidence you will gain.

In Region II, *the required effort seems relentless.* Doing new things is a big production. Planning, executing and evaluating new activities is stressful; enlisting others or joining those already involved in some new activity creates anxiety. In Region II, expectations are not yet strong, and you may lack a clear vision of success. Consequently, attention is captured by the size of the effort rather than the hoped-for result. For example, in approaching the task of achieving a healthy and attractive weight, it is natural to think more about the pain of dieting than about the joys of attractiveness and vigor. While struggling in Region II without a swift, sure and valuable reward, it is natural to wonder, "Why bother with the effort?" Day after day of struggling to get to some unknown goal seems like wandering in the desert on the way to a mythical promised land. It tests your patience.

In Region II, *weary with the effort, you may question the value of trying.* Too much sacrifice brings too little reward. In order to enter Region II, you may have had to give up old habits, including destructive ways of being close to the addict (e.g., drinking together), ways of soothing yourself, ways of getting attention and ways of finding excitement. Whereas Region I may have been painful, it was also familiar and predictable. When you enter Region II, you trade familiarity and predictability for the vague hope of a better life. If the results do not come quickly—and they often do not—you may find yourself suddenly wishing to revert back to old habits. If you can hang in there long enough to answer the four questions in different parts of your life, your impatience may eventually work in your favor. It will motivate you to take the risks needed to take charge of your life and move into Region III.

In Region II, responses to the four questions are sharper than they were in Region I. Characteristic ways of responding are described below.

Effort. Question 1: What Kind of Experiences Do I Want Right Now?

The individual seeks out safe pleasures. He does not understand most of his deeper emotional needs and passions. Typically, he dismisses those needs that do enter conscious thought by telling himself:

a. "I'd have to be high to do that"
b. "Maybe other people can do that, but not me"
c. "Other people would object if I tried to do that"
d. "Maybe if I came from a normal family, I could do that"

The world is grey, and pleasures are either muted or they are viewed as beyond reach—impractical or unacceptable.

Effort. Question 2: What Choices or Actions Would I Admire in Myself in This Situation?

The individual relies on others to set his standards and to make him feel worthwhile. Typically, he does not fully:

a. Recognize when he has succeeded in doing something worthy of admiration
b. Have confidence in his plans for improvement
c. Enjoy recognition of his successes
d. Share successes with others
e. Believe that others admire his actions

The individual becomes compliant, a "people-pleaser."

Successes and failures are remote. They often make the individual feel hollow, empty and perhaps anxious even when they lead to superlative praise from others. Praise feels as if it is undeserved and soon will be withdrawn.

Effort. Question 3: What Strengths Do I Have That Would Be Valuable in This Situation?

The individual's internal picture of his own strengths is dim and unstable. Typically, he lacks confidence in his judgment about his own skills and abilities.

Acknowledging strengths seems very risky. The idea of having false confidence and false hope is frightening.

The individual feels increasingly responsible to be the judge of his own strengths and resists outside evaluations, particularly compliments. But, because he does not yet know how to evaluate himself, he still feels dependent on the opinions of others. He is in limbo.

Effort. Question 4: What Do I Feel Right Now?

Prevailing negative feelings are weariness, sadness, emptiness and fear. Positive feelings are blunted because the individual is skeptical about the meaning of positive actions and events. As he experiments with new actions and begins to get good results, mild positive feelings develop. For Shel, these included relief, hope, anticipation, excitement and affection among others. Strong feelings may exist under the surface without being understood or accepted.

REGION III: EMPOWERMENT

It is uplifting and empowering to pursue the experience you wish for, in a way you admire, using strengths you can count on, with full awareness of your feelings. When Region II becomes too monotonous and you feel as if you are at the end of your rope, you take the risk of taking charge of yourself, first in a single situation. If the time is right, the hope and information gained through your exploratory efforts in Region II come together for you in a new way. You recognize the direction you need to take. You have an intuitive understanding of the "next right thing." You enter Region III by taking charge and taking action. At that moment, you are no longer merely struggling to survive; you are empowered.

Particularly if you get the results you wanted, early experiences in Region III are memorable; they are the beginnings of flourishing. Success (e.g., a successful business transaction, an intimate conversation with a friend, a tender and loving romantic evening, a relaxed outing with the kids) gives rise to a sense of determination to live well, to feel alive and lively. Shel, the young man whose experiences in Region II are described on pages 31–32, succeeded in entering Region III, first through experiences at work, then through friendship and finally through romance.

It seemed as if my boredom and emptiness would go on forever. I got up every morning, went to work, did my best, often worked late or went to a class, then crashed. One day, I was at a meeting and noticed that I was sitting on some very interesting ideas. We were putting together an ad campaign. I sat, listened and made trivial comments. I started to doodle. The ideas started coming out. I was afraid to say anything, thinking, "I'm not good enough. If

I say something, everyone will know it. . . ." "Wait a minute," I argued silently, "these ideas are great. I can't go on acting like a weird little guy with nothing to say." With surprising calmness, I presented my idea. The group loved it. Later, when the client bought it, I let myself believe that I might have some talent. After that critical meeting, I began to contribute more and more regularly. The creative process got very exciting. I often felt elated at work. After several months of solid performance, I started getting interested in leading the creative process, and I sheepishly asked my boss to send me for training. I was shocked when he encouraged me.

One night, after a particularly exciting and creative day at work, I went to my acting class and met a lovely woman named Dee. The instructor set up a scene for the two of us, making it necessary for us to interact. The success and excitement of the day had not yet subsided, and I was conscious of feeling lovable, attractive and worthwhile. Without those feelings, I would have been tongue-tied during the scene. But, with those feelings, I was able to relate to Dee. I could focus on her and I liked her instantly. She was quick, very bright, and very strong but feminine—a heady combination. After the class, I went over to her and asked her out for a drink. Later, over coffee, I felt that we were drawn to each other. I got her phone number. We've been dating five months. The lonely, empty feeling I had months ago is long gone. I think now that those feelings were my way of telling myself that I was missing what I have now, a loving relationship with Dee.

In Region III, *you take charge of your life.* The negative emotions that remain a part of everyday life no longer paralyze you. Instead, you take responsibility to identify your needs, you accept them and you act upon those you deem worthwhile. You are no longer overwhelmed by confusion. In fact, you expect to feel confused at times, see yourself as capable of resolving confusion and expect to benefit from what you learn in the process.

In Region III, *you find purpose, meaning and direction in your life.* Exploring in Region II helped you expand your understanding of yourself and your knowledge of the world. You now find more consistency in the meanings of the events in your life. You understand and accept your motives so that you feel a sense of purpose in familiar situations. In new situations, you recognize that it may take some time to establish a sense of purpose, as when Shel went to his first leadership workshop. He wondered if he was good enough, whether he would get anything out of the class and whether he was silly in even trying. But he was able to hold on to his goal and give himself time to get his bearings.

In Region III, *you actively seek out involvement with others and make commitments to shared goals.* Because you now trust yourself to take charge, you no longer need to fear commitments. You no longer permit others to impose their wishes and values on you. And you no longer let yourself get trapped or feel suffocated. Since you know yourself better, you now have enough information to feel confident that you will want to live up to the terms of your commitments on a consistent basis.

Answers to the four questions in Region III are clear and firm.

Empowerment. Question 1: What Kind of Experiences Do I Want Right Now?

The individual typically feels confident in his knowledge of his wants and needs. He feels entitled to pursue happiness openly and to share his pleasures with others. He expects others to be happy for him when he succeeds.

He is consistently involved with others in ways that gratify his needs. Depending on the situation, relevant needs may include love, intimacy, sex, power, achievement, material objects, financial security and spirituality, among others.

When he is uncertain about his needs, he takes the time to figure them out. Confusion is accepted as a normal precursor of growth and change.

He asserts himself by expressing his desires and his reactions in ways he finds appropriate. He has learned enough about himself and his world to set goals and to express them in ways that do not alienate others. For example, Shel knew intuitively he should ask Dee out for a drink after his class. The words just came to him. He knew that he wanted to spend more time with her and to hint that he was interested in her. The invitation was only a small risk for him; in that class members often went out in small groups. Aware that he knew nothing about Dee, Shel was not ready to ask her out on a formal date. Was she already involved with someone else? Would she be interested in him? He was certainly not ready to tell Dee about his more intimate desires without knowing her better first. To do so would have been inappropriate in *his* eyes.

Empowerment. Question 2: What Choices or Actions Would I Admire in Myself in This Situation?

Rather than giving away the power to define admirable behavior, the individual follows his own values as he makes decisions and takes action.

He takes pleasure in achieving his own standards. At times, he feels particularly worthy of love, respect, liking, praise or honor.

When he is in conflict about which courses of action would be admirable, he thinks through his dilemma, talks to others and resolves his ambivalence as well as he can.

When he experiences disappointment or shame, he is capable of examining his own behavior. He can identify the ways in which he fell short and envision a more admirable course for future conduct.

He finds ways of getting what he wants in ways he admires.

Empowerment. Question 3: What Strengths Do I Have That Would Be Valuable in This Situation?

The individual perceives his current strengths accurately and maintains a stable view of them. He learns to count on them when under fire or as he enters challenging situations. He recognizes many of the contributions he makes to the achievement of individual and group goals.

He recognizes the need to develop new strengths and to remedy weaknesses.

When appropriate, he accurately communicates his understanding of his strengths to others.

He views himself as capable of adapting to change.

Empowerment. Question 4: What Do I Feel Right Now?

The individual experiences a full range of positive and negative emotions and sensations. Events stimulate, exhilarate and please him when they are desirable. Conversely, he is shaken up or hurt when life does not go his way. The individual feels genuine disappointment, anger, hurt and other negative emotions when he fails and when he experiences important losses. But his sense of purpose and autonomy withstand the pressure caused by disappointments.

The individual in Region III can name the different types of feelings he experiences. At different times, he can be joyful, sad, angry, affectionate, confident, scared, embarrassed or proud. He often understands the connection between his feelings and his perceptions of himself and his environment.

He expresses feelings appropriately to others. For example, when Shel was in a state of exasperation in Region I, he was very isolated. On the few occasions when he spoke up about his feelings, he did so almost randomly. He could not take into account the type of relationship he had with his listener, the degree of risk and the situational context. One day he found himself talking bitterly about how he was just a worthless victim of office politics. Shel could not have chosen a worse audience in a riskier situation. His listener was the new president of the ad agency who was wandering around the office, meeting people for the first time.

One year later, when Shel had begun to feel empowered at work, he had many occasions to express himself more appropriately. He became familiar enough with his feelings so that he knew what they meant, he learned how to use appropriate channels, he developed mutually supportive relationships at work and knew whom to talk to there when he needed emotional support, and he acquired a sensitivity to the level of risk involved in expressing his feelings. Ultimately, when he had feelings that required the attention of the agency president, he prepared an outline focusing on the consequences *for the agency* of his concerns and presented creative ideas about how to resolve the identified problems.

Individuals may find themselves in one region with some people, in another with others and in a third in solitary activities. For example, a person may be flourishing at work in an empowered Region III existence, dislike going home to a chaotic Region I family life and find himself in a solitary Region II effort to change self-destructive habits. This individual may have a lot to look forward to at work, a lot to avoid at home and a lot to learn about himself alone.

Families who move from Region I to Region II and then to Region III may slip back periodically to an earlier stage of development. For example, even a brief return to drinking by the addict can bring back some of the chaos, humiliation and uncertainty of an earlier stage.

The remainder of the book describes steps struggling families take to move from a state of exasperation to one of empowerment. In it, you will find:

- An overview of each stage of the journey
- Examples drawn from the experiences of families who have made the journey successfully
- The concrete tasks that comprise each main step to recovery
- Examples drawn from case histories in which individuals successfully completed each task
- Specific exercises to help your family understand each task
- Sample action plans in the appendices for you to consider as models
- A log in the appendix to help you summarize insights you gain along the way
- A separate appendix to teach you, in detail, about the history, use and effects of commonly abused drugs

Chapter 2

Defining the Problem

Coming to grips with the pain addictive families face may initially be up to you, the nonaddicted members. Only you can develop the concentration and disciplined thought to tackle what seems, at first, to be a hopeless tangle of problems.

The first task in untangling family problems is to define very clearly what those problems are. In our experience, families often define their problems in such a way as to feel overwhelmed and helpless to do anything about them. For this reason, we will start by suggesting ways to break your large and complex family problems into manageable components. This will produce a series of small, visible steps along your recovery route. Now, you might say at this point that the problem is clear to start with: "John has been an addict so long, he has wrecked the family." But that is not a clear definition of the problem. It is not specific enough.

Defining the problem clearly is a four-step process. It starts with the general and goes to the specific, as illustrated in the chart shown here (see next page) and as we shall see as we go through it step by step.

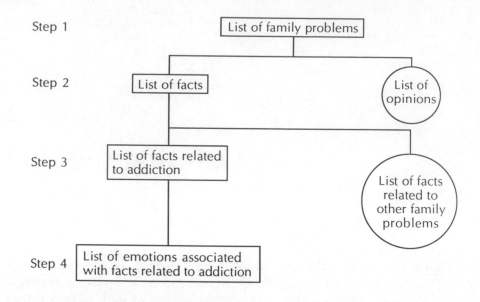

STEP 1: IDENTIFYING FAMILY PROBLEMS

The first step is to get the family together to talk about the problems everyone has noticed. Though what you have noticed may be clear to you as an individual, it does not necessarily follow that everyone in the family has seen the same things you have or that they have seen those things in the same way. Sit down as a family—minus the addicted member—and make a list of your observations about the family's problems. Include the addicted member only if you feel confident in his ability to contribute and in your ability to be open in his presence. Be sure to include the difficulties the addicted person contributes to family life. Try to make the list complete. Include everyone's observations and opinions even if some family members may disagree about their importance, their relevance or their accuracy, and even if they all do not relate directly to addiction.

Try to consider each area of family life, including financial, vocational, emotional, spiritual, interpersonal and community activities. For example, one father's intoxicated behavior contributed to financial losses for his family, strained relationships among family members and caused an alienation of the family from the church. This same family also had a teenager who was pregnant and unprepared for motherhood, and members had experienced serious illnesses. What follows is the first draft of a list another family created during Step 1. It includes some extremely demoralizing problems.

The First, Unrefined List

1. John (the father) is a drunk and a drug addict.
2. John yells at the kids too much and hits too much.
3. John has a girlfriend besides Mom.
4. John never comes home.
5. Mary (the mother) is sad a lot; she cries.
6. When John is high, it embarrasses everyone.
7. Tim (the middle child) is flunking out of school, and John does nothing about it.
8. Mary can never help the kids with their homework.
9. John lost feeling in his fingers.
10. Susan (the youngest child) is very shy and afraid.
11. John, Jr., (the eldest child) is too perfect.
12. Mary works too many hours and is afraid.
13. John, Sr., and Mary no longer sleep together.
14. John, Sr., has had three injuries when high on drugs or drunk.
15. The people at church look down on us.
16. Our friends do not want us over anymore.
17. John, Sr., no longer talks to his brother-in-law.
18. John, Sr., is an unsafe driver and an unsafe handyman around the house.
19. The house is a mess.
20. John, Sr., and Mary have never loved each other, even before the drinking.
21. The family is embarrassed because John, Jr. is illegitimate.
22. John, Sr., was always a terrible son; even today he does not visit his parents in the nursing home.
23. Mary is fat.
24. Nobody in the house knows how to fix anything when it breaks.
25. Susan reads too much and still sucks her thumb.

Without having to think long, this family was able to identify a host of serious problems. If they had stopped at this point, these problems might well have seemed hopeless. But this was only Step 1 for them, as it will be for your family.

As you ponder your list, imagine a home in which tidiness is preserved by putting scattered objects in the closet at the end of each day. Close the closet door and everything looks neat and in order. But, if you open the door, what you see is disarray. The disarray contains nothing new; you have seen it all before.

The problem is that it may look overwhelming because you see the sum of all those little objects you stashed away over the weeks. You see it all at once just because it is all in one place. And so it is with family problems on your list.

Once you have made your list, have a look at it. Try not to be taken aback by its length. It is probably not too long. In fact, its length is not significant at this stage. Try not to give up if your list seems long or horrifying on the one hand, or too vague and trivial on the other hand. Many people, after years of ignoring problems, have great difficulty identifying them. You will whittle the list down (or build it up) to a manageable size as you move on to Step 2.

STEP 2: SEPARATING FACTS FROM OPINIONS

It is important as we look at the world around us that we be able to distinguish the realities we observe from our conclusions and opinions about them. But although it is important to distinguish these things, sometimes we do not.

Step 2 of defining the problem clearly is to learn to describe your observations and to distinguish them from your opinions. When we talk about facts in our lives, we are referring specifically to those things we can know through our five senses. In other words, facts are things we know about from seeing them, hearing them, tasting them, smelling them, or touching them. Opinions, on the other hand, are conclusions we draw or assumptions we make from the way we assemble those facts.

Consider this example. Look at the preceding drawing for a moment.

How would you describe it? What would you call it? To describe it is to view it factually. You might make note of the curved shape and positions of the lines. You would be describing what you see.

To name the figure, though, is to put your observations together and to reach a conclusion. The closest category it fits is the category of circles. "I'd say it's a circle," you might reply, qualifying your conclusion perhaps with a comment about its unique or incomplete nature. The important step in reaching that conclusion is that you chose to assemble your observations into a particular shape. You could not do that, however, if someone required "just the facts" of you. Facts are direct observations; opinions are subsequent inferences.

Let's return to the first, unrefined list. In item 18, the sample family listed their opinion that John is an unsafe driver. One observation that led to this opinion occurred at the family's previous Christmas gathering. John, Jr., remembered that his father had drunk a pint of scotch, had yelled loudly at Mary's brother and had stormed out of the party with Mary and the kids in tow. Mary, Tim and Susan had been seated in the car when John floored the accelerator. John, Jr., had one foot in the car and one foot out, and three of the doors were open when the car took off. Fortunately no one was injured. Everyone reported feeling a mixture of panic, humiliation and rage. The feelings are also facts. The inference that John was a poor driver was an opinion.

Go back over the list that you made in Step 1 and try to separate the observations that you listed into facts and opinions.

As you look at the list, take a look at each of the entries, one at a time. As you look at each entry, ask yourself whether it was the result of something you saw, heard, smelled, tasted, or felt, or whether it was a conclusion you drew based on your observations. Label each as either a fact or an opinion. When you have finished, prepare a second list on which you write the facts (but not the opinions) that you have now identified from your first listing. We will further refine the list in a moment as we get closer to defining your family problems and corresponding emotions directly related to the addiction.

As you prepare your revised list of facts, try to recall particular incidents in vivid detail. As you do, you can list them using shorthand and abbreviations. Vivid images are easy to remember, but it is not necessary to write them out in detail. Look at the next list. It shows observations related to some of the items in the first, unrefined list. It then gives examples of shorthand factual descriptions. Remember: Quality, accuracy and specificity are more important than quantity. Even a handful of pertinent observations can start the family on a road to understanding the problem. Many therapists are equipped to facilitate and improve this process.

Refining Opinions to Identify Facts

Detailed Observations

1. One night last year, John came home smelling like whiskey; he threw up in the kitchen; he had blood coming out from a cut over his eye. The car looked wrecked.

2. The toilet has been on the blink for months.

3. Susan still sucks her thumb.

4. John's secretary called to say that we had to pick him up at work. When I got to his office, his boss was yelling that John had fallen asleep in his chair while a major account representative was in his office. John stopped working there two months later.

5. Susan, John, Jr., and Tim have never seen John, Sr., and Mary kiss or touch.

6. I saw John snorting some white powder with his friend.

Shorthand Descriptions: Practical Examples

1. Last year, car wreck, cut on head, vomit.

2. Broken toilet.

3. Thumb sucking.

4. Asleep at work; lost job

5. No open affection between Mom and Dad.

6. Snorting cocaine in the basement.

7. Mary weighs 220 pounds.

8. Kathy's wedding, wailing loudly and embarrassing the family.

9. Slurring words at the graduation.

10. Dirty and cluttered house.

11. John, Jr., is illegitimate.

12. Last Wednesday, talking fast, saying words we did not understand, bragging.

13. Losing the mortgage money and "finding cocaine," January.
14. Mary works 60 hours a week.
15. John complained last year that he had lost feeling in his fingers.
16. John had three injuries while he was intoxicated: last February, two years ago, and at the football game.
17. Nancy and Dave told me that John's cocaine use at parties offends them.

STEP 3: IDENTIFYING FACTS RELATED TO ADDICTION

It is important at this point to pare your list from Step 2 a bit further. The next step is to distinguish between problems related directly to addiction and those related only indirectly to addiction. In this second category might fall such things as longer-term, chronic family problems, disagreements or misunderstandings. In the former category are your observations and experiences which relate exclusively to the addict's drug use.

Go over your list in Step 2 entry by entry and ask yourself whether each fact listed there is related to addiction or to some longer-standing family problems. As a conclusion to Step 3, prepare one list of those facts related to drug use and a second list of those facts related to other family problems. We have provided an example from our sample family in the following lists. As we talk about changing the addict's impact on the family, we will be looking at those facts that help you define the problem, because they are related most specifically to the addiction.

Separating Addiction-related from Other Problems

Addiction-related Problems
1. One night last year, John came home smelling like whiskey; he threw up in the kitchen; he had blood coming out from a cut over his eye. The car looked wrecked.
2. John's secretary called to say that we had to pick him up at work. When I got to his office, his boss was yelling that John had fallen asleep in his chair while a major account representative was in his office. John stopped working there two months later.
3. I saw John snorting some white powder with his friend.
4. Mary is overweight.

Shorthand Descriptions: Practical Examples

1. Last year, car wreck, cut on head, vomit.
2. Asleep at work; lost job.
3. Snorting cocaine in the basement.
4. Kathy's wedding, wailing loudly and embarrassing the family.
5. Slurring words at the graduation.
6. Last Wednesday, talking fast, saying words we did not understand, bragging.
7. Losing the mortgage money and "finding cocaine," January.
8. John complained last year that he had lost feeling in his fingers.
9. John had three injuries while he was intoxicated: last February, two years ago and at the football game.
10. Nancy and Dave told me that John's cocaine use at parties offends them.

Problems Not Directly Related to Addiction

1. The toilet has been on the blink for months.
2. Susan still sucks her thumb.
3. Susan, John, Jr., and Tim have never seen John, Sr., and Mary kiss or touch.
4. John, Jr., is illegitimate.

STEP 4: IDENTIFYING FEELINGS ASSOCIATED WITH THE FACTS

It is the emotions stirred up by a problem that alert us to its importance and the need to tackle it. The next step in developing a clear understanding of the problem is to discuss and record the emotions related to that problem. For example, "When Dad sped off with the doors of the car open, I was scared, angry and disgusted."

Go back over your list, entry by entry, and discuss each observation among yourselves. As you focus on each observation, write down a list of the emotions that each member experienced when confronted by the particular observation. These emotions are one source of the family's discomfort and something that has brought you to the point of wanting help. It will be important for the family to identify the emotional aspects of their difficulties with the addict in order to understand later portions of the book.

Refinements of the preceding list looked like this for Mary and the kids:

Relating Feelings to Facts

Shorthand Descriptions	*Feelings*
1. Car wreck, cut on head, vomit	Fear, revulsion
2. Lost job	Anger, fear
3. Snorting cocaine in the basement	Fear, loneliness
4. Behavior at Kathy's wedding	Embarrassment, rage
5. Slurring words at graduation	Embarrassment, anger
6. Talking fast . . . bragging	Pity, impatience
7. Losing mortgage money . . .	Rage, fear, frustration, insecurity
8. Lost feeling in fingers	Hope, vindication, fear, pity
9. Three injuries while intoxicated	Panic
10. Nancy and Dave took offense	Embarrassment, loneliness, anger

Now take a moment to make refinements in your own list.

The product of the four steps you have just completed is a concentrated view of family pain related to the addiction. Before turning our attention away from the addict, it is vital that we round out a perspective on the addict's positive contributions to family life. This is important because these will be primary factors in deciding ultimately whether to seek a reconciliation with the addict. If the family ignores them, it will be more likely to become entangled in a web of blame and rejection of the addict, the outcome of which can only be frustration.

An awareness of positive family emotions associated with the addict is a necessary backdrop for discussion with the addict. Few addicts will accept an invitation to be the guest of honor at a lynching party. Negotiating with an addict when your emotions are overwhelmingly negative may ensure failure.

POSITIVE CONTRIBUTIONS TO FAMILY LIFE BY THE ADDICTED MEMBER

The steps involved in creating a positive list are similar to those required in defining problems. The objective is to develop a list of these emotions and related facts. Just as an open family discussion provides an excellent starting point for the definition of problems, it is often helpful to bring the family together to discuss positive emotions about the addicted member.

Assuming that the family now has experience with the fact/emotion format, it may be possible to be more flexible in creating the first, unrefined list. Emotions, events, facts and opinions that are positive can all be included in the unrefined list.

Unrefined List of Positive Contributions

Dad is a great guy down deep.

Dad pays the rent most of the time.

Last year, Dad took me to four baseball games.

John is still very assertive at times.

I love my Daddy.

Last week, Dad helped me build a car for the soapbox derby.

When he's sober, Dad does a good job at work.

The next step is to translate each item into a fact/emotion pair as in the table "Relating Feelings to Facts." (See the instructions given earlier in the chapter for steps 2, 3 and 4.) The steps will lead to a refined list of positive facts and warm emotions, as in the table "Positive Facts and Warm Emotions."

Now you have lists of the nitty-gritty, concrete problems associated with the addict's drug use and of some of the positive contributions made by the addict to family life. More importantly, you also have a concise listing of your emotional reactions to his behavior—both positive and negative—and a more precise account of his effects on the family. It is a far cry from the general level of discomfort you were able to describe earlier, in Step 1. It will be important now to define the solution to those problems clearly. That will begin the process of resolving those problems so the family can return to normal functioning.

Let's consider how defining the problem fits into the journey we pro-

Positive Facts and Warm Emotions

Fact or Event	Emotion
When Dad is sober and holds me, like last week	I feel hope and love
When Dad pays the rent	I breathe a sigh of relief
When Dad takes me to the baseball games and doesn't drink beer	I feel "normal," proud
When John outlines his rather creative business plans and describes the steps he is taking to carry them out	I feel respect, pride and hope

posed in Chapter 1. Diagram 1 gives examples of possible actions in each of the three regions. We will present similar diagrams throughout the book to help you relate our concepts to the journey to recovery.

As you look at Diagram 1, we invite you to imagine that you could place yourself in it. Defining the problem creates a solid boundary between Region I and Region II. The tasks in this chapter require you to look down on the chaos. In this chapter, we have described the steps in

Diagram 1
DEFINING THE PROBLEM

Region	Examples of Possible Actions
III Empowerment	Family members quickly and clearly discuss the facts and feelings of their lives.
II Effort	Making lists of positive facts and feelings. Making lists of negative facts and feelings.
I Exasperation	Dishonest with oneself and others about the addiction. Hiding from the problem. Jumping to conclusions and not discussing them.

which a family builds a floor over the chaos of Region I, pulls up chairs, looks down and has a frank discussion.

Before we proceed to the task of defining the solution clearly, consider these points. What you have begun to do is to look at yourself and your family and to make certain observations. You may have concluded that some things about yourself and your family are not to your liking. They may seem strange, they may seem abhorent, they may seem intolerable. They may even have violated some of your cherished values for family and personal life. You may, in short, have begun to conclude that the situation is far worse than you had originally believed, and you may be asking yourself, "How could we ever have allowed things to go this far and have done the things we did?"

One answer is that the addictive process has distorted your family's perceptions and functioning. In response to the distortion, you may have done things that are humiliating to admit. These are things you may have done in public (with other family members, friends or work partners) or they may be private thoughts or actions that violate some of your cherished values. Indeed, many of your goals may remain unfulfilled because it has been so difficult getting anything done in your life in the midst of the chaos surrounding the addictive behavior. As you begin your journey, it will be important to remember your goals and values and standards. As you proceed, your world will likely expand again. You will become concerned with more productive endeavors than previously, and you will become less concerned with such matters as when your addict will return to his addictive behavior. You will see your hopes and your goals reemerge. Hang on for now.

PART II

Strengthening the Family

Once you have defined the problems related to the addiction, the process of setting realistic goals begins by focusing on you. Set the addiction aside, and discover what you and your loved ones can do to help *yourselves*. We will start with your wants, standards, feelings and strengths. Only after getting better answers to the four questions we introduced in Chapter 1 will it be helpful to start thinking about the addiction itself. This kind of self-knowledge will be your most powerful source of leverage in the recovery process. Knowing your wants, abilities, commitments and good points will help you counteract the feelings of helplessness that bog down the family. By acknowledging areas of strengths, the family equips itself to make use of them.

As despair increases, the world appears to shrink. Eventually it may seem that the only important events in the family have to do with the addiction: "Did he seem high when he came home?" "Will she overdose tonight?" "Will she even come home?" Reversing this process is critical to recovery. You must learn to see beyond the addiction to other non–addiction-related desires and values. In so doing, you will refresh yourselves and renew your vitality and your spirits.

In her autobiography, Lauren Bacall discusses the process of recovering from a crippling involvement in her ex-husband's (Jason Robards, Jr.'s) addiction. In the excerpt below, she describes how she became aware that she had allowed herself to lose touch with important values (her own health and beauty and enjoyment of life).

Katie [Hepburn] came over one afternoon, took one look at me, and pronounced me a damn fool. "You're too thin—a wreck—you should be on the beach. The marriage is no good for you—get out, forget it, think of yourself again. You've forgotten about living." She was dead right. I realized I'd been trying to beat the drink problem by talking logically, or by threatening to leave. Spence told me, "No one ever stops drinking because someone asks them to. You can't make him stop—he will, but only when he wants to, only when he has no choice. I know." . . .

I'd forgotten to notice the sky, the trees, flowers, grass—to just enjoy a beautiful day. I'd forgotten how to laugh, to relax, to have any sane social exchange. I had no peace. My only pleasure was my children.

Bacall's awareness that she had neglected some important assets, pleasures and values was pivotal in her choice of a new direction for her family. The confrontation with Hepburn was not the first for Bacall, but it came at a time when she was willing to hear it. Bacall then could imagine getting involved again in the richness of life.

Your family may or may not be at that point. Indeed, many members of addictive families feel depressed and hopeless about their situations and the probability that things will change. Many potentially positive experiences and strengths go unnoticed; the world seems too bleak to imagine constructive changes.

In the three chapters that follow we will help you take a systematic look at your family, with an eye to helping you discover and use your answers to the four questions. This process has helped other families climb out of their valleys of despair. We will follow a simple path. We will help you explore significant aspects of your family's emotional and physical characteristics—one by one—to help you extract useful observations that, with appropriate professional consultation, can lead to action. We will encourage you to complete a number of exercises in which you will analyze your family. Through the use of the appendices, we will help you transform the results of each exercise into helpful family concepts that you can use later as blueprints for action.

TAKING AN INVENTORY OF EXPERIENCES RELATED TO THE FOUR QUESTIONS

We invite you to confront yourselves by taking an inventory of your wants, standards, feelings and strengths. What choices and actions will help you restore sanity and vitality to family life?

Strengths, wants and standards can be difficult to pin down. Therefore, we direct your attention to three crucial areas of your life:

I. Increasing self-care activities
   a. General health and hygiene

    b. Maintenance of safety, well-being and comfort
    c. Management of stress
  II. Living a full life
    a. Clarifying values, desires and commitments
    b. Overcoming barriers to a full life
 III. Developing support
    a. Building supportive relationships
    b. Overcoming barriers to developing support

The following three chapters deal with areas in your life that influence your confidence and vitality. By increasing self-care, living a full life and developing support, you will prepare yourself to rid your life of the destructive effects of addiction. By preparing yourself in this way, you will be in a stronger position to help your family get better.

The information and exercises in the chapters that follow are for you and your family to consider and work through. It will help strengthen the family for every member to participate in the process of completing these steps to recovery. After reading these next three chapters and completing the exercises, you and your family will be in a position to turn your attention back to the addict.

Chapter 3

Increasing Self-care Activities

Families of addicts are frequently less physically healthy than families in which there is no addiction. According to some researchers, there is a much higher incidence of stress- and trauma-related disorders in such families. A story, told by a popular Al-Anon speaker, whom we will call Annie, illustrates some aspects of deteriorating self-care (for more information about Al-Anon, see Chapter 11):

It was twenty below zero and my husband called to arrange to take our kids to a Saturday matinee movie. We were then working on one of our many separations, and I agreed for him to come and get the kids on the condition that he promise to stay sober all afternoon. He looked pretty good when he arrived to get our two boys, ages five and eight. Several hours passed and I sat around the apartment doing nothing. I began to worry and pace soon after the movie ended. Where were they? I *knew* he was drunk and that they were lying in a ditch somewhere on the side of the road freezing. When the phone rang, I was blinded with fear and grief, expecting the sheriff. It was our five year old, calling from the lobby of the theatre. He said he was scared, that his daddy had left them at the theatre and was late picking them up. Panic turned to rage. In my bathrobe, curlers, and slippers, I ran out into the snowy, frigid twilight. I sped to the theatre, screamed at my kids, and raced to the bar with the kids flying behind me, one in each hand. I saw him. Making what must have sounded like an inhuman war cry, I grabbed him behind the neck and yanked him onto the floor. I knew then I was as sick— or sicker—than he was.

Deteriorating self-care can damage a family. This story illustrates Annie's disregard for her own welfare and the unhealthy conditions to which her children were exposed. Annie put herself in a stressful position in which her children's welfare depended on a dubious promise from her husband. Her resulting panic and feeling of helplessness led her to respond in a disordered manner: She went out in the cold inappropriately dressed, sped on snow-covered highways, publicly screamed at her children and physically attacked her husband. The children were exposed to their father's neglect and abandonment, their mother's humiliating behavior in public and a violent confrontation between their parents. This single lapse in self-care weakened and damaged the family. A more chronic and general breakdown in self-care is common in addictive families.

Habits of self-care, vigorously maintained, provide a family with strength and a sense of dignity and well-being. There are three important aspects of self-care: (1) general health and hygiene, (2) maintenance of safety, well-being and comfort and (3) management of stress. Each individual assumes some responsibility for himself in these areas, and the adults in a family assume additional responsibility to establish routines for the children. Exercise 1 on pages 60–63 provides you with one method of assessing the ways in which the members of your family care for themselves.

TAKING CARE OF YOUR GENERAL HEALTH AND HYGIENE

Many books have been written on the importance of good general health and hygiene practices. Included in this category are such things as good dental hygiene, sound nutrition, regular exercise and sleeping habits, abstinence from cigarettes and other harmful substances, moderate use of caffeine and alcohol (by non-problem drinkers) and healthy sexual activity. Another important ingredient is good care for ill family members (e.g., increased rest, compliance with physicians' instructions) and the overall valuing of good health. Clothing should be comfortable and appropriate for the weather. Although this recital may sound basic and familiar, many families fall short of basic standards. Addictive families usually do worse.

Organizing the health and nutrition habits of the family may provide you with one direct way to progress in your journey from Region I to Region II. By completing the following checklist, "General Health and Hygiene," you will gain more information about your wants, standards, strengths and feelings. Based upon this information, you may be in a position to make better decisions regarding your family's health so that you may then adopt a small, manageable number of new practices, and learn to maintain them. Adhering to a new, healthy discipline takes you out of Region I and places you in Region II: expending effort with the hope of improving health, vigor and fitness.

EXERCISE 1

GENERAL HEALTH AND HYGIENE

A. *Nutrition*

1. Place the first initial of each family member in the appropriate slot on the scale below. More than one person's initial may go in a single slot.

Underweight		*Healthy*		*Overweight*
1	2	3	4	5

Initials: _____ _____ _____ _____ _____

2. Do you eat a balanced diet?

_____ Yes. I draw foods from all four food groups each day.

_____ Not consistently.

_____ I don't know.

_____ No. My diet is unhealthy.

3. Do you promote sound nutrition in your children?

_____ Yes. They eat a balanced diet.

_____ Not consistently.

_____ I don't know.

_____ No. They primarily eat junk foods or otherwise incomplete meals.

4. Do any members of your family engage in destructive eating patterns? (Place the initial of each person next to his or her pattern.)

60

_____ Overeating   _____ Overuse of laxatives

_____ Binge eating   _____ Undereating

_____ Vomiting to purge calories

B. _Exercise_

Do you: _Yes_   _No_

1. Know the types of exercise that may help prevent heart attacks and increase your physical stamina?   _____   _____

2. Seek your physician's advice regarding an exercise program?   _____   _____

3. Know how to take your own pulse and monitor the effects of exercise?   _____   _____

4. Get regular strenuous exercise such as jogging, swimming or racquetball, for at least twenty minutes three times per week, with your physician's OK?   _____   _____

5. Get exercise of any type as a consistent part of your life?   _____   _____

6. Provide regular opportunities for your children to exercise?   _____   _____

7. Provide your children with regular instruction to increase their physical skills?   _____   _____

C. _Miscellaneous Hygiene_

Do you:

(Place the first initial of each family member in the appropriate column.)

Yes	_Sometimes_	_No_	
_____	_____	_____	1. Smoke cigarettes?
_____	_____	_____	2. Abuse alcohol?
_____	_____	_____	3. Abuse mood-altering drugs?
_____	_____	_____	4. Suffer from insomnia?
_____	_____	_____	5. Maintain consistent bedtimes on school or work nights?
_____	_____	_____	6. Dress appropriately for the weather?

	Yes	Sometimes	No	
	_____	_____	_____	7. Shower or bathe regularly?
	_____	_____	_____	8. Wear clean clothes?
	_____	_____	_____	9. Wash your hair regularly?
	_____	_____	_____	10. Fear that you have offensive breath or body odor?
	_____	_____	_____	11. Depend upon many cups of coffee to keep you alert during the day?
	_____	_____	_____	12. Dress neatly?
	_____	_____	_____	13. Dress attractively?
	_____	_____	_____	14. Maintain good grooming habits?
	_____	_____	_____	15. Get enough rest during illnesses?
	_____	_____	_____	16. Follow doctors' advice when ill?
	_____	_____	_____	17. "Borrow" medications prescribed for friends and family members?
	_____	_____	_____	18. Get angry at family members when they say they are sick?
	_____	_____	_____	19. Pretend to be sick to receive special privileges or to be excused from responsibilities?
	_____	_____	_____	20. Maintain good dental hygiene?

D. *Parental Guidance on Self-care*

Do you promote habits of good health in your children? (If you respond differently to each of your children, mark your response to each by using the child's first initial rather than a check mark in the items below.)

Do you:	Yes	Not Consistently	No	Does Not Apply
a. State rules concerning hygiene?	_____	_____	_____	_____
b. Provide reminders when necessary?	_____	_____	_____	_____

62

	Yes	Not Consistently	No	Does Not Apply
Do you:				
c. Praise or acknowledge the children's efforts?	____	____	____	____
d. Through your behavior, act an example of good hygiene?	____	____	____	____
e. Provide corrective feedback when the children fall short of standards?	____	____	____	____
f. Furnish the necessary resources (e.g., vitamins, toothbrushes, transportation, etc.) to enable the kids to remain fit and healthy?	____	____	____	____

PROTECTING SAFETY, WELL-BEING AND COMFORT

Maintaining safety, well-being and comfort may be impossible at all times in some families and at some times in every family. Addictive families are at risk for incest, family violence, serious accidents, verbal abuse, neglect and other threats to well-being. The mere fact that one person is emotionally unavailable to his family during (and sometimes between) periods of intoxication increases significant distress. A family can strengthen itself by evaluating sources of discomfort and safety risks like fire, leaving kids with an intoxicated care-taker, driving while intoxicated, violence and incest. Steps already taken by the family to promote safety and well-being are well worth noting. They may include such things as family rules governing bedtimes, playing with matches and sobriety of drivers. An understanding of steps already taken is the platform upon which new initiative can be launched.

Any rule that eliminates needless risks allows the family to feel stronger. For example, one family drew up a contract with its eighteen-year-old hashish-dependent daughter. It provided that she would move out of the home—either voluntarily or with police assistance, if necessary—if she were to abuse other family members either verbally or physically. After the contract was signed, her chronic physical abuse of her mother stopped completely, even though her drug use continued.

Steps taken to increase security, comfort and well-being will bolster

63

the family's self-esteem and confidence. Changing dangerous family patterns, especially those pertaining to incest and abuse, will require outside assistance. Many families struggle in isolation, shame and despair because they fear that if they ask for help they will have to face a sudden, horrifying public exposure of family secrets, that outsiders will take control and that the destructive forces in the family will be unleashed.

If you find yourself in a dangerous situation, we urge you to seek a confidential assessment from a professional you trust. Taking the initiative will give you more control in the situation than you will have if you wait until abuse or incest is accidentally discovered by the outside world. You may be in a position to prevent an acute catastrophe or the destruc-

Diagram 2
INCREASING SELF-CARE ACTIVITIES

Region	Examples of Possible Actions
III Empowerment	Maintaining close and lively contact with other people Regularly planning things to look forward to Taking direct action on problems Practicing sound health and exercise habits to maintain fitness and vigor Living a balanced lifestyle
II Effort	Trying new ways to relax Exploring new hobbies and outlets Focusing attention on problems as they arise Teaching safety and health habits to the children Beginning to exercise Learning to eat a balanced diet
I Exasperation	Remaining isolated Living carelessly Neglecting personal hygiene Failing to provide adequate supervision for children Ignoring signs of problems

tion of the spirit that occurs when you live in a dangerous situation for a long time. Eliminating sources of danger and chaos is essential in moving from Region I to Region II. Actions taken to increase your level of comfort and well-being eventually can take you into Region III. Take a look at Diagram 2 for some ideas.

The second part of Exercise 1, "Safety, Well-being and Comfort," found below, provides you with an opportunity to evaluate the ways in which your family maintains its health, safety, and general well-being.

SAFETY, WELL-BEING AND COMFORT

A. Safety: Following is a list of habits, practices or conditions that either protect family safety or jeopardize it.

Does it happen in the family?			Is it permitted by the family?			
Yes	Some-times	No	Yes	Some-times	No	
___	___	___	___	___	___	1. Driving under the influence of alcohol or drugs
___	___	___	___	___	___	2. Carrying weapons
___	___	___	___	___	___	3. Hitchhiking or picking up hitchhikers
___	___	___	___	___	___	4. Arguing with hostile strangers
___	___	___	___	___	___	5. Driving without seatbelts
___	___	___	___	___	___	6. Living, working or playing in a high-crime area
___	___	___	___	___	___	7. Leaving chidren under the age of ten at home unsupervised

	Does it happen in the family?			*Is it permitted by the family?*			
	Yes	Some-times	No	Yes	Some-times	No	
	——	——	——	——	——	——	8. Leaving children unattended in parks, outdoors and in other public places
	——	——	——	——	——	——	9. Keeping weapons in the home
	——	——	——	——	——	——	10. Associating with violent people
	——	——	——	——	——	——	11. Physical abuse
	——	——	——	——	——	——	12. Leaving kids with intoxicated care-taker
	——	——	——	——	——	——	13. Engaging in sexual activity with children
	——	——	——	——	——	——	14. Exposing children to poisonous substances, paint chips and electrical sockets
	——	——	——	——	——	——	15. Playing with matches

It may seem very basic, even to the point of insult, to be asked to consider whether your family follows elementary health and safety practices. We encourage you to complete the exercise even if it seems too basic for your family. Many addictive families are unable to sustain the basics of self-care. Be sure to acknowledge the strengths indicated in your answers to items.

Exercise 1 is the first of several exercises in this section of the book. Each is designed to increase understanding of an important aspect of family life. To add to the value of this experience, we have provided summary tables in Appendices 4, 6 and 8 so you can compile examples from the various exercises. One look at a completed appendix will give you a quick overview of the journey you have undertaken. Review your answers to Exercise 1. For each family member, select one example of a *current* want, standard and strength, a *neglected* want, standard and strength (one that is no longer active), and a *new* want, standard and strength that could be developed with some effort.

To help you think about self-care in terms of wants, standards and strengths, consider the example of a client whom we will call Cathy. She submitted the following list two weeks after her husband stopped drinking:

Examples from Cathy's Appendix 4 List
A. General health and hygiene
    1. Current habits, standards and strengths
        a. I want to be fit so I watch my calories, exercise and keep myself at 135 pounds.
        b. I want my son to be healthy and I take pains to feed him three well-balanced meals a day.
    2. Valuable old habits currently neglected
        a. I want to be alert and to provide consistency for my son, but I no longer get him to bed at a regular time and I stay up most of the night. We are often cranky.
        b. I used to make him brush his teeth twice a day, but lately I've neglected dental hygiene.
    3. New habits to be developed
        a. I want to look attractive and I'm going to learn how to use makeup more artfully and tastefully.
        b. I want my son to feel more comfortable when he has colds, so I am going to learn to give him more T.L.C.

Record your own answers in items A and B in Appendix 4 on pages 268–70. Then we will proceed to the last self-care area.

MANAGING STRESS IN THE FAMILY

Working together, two researchers (Drs. Ayala Pines and Elliott Aronson, in their pamphlet entitled *Burnout*) have developed an excellent framework for understanding the tasks involved in coping with stress. They argue that stress reduction activities can be either passive or active and either directly related to the problem causing the stress or only indirectly related. The "Stress Management" table provides a convenient grouping of these activities. All four groups of activities are useful in reducing stress.

Stress Management

	Type of Activity	
	Active	Inactive
	Purposefully working to reduce stress	*Thinking and talking*
Activities Directly Related to Stressor	Solving problems Eliminating stressors Speaking up Taking action Implementing solutions Learning about the problem	Complaining Thinking about the problem Talking with supportive friends or therapist
	Growing and having fun	*Escaping*
Activities Indirectly Related to Stressor	Recreation/leisure Spiritual activity Exercising Having sex Developing hobbies	Sleeping Daydreaming Idle thinking Resting

Active, Direct Methods of Heading Off Stress

Active, direct methods reduce future stress by getting directly at the source. For example, when the family prohibits drunk driving among its members, it prevents worry and suffering. But when the family procrastinates in tackling a problem—that is, ignores the problem—the situation deteriorates, injuries can result and the suffering continues. One family ignored the problem until after the eighth drunk driving arrest. The father was charged with driving under the influence of alcohol just after the ambulance left the scene with his severely injured passenger—his nine-year-old son.

Successful stress reduction depends on effective problem solving. The seven components of active, direct stress reduction are given in the second part of Exercise 2, on pages 75–76.

Mr. and Mrs. Davis's struggle with son Brad's drunk driving illustrates how each problem-solving component helps reduce family stress. The Davises finally were forced to conclude that Brad had a problem after he pulled into the garage when the garage door was only halfway up, staggered into the house and sneaked into bed. He left the keys in the car, and the engine was still running when his parents went out to inspect the damage. The next morning, Brad was late in getting up and skipped breakfast. As he shot out the front door to avoid talking with his parents, he was confronted by his enraged father. "Your mother and I are furious about your dangerous habits. We have your keys and will hold onto them until we solve this problem." Mr. and Mrs. Davis talked about their dilemma and were baffled. They decided to talk with Mr. Davis's brother, a recovering alcoholic who had been sober for the past four years. At first, he did not give much advice; he mainly listened. The problem got much clearer to them as they talked. Mr. and Mrs. Davis were afraid their son was developing a drinking and drug problem, that he would harm himself and others, that he would seriously jeopardize his future. They decided to focus on the immediate problems first: Prevent an auto fatality and instill in Brad a sense of responsibility that should be a prerequisite for the privilege of driving.

But, how could they do this? As angry as they felt, Mr. and Mrs. Davis's first ideas were punitive: no driving for one year, being grounded for two months, a "trip to the woodshed." Ultimately, they decided to suspend driving privileges until Brad demonstrated an understanding of the dangers of drunk driving, gave a verbal commitment to remain sober and clear-minded whenever he was behind the wheel, and paid for at least half the damage to the car and garage door.

To implement their solution, Mr. and Mrs. Davis had to confront Brad and remain firm. They had to make arrangements for Brad to get to school, work and band practice. They had to get estimates for the necessary repairs. They had to stay alert to any signs of intoxication and learn how to respond. Once Brad earned the right to drive, he complied with the new rules . . . for three weeks.

The night of Brad's senior prom, Mr. and Mrs. Davis detected the faint odor of marijuana smoke as Brad was leaving. If they had confronted him, they would have placed themselves in the position of having to stop him from attending his prom. Sheepishly, they avoided saying anything to him, and neither parent commented on their collusion with Brad's problem. Later that evening, they received a call from Brad. He was at the police station. He had not injured anyone, but he had totaled the car and had been charged with driving under the influence.

Mr. and Mrs. Davis chose not to provide bail until the next morning. They selected a lawyer with a reputation for helping drunk drivers get treatment. Ultimately, with the help of a treatment center, Brad and his parents solved the problem of Brad's drinking and drug use. They were confident that if Brad slipped into his old destructive habit, they knew exactly what to do, and that they were determined to do the right thing. Taken together, these developments significantly reduced the stress that Mr. and Mrs. Davis felt.

During recovery, the family learns to discuss and identify problems, develop solutions, and change its patterns so that stress is reduced.

Inactive, Direct Methods of Relieving Stress

The second part of the table "Stress Management," on page 68, contains examples of direct but inactive coping methods. For instance, complaining is a highly underrated activity. It promotes ventilation of feelings, reorganization of thoughts, clarification of goals and wants, and identification of stressors. Complaining can be extremely valuable. To move forward, families must give themselves permission to complain. This type of stress reduction has gotten a bad name ("You're just feeling sorry for yourself"; "Quit complaining"; "Cut the beefing and *do* something"), because talking can be a way of avoiding action. No single stress-reducing activity is enough to get the job done, yet none can be eliminated. When complaining replaces suffering in silence, the family is getting better.

Increased complaining may create an illusion that things are getting worse, because this form of progress hurts. Hearing a ten-year-old child say, "I hate Daddy. He's always smoking grass with his stupid friends," is difficult, but necessary, for a family. If no one is opening up to complain, developing this form of stress reduction activity is a worthwhile goal for the future.

Active, Indirect Methods of Relieving Stress

Most popular books on stress reduction emphasize relaxation, leisure and physical exercise; the individual is active but is not directly working on solving stressful problems. One of the early beneficial effects of self-help groups or therapy is that family members learn that it is all right to develop their lives. The mother of a thirty-year-old cocaine addict presented this issue directly to one of the authors in the form of a question, "Is it OK that I'm continuing work and that my husband and I play bridge? I feel so guilty playing while my son may be dying." Our answer is an emphatic "Yes!" There is no way to help the addict if *you* stop living, if you let yourself be consumed by the problem.

Building active, indirect stress-reduction outlets will have immediate beneficial effects for you at this point. Resuming neglected exercise routines, attending religious services or picking up discarded hobbies, for example, provides a much-needed reminder that you are alive. These activities remove you from the daily grind, strengthen your sense of purpose and allow you to resume coping with greater strength and self-confidence. The parents of a young adult heroin user reported that through all the horror of their son's addiction, they kept themselves sane by running, swimming, remaining active in community affairs, maintaining an active sex life, socializing with friends and traveling. Children require assistance from their parents to arrange age-appropriate activities. Parks, religious organizations, community centers and clubs are brimming with opportunities.

Inactive, Indirect Methods of Relieving Stress

The fourth and final stress reduction activity is that of escape. Judeo-Christian tradition teaches that even the Almighty rested on the seventh day. But some of us mortals feel compelled to remain productive every waking moment.

Mortimer Adler, the philosopher, argues that three forms of passive experience are essential: idling, rest, and sleep. Adler describes idling as something akin to daydreaming; the mind is active but responds to its own internal agenda, oblivious to the world. His metaphor is that of a car sitting in the driveway with its engine running, disengaged. Thoughts easily enter and leave consciousness. Adler conceives of rest in spiritual terms; he describes it as a state in which an individual opens his mind to the elevating and relaxing effects of, for instance, art. For the secular individual, rest occurs when he contemplates secular images (e.g., paintings, sculpture, philosophy, dance, fantasy), while the religious individual may find rest in prayer, rituals and religious symbols. Few of us challenge the basic human need for refreshing sleep, the last of Adler's passive experiences.

Other familiar indirect, passive methods of relieving stress include television watching, napping, reading and listening to music. Like the other three categories of stress-reducing activity, this group is helpful and enhances family strength. However, overreliance on escape can be counterproductive, primarily because the source of the stress is unchanged.

Now it is time to define the family's strengths in coping with stress.

EXERCISE 2

COPING WITH STRESS

The first step in managing stress is to reflect on the things that have happened to you over the last six months. Unwelcome, uncontrollable, unpredictable, painful changes that affect your everyday life produce the most stress. Desired changes that are under your control and produce few changes in your daily routine create the least stress. Although it is often said that these are stressful times, recent studies indicate that few of us experience more than three of the events on the list below during any six-month period. From our clinical experience, it appears that relatives of addicted individuals lead more stressful lives than their counterparts in nonaddictive families.

The following exercise was developed by Drs. Holmes and Rahe and may give you more perspective on the stressors in your life.* Please note that this list contains dramatic examples of stressors but is not intended to be complete. As you read the list, you may note that when you come across a traumatic event that occurred long ago, you still feel shaken up. If so, you may be suffering the aftereffects of early stressors, thus adding to the difficulty of coping with new problems.

Next to each item below, place the initials of the family member(s) who experienced it during the past six months.

* T. H. Holmes and R. H. Rahe, "The Social Readjustment Rating Scale," *Journal of Psychosomatic Research*, 1967, Vol. II, pp. 213–218.

Initials	Event
_____	Getting married
_____	Troubles with the boss
_____	Detention in jail or other institution
_____	Death of a spouse
_____	Major change in sleeping habits (a lot more or a lot less sleep, or change in part of day when asleep)
_____	Death of a close family member
_____	Major changes in eating habits (a lot more or a lot less food intake, or very different meal hours or surroundings)
_____	Foreclosure on a mortgage or loan
_____	Revision of personal habits (dress, manners, associations, etc.)
_____	Death of a close friend
_____	Minor violations of the law (e.g., traffic tickets, jaywalking, disturbing the peace)
_____	Outstanding personal achievement
_____	Pregnancy
_____	Major change in the health or behavior of a family member
_____	Sexual difficulties
_____	In-law troubles
_____	Major change in number of family get-togethers (e.g., a lot more or a lot less than usual)
_____	Major change in financial state (e.g., a lot worse off or better off than usual)
_____	Gaining a new family member (e.g., through birth, adoption, older relative moving in)
_____	Change in residence
_____	Son or daughter leaving home (e.g., marriage, attending college)
_____	Marital separation from mate

Strengthening the Family

Initials	Event
_____	Major change in church activities (e.g., a lot more or a lot less than usual)
_____	Marital reconciliation with mate
_____	Being fired from work
_____	Divorce
_____	Changing to a different line of work
_____	Major change in the number of arguments with spouse (e.g., either a lot more or a lot less than usual regarding child-rearing, personal habits)
_____	Major change in responsibilities at work (e.g., promotion, demotion, lateral transfer)
_____	Wife beginning or ceasing work outside the home
_____	Major change in working hours or conditions
_____	Major change in usual type and/or amount of recreation
_____	Taking on a mortgage greater than $10,000 (e.g., purchasing a home, business)
_____	Taking on a mortgage or loan less than $10,000 (e.g., purchasing a car, TV, freezer)
_____	Major personal injury or illness
_____	Major business readjustment (e.g., merger, reorganization, bankruptcy)
_____	Major change in social activities (e.g., clubs, dancing, movies, visiting)
_____	Major change in living conditions (e.g., building a new home, remodeling, deterioration of home or neighborhood)
_____	Retirement from work
_____	Vacation
_____	Changing to a new school
_____	Beginning or ceasing formal schooling

List below any major changes you experienced in the last six months that do not appear above.

_____

_____

_____

_____

_____

Methods of Reducing Stress

ACTIVE, DIRECT

When faced with an important problem or opportunity, how effectively do you approach each of the following steps? Rate each item below by checking how effectively you tackle each step.

When a situation calls for me to: *I am:*

	Effective	Sometimes Effective	Often Ineffective
1. Quickly and naturally focus my attention on problems as they arise	____	____	____
2. Define problems clearly to promote problem solving	____	____	____
3. Talk with others to get information, support and help in organizing an approach to the problem	____	____	____
4. Think of alternative solutions	____	____	____
5. Take direct action by asserting myself and making arrangements with others	____	____	____
6. Take direct action by doing independent work (e.g., writing, working with my hands)	____	____	____

When a situation calls for me to: *I am:*

	Effective	*Sometimes Effective*	*Often Ineffective*
7. Follow up and stick with routines designed to prevent problems in the future	_____	_____	_____

8. List three examples of problems you have solved in time to prevent stress. Which of the steps listed above, if any, did you use?

9. List three examples of problems that got out of hand and led to more stress than was necessary. Where did the process break down? Was it in one of the steps listed above? Was it some other problem?

INACTIVE, DIRECT

Think about your average weekly routine. How often do you focus your attention on stressors in each of the following ways?

	Often	*Sometimes*	*Rarely or Never*
1. Talking with friends	_____	_____	_____
2. Talking with family members	_____	_____	_____
3. Talking with coworkers or colleagues	_____	_____	_____
4. Talking with a therapist	_____	_____	_____
5. Writing letters or in a diary	_____	_____	_____
6. Reflecting in a setting that allows for focused, uninterrupted thinking (e.g., a sanctuary, bathtub, health club)	_____	_____	_____

ACTIVE, INDIRECT

In many families, particularly those that contain an addict, we have observed that family members have little or nothing to look forward to. They lack activities or involvements that would increase their sense of vitality and equip them to deal with stress more productively. The questions below first examine routine activities, then later examine activities you can engage in specifically during stressful times.

How often do you engage in the following activities?

	Twice or more a week	Once a week	One to 3 times a month	Less than once a month	Less than once a year
1. Engage in strenuous exercise	___	___	___	___	___
2. Participate in social sports (e.g., tennis or basketball)	___	___	___	___	___
3. Engage in sexual activity	___	___	___	___	___
4. Go out on a "date"	___	___	___	___	___
5. Attend public events	___	___	___	___	___
6. Go to meetings of religious or community groups	___	___	___	___	___
7. Attend religious services or engage in religious ritual	___	___	___	___	___
8. Attend public lectures	___	___	___	___	___
9. Attend artistic performances or movies	___	___	___	___	___
10. Listen to music	___	___	___	___	___
11. Go to restaurants	___	___	___	___	___
12. Work on a hobby	___	___	___	___	___
13. Receive instruction in a class or in private lessons	___	___	___	___	___
14. Take vacations	___	___	___	___	___
15. Practice a skill for enjoyment and learning	___	___	___	___	___
16. Learn through reading	___	___	___	___	___

	Twice or more a week	Once a week	One to 3 times a month	Less than once a month	Less than once a year
17. Explore new environments	____	____	____	____	____
18. Donate your time to a community group or professional society	____	____	____	____	____
19. Go out with friends	____	____	____	____	____
20. Engage in a spiritual discipline (e.g., yoga, meditation, prayer, confession, study)	____	____	____	____	____
21. Play with children or other family members	____	____	____	____	____
22. Work around the house	____	____	____	____	____
23. Build something	____	____	____	____	____
24. Take a walk (alone, with a friend, with a pet)	____	____	____	____	____

When feeling under pressure, which of the above activities help you relieve tension?

INACTIVE, INDIRECT

How much time do you devote to each of the following activities? Rate only those activities that apply to you.

	Too much	Generally an appropriate amount	Too little	Does not apply
1. Watching TV	____	____	____	____
2. Drinking alcoholic beverages	____	____	____	____
3. Smoking	____	____	____	____
4. Forcing myself to forget about problems	____	____	____	____

	Too much	Generally an appropriate amount	Too little	Does not apply
5. Daydreaming	____	____	____	____
6. Shopping (to relieve anxiety) for things I don't need	____	____	____	____
7. Taking baths or showers	____	____	____	____
8. Sleeping	____	____	____	____
9. Eating	____	____	____	____
10. Using street drugs	____	____	____	____
11. Using prescribed tranquilizers	____	____	____	____
12. Resting quietly	____	____	____	____
13. Clearing my mind	____	____	____	____
14. Going to the movies	____	____	____	____
15. Praying or meditating	____	____	____	____
16. Looking at pictures or photos	____	____	____	____
17. Listening to music	____	____	____	____

Now review your ratings in each of the four portions of the table. Select one current, one neglected, and one potential new strength from each. Record each example in the appropriate space in Part C of Appendix 4. It will be useful for each family member to complete this task, even the children. Having gained a richer understanding of self-care, you may be ready to think about how others have put their insights to work. Now look at Appendix 5, which focuses on stress management and provides a format that others have used to develop successful action plans. It may be a useful guide for organizing your own thinking as you plan your efforts to manage stress more effectively.

Chapter 4

Living a Full Life

Families vary in their determination to live a full life and maintain their values. As a result, they also differ in the way they decide when enough is enough and when to take decisive action. Some go so far as to allow the addict to ruin their lives, to cut off all ties with the outside world. For example, Allen permitted his son to destroy his home—four times—including priceless family heirlooms and antiques, before taking definitive action. Joan quit her job, left her church and cut off relationships with friends before presenting her husband with the choice of treatment or a divorce. It took his drunken attempt on her life to prompt her to take firm action.

Other families act much sooner. One woman who maintained active relationships and pursuits took action at the first sign that her husband's drinking threatened her relationships with others. Helen sought help after a party in which her husband drunkenly screamed insults at her. She had allowed herself to endure twelve years of infidelity, nightly drinking, irrational tirades, long absences and other private horrors. But when her husband's drinking threatened her ties to the outside world, when it prevented her from being the kind of person she needed to be in public, she acted boldly. She confronted him about his unacceptable behavior and demanded that he enter treatment as a prerequisite for continuing the marriage.

Lauren Bacall described her breaking point in her 1979 autobiography. Like Helen, she knew she had to act decisively after a critical incident in which her own feelings and behavior were abhorrent to her. No longer could she smother her self-respect.

It all came to a head in the summer of 1963. He'd had a two-day siege and come home feeling very sick. I had made up my mind by then that he would have to do something positive. Life was becoming unbearable. Success didn't help—reassurance, love, the children. Nothing did. And I was turning into someone I didn't like. I'd continually lie to Mother—try to keep her from coming over without telling her why. I'd gathered our friends at home for a surprise party for Jason's fortieth birthday, telling him only that a couple of people were coming by for a drink after his show. I had a cake all ready. When the clock struck two, it was clear he had made other plans—and who knew when he'd show up? A few stalwarts stayed, the others left. When he finally did walk in, loaded, I was in such a state that I grabbed a bottle of vodka, turned it upside down, and smashed it into the cake. "Here's your goddamn cake!" When I realized that what I wanted to do was slam it over his head, that I was capable of violence, it frightened me so that I knew I would finally have to act.

The effects an addict may have on his family exist along a continuum that increases steadily in seriousness. Families sometimes feel helpless to stop the progression of the reign of terror along the continuum. On one end may be simple distaste for the addict's private antics. Further along may come public embarrassment at his behavior. As the effects escalate in seriousness, families sometimes fear that, actively or by mistake, the addict may threaten their safety or property. At the extreme, family members may believe their lives are in danger.

Continuum of Escalating Effects:
When Do People Act?

Distaste for addict's behavior	Public embarrassment; distaste for own behavior	Threat to safety/property	Endangered lives
	Helen Lauren Bacall	Allen	Joan

—————————— seriousness increases ——————→

Sometimes family members must rely on others to help them see what is going on. Frequently, outsiders are more aware than family members when they allow their lives to shrink and when they abandon their values and aspirations.

Whether their motivation comes from their personal experiences or in reaction to comments made by people outside the family, when do families decide to act? When do they become determined to fight their way out of the exasperation and chaos of Region I? In Alcoholics Anonymous, it is said that the alcoholic stops drinking when he hits bottom; that is, when he undergoes so much loss and humiliation that he no longer can maintain the illusion that his drinking is under his control. He is forced to recognize that alcohol has made his life unmanageable. How quickly a family hits bottom (i.e., recognizes that addictive behaviors are making family life unmanageable and that the addict is not under their control) depends on how accurately family members answer the four questions. To the extent that you know which experiences you want and which you detest, which of your choices and actions make you proud and which shame you, which situations stir feelings that enrich your life and which detract from it, you will feel the motivation to take action to leave chaos behind you. To the extent that you know and exercise your strengths, you will feel confident in your ability to live a full life. The strength and vitality you gain from living a full life will help you confront the addiction. Conversely, to the extent to which you are unable to answer the four questions, you will be mired in confusion. To the extent that you settle for an empty life, you will feel helpless, and you will lack the energy and confidence to confront the addiction. Your bottom will be very low. Living a full life is at the core of recovery. Knowing how to live a full life and insisting on doing so made it possible for Helen to act so soon while Joan had to wait much longer. Diagram 3 gives some sample actions to help you live a fuller life.

Task A—Clarifying Wants, Standards, Strengths and Feelings

Exercise 3 provides you with an opportunity to examine some of your opinions about yourself. Such an examination will help you lay the foundation for a fuller life.

The emphasis here is to flesh out your idea of a full life. Go over your

Diagram 3
LIVING A FULL LIFE: ENDING THE PAIN

Region	Examples of Possible Actions
III Empowerment	Relaxing with friends at home after making the house comfortable and inviting. Feeling confident and being assertive when under fire at work. Going to a family gathering feeling proud and energized.
II Effort	Remembering a few proud moments, not knowing how to find them again. Searching memory for fulfilling past experiences. Forging a boundary between Region I and Region II. Feeling determined to prevent one more loss, one more scene, one more humiliation, one more terrifying fight, even if it means kicking the addict out of the house.
I Exasperation	Feeling enraged when the addict fails to show up at his own party. Being humiliated at a family gathering. Being afraid of the addict's rage. Watching the addict trash family heirlooms.

replies to the items in Exercise 3 and pick out the implied wants, standards, strengths and feelings as they apply to your family. Then turn to Appendix 6 to record examples in the summary table. Children may be able to add their own items to the list, depending on their level of psychological development and the level of communication achieved by the family. Methods of getting started are presented in Appendix 7. In a later chapter and exercise, we will examine some of the ways in which you can stop addiction from interfering with your attempts to enrich your life.

EXERCISE 3

CLARIFYING WANTS, STANDARDS, STRENGTHS AND FEELINGS

1. I see people in the following settings on a consistent basis: [List places (e.g., school, work, health club) or groups (e.g., a circle of friends, parties, the Shriners) in the columns below to indicate how regularly you see people in each. One item per column is sufficient.]

	At least weekly	At least monthly	At least quarterly	At least annually	Less than once a year
Example	Work	Health club	Church	Hometown	Old high school friends

2. Complete the following sentences:

    a. My favorite people _____

    _____

    b. My favorite activities are _____

    _____

    c. I will not let anyone or anything interfere with _____

    _____

    d. The people closest to me are _____

    _____

    e. My favorite pleasures are _____

    _____

    f. I enjoy _____

    _____

g.   I did the right thing when I _____

_____

h.   When I am at my best, I am _____

_____

i.   I am committed to _____

_____

j.   I like myself best when _____

_____

k.   I want _____

_____

l.   If only [addicted person] were sober, I would _____

_____

_____

m.   Without [addicted person] as an active part of my life, I am _____

_____

_____

n.   I am good at _____

_____

o.   Other people think I can _____

_____

3.   Describe a situation in which you did at least one thing well. Highlight the aspect of your behavior you most associate with a feeling of self-respect.

_____

_____

_____

_____

_____

Task B—Overcoming Barriers to a Full Life

To appreciate the fullness of one's life, to revive desirable commitments that have been cast aside, to protect existing values from the chaos of addiction and to enrich family life in new ways, some families must challenge opinions they have of themselves that inhibit bold action. We offer the items in the table "Overcoming Barriers to a Full Life" as examples of opinion changes that often help build momentum toward recovery.

Overcoming Barriers to a Full Life

Opinions That Weaken	*Opinions that Motivate*
1. I failed myself and my family, and I do not deserve to live a good life.	1. I did the best I knew how to do. I want to live the best life I can. Hurting myself, holding back or being miserable will help no one. I am human and will make mistakes. For now, I'll do the next right thing.
2. There is a blight on my family. We'd better not show our faces. We are pariahs.	2. All families endure pain, shame or vulnerability at some point. There is dignity in accepting and coping with family problems. Some people may "throw stones," but others will respect what we are trying to do.
3. Our lives are awful because of the addiction. They will get better only when the addict learns how terrible he is and pays us back for our trouble. There is nothing I can do until then.	3. Our lives are what we make of them. If I am frustrated, I must want something. If I feel inadequate, there must be something I want to do better. If I feel unfulfilled, there must be something I want to accomplish. I cannot wait for the addict, I must live my life now (and help my children live their lives now). My values, my satisfactions, my problems are my responsibility.

Opinions That Weaken	*Opinions that Motivate*

4. My satisfaction will come when I reform the addict. Then I will have done something really important. The addict has such potential, so much more than I do! If I could be the one to help him, he would take care of me and accept my weaknesses.

4. I cannot save anyone. I have to develop my own strengths, be the best person I can be.

5. The addict is only hurting me, and that does not really matter. If he were hurting others in our family, then I would have to do something. My welfare is unimportant.

5. I will no longer permit anyone to damage me or to stop me from living a full life. I am important, every bit as important as any other member of my family.

6. I am—for the addict—the patient and loving person I myself needed all these years. To be firm right now would be harsh and cruel. It would create, for the addict, the same lousy conditions I have had to live under my whole life.

6. I want support and will seek it. I want to give support, but I can only support health. I can no longer cater to abuse. To coddle an addict is not to help him.

Chapter 5

Developing Support

Families grow stronger as their members develop relationships with people outside the family. Despite stereotypes to the contrary, even people who feel powerful depend on many other people and institutions. Getting support is a sign of strength, not weakness. As you begin the process of recovery, you will become more effective by forming relationships and joining groups.

BUILDING SUPPORTIVE RELATIONSHIPS

Supportive relationships greatly increase the strength of the family in coping with any crisis, including addiction. Each positive relationship with another person or group adds to the vitality of the family. Support, in the form of such positive involvement with other people, is important for four reasons:

1. It strengthens personal identity.
2. It enhances positive aspects of our lives.
3. It increases emotional support and challenge.
4. It increases informational support and challenge.

Strengthening Personal Identity

Other people remind us of who we are, what we do, and when we do it. When asked "Who are you?" most people respond by listing the roles they assume: I am a mother, a husband, an engineer, an American, a son, a sailor, etc. Since addiction and social isolation go hand in hand, family members are often stripped of their roles, and therefore stripped of their identities. For example, the wife of an addicted businessman felt too embarrassed to go to church. For her, this meant that she no longer was a member of her community, and that part of her identity was lost. In recovery, families reverse this process by joining groups and building relationships with others. When we perform our roles well, we think of ourselves as competent. Members of healthy relationships acknowledge each other's competence and enhance each other's self-esteem.

Enhancing Positive Aspects of Our Lives

Relationships and social contacts provide stimulation, variety, recognition, communication, closeness, attraction, intimacy, sense of purpose, useful activity, practical help, challenge and structure, among other satisfying experiences. Many of the best things in life occur with other people. Without contact with others, life can be barren, empty and painful.

Increasing Emotional Support and Challenge

Addicts sometimes command most of the attention in the family, interfering with the family's attempt to understand its everyday world and blinding family members to the possibility of finding support through involvement with others. Events in a chaotic family are difficult to think about and comprehend. In order to develop an understanding, family members must first put their experiences into words that may sound disloyal, provocative or offensive. Without access to supportive listeners, family members can never get past the numerous dead ends in their thinking. Consequently, the family becomes ensnared in its own lack of understanding and its misguided sense of loyalty.

With support, however, experiences—no matter how painful—are accepted, discussed and incorporated into the family's understanding of itself. Families can then describe their everyday life in terms that stick. Today and tomorrow are connected and consistent. There is continuity. In the words of one recovering mother of an addicted child:

Getting support made me feel like I was stepping out of a steel garbage can. Everyone had been beating on the can. I could not hear myself think. My ideas bounced off the walls. They didn't seem real. Learning to talk to my therapist, my [Families Anonymous] group, my husband and finally my daughter helped me out of the drum. I could see. I could describe what I saw.

As family members become involved with people outside the addictive environment, they get sufficient support to understand their dilemma more accurately. Emotional support is a process in which one person listens to another, understands and responds, but does not judge. The speaker learns about his feelings and ideas as he talks (rather than knowing them fully before he talks). Emotional challenge occurs when the listener is more active, confronting the speaker with his own perceptions, without judging or rejecting. Friends can offer both. The two examples in the following dialogues may help to clarify these concepts.

Emotional Support
Pat: Jim slugged me last night.
Joan: Are you OK?
Pat: Yeah, I'm always OK. It just shook me up to see him so angry.
Joan: Oh, how frightening!
(Joan reaches over to touch Pat's arm.)

Emotional Challenge
Pat: Well, I'd better get home. Maybe if I bake Jim a special cake, he won't be so angry tonight.
Joan: Yeah, maybe if the frosting is made out of Valium.
Pat: Jim doesn't have that kind of problem!
Joan: If you want me to butt out I will.
Pat: No, I'm sorry. It's just hard to face the truth.
Joan: I haven't seen Jim sober for two years, and I'm worried about you.
Pat: Thanks.

Increasing Informational Support and Challenge

Informational support and informational challenge are also important. This type of support pertains to information about the way the world works, practical knowledge that helps in problem solving or in accomplishing things. For example, the very sociable wife of one drinker explained her need for informational support during the planning phase of treatment: "I need more than an understanding listener. I've got four very close friends. Talking to them used to help. They are very smart and very caring. But I need more. I need someone to give me information, to tell me my options and to tell me when I screw up." Another example comes from a family in which the drug-addicted husband forced his wife to have sexual relations with one of his friends. When she threatened divorce several years later, he intimated that he would expose her "perverse conduct" in court and take custody of their son. She did not pursue the divorce issue again until two friends convinced her that her husband's threat was ridiculous. She then contacted a lawyer and got her divorce.

Involvement with friends and groups naturally increases our access to expertise generally. When you are involved with people, chances are better that someone will notice if you are doing something dangerous. This principle holds in every problem area, including recovery from addiction. You can be much more effective when you are exposed to others who can provide practical, realistic information, confirm or challenge your ideas and serve as models of competence.

Some family members who have temporarily held themselves back from involvement with others in order to deal with an addict will readily become involved once again with friends and groups. They have already developed the confidence, skills and self-awareness to venture out again, to rebuild their social lives. For others, the process may be far more difficult. Feeling stymied in your attempts to deepen or broaden your involvement with others is another good reason to seek out a self-help group or therapist. Alcoholics Anonymous, Al-Anon and other organizations (see Chapter 11) are extraordinarily open to new people.

Diagram 4 provides one example of how social support may develop over the course of the journey from exasperation to empowerment. Diagram 5 gives a specific example of the romantic journey made by one woman, Barbara, an adult daughter of an alcoholic father. There are many different paths to involvement with other individuals and groups of people. The key is to find ways to have the experiences you want to have with other people, in a way you admire, by using strengths you have, while remaining open to your feelings.

Diagram 4
DEVELOPING SUPPORT

Region	Examples of Possible Actions and Consequences			

III
Empowerment
	Commitment
	Intimacy
	Passion
	Companionship
	Stimulation
	Lovability
	Support
	Responsibility
		Achievement
		Financial
		   security
		Teamwork
		Pride in
		   excellent
		   perfor-
		   mance
		Recognition
		Power
		Responsi-
		   bility
			Commitment
			Intimacy
			Support
			Shared interests
			Understanding
			Responsibility
				Contribution
				to achieve-
				   ment of
				   worth-
				   while
				   goals
				Leadership
				Recognition
				Friendship
				Spirituality

	Loving Ro- mance	Productive work	Friendship	Community involve- ment

⇑ ⇑ ⇑ ⇑

PASSAGEWAYS TO REGION III

—Begins to feel drawn to groups and
   individuals

—Begins to feel accepted and to look forward
   to going to meetings or other activities

—Surprise. Finds a promising group or possible
   friend

—Keeps on trying despite weariness and "mistakes"

—Tries new groups but feels pessimistic about them

—"Racks his brains" to find things to do

—Good experiences appear random, haphazard, unreliable

—Forces self to go to self-help groups, despite shame, fear,
   pessimism, alienation

II
Effort

⇑ ⇑ ⇑ ⇑

Isolated and ashamed

Jealous, easily
   threatened

Stripped of all
positive social roles

Bored and empty. Does not
   know who he is or what to do

I
Exasperation

No one to talk to;
confused

Lacks
information
about how to
get things
done. No one
to turn to.

Diagram 5
**FROM EXASPERATION TO EMPOWERMENT IN ROMANTIC RELATIONSHIPS:
BARBARA, AN ADULT CHILD OF AN ALCOHOLIC**

Region	Examples of Possible Actions
III Empowerment	Knowing different ways to relax and get close to one special person Feeling closer and closer to one special person Knowing what kinds of choices and actions she admires on a date Accepting her sexual, romantic, intimacy and companionship needs Knowing what kinds of romantic experiences she looks forward to Knowing what makes her lovable in her own eyes Having a great date with one special man
II Effort	Meeting available, functional, sober men, without making commitments, by attending classes and by joining groups Discovering bit by bit what makes her lovable in her own eyes Discovering her own tastes in clothes and makeup Exercising Dieting No more attempts to join futile battles
I Exasperation	Giving men power to judge worthwhileness Feeling guilty about sexual needs Having panic attacks in sexual encounters Feeling overweight, frumpy, homely Finding dysfunctional men and taking care of them, only to be rejected Dating married men

OVERCOMING BARRIERS TO DEVELOPING SUPPORT

As we think about families we have known, there are relatively few who did not encounter intense resistance from the addict when they began reaching out for support and friendship. One cocaine-addicted mother fined her young adult daughter the amount of the fee every time the daughter went to see her therapist ("one for her and one for me!"). Another woman "drank at" her husband whenever he attended Brotherhood meetings at their church. She also exploded when her husband took their children to Al-Anon meetings, and she insisted on grilling each of them in an intoxicated rage. Jealousy is a common theme that persists even after addiction has stopped. We know many families in which the spouse, child or other family member has tried to talk on the phone to friends (or employers or relatives) while the addict launched a humiliating attack in the background.

Through exploration in therapy, we often have found that addicted individuals react so intensely for a number of reasons. First, outside contacts are viewed as extremely threatening. To maintain the status quo, the addict must continually overwhelm, manipulate or badger family members so that they continue to accept the unacceptable. Relationships with others threaten the addict's grip on the minds and behavior of family members. Second, outside relationships stir up feelings of inadequacy in people who suffer from low self-esteem. Any satisfaction acquired outside of the relationship becomes a symbol of failure, to be opposed or destroyed. Family members often do not know what they want to achieve in the family; they rarely know how to come together in a pleasing way. It is natural for the addicted member to become jealous of outside relationships and to form deep resentments ("Why can't she be that way with me?"). In Region I, addict and family members alike typically feel incomplete as people and view each other as extensions of themselves. Any independent activity may be viewed as foreign and as taking the loved one away, thus producing an unconscious injury to self-esteem. Extreme forms of jealousy are found in people who are not addicted as well as in those who are. We highlight the problem here because it so often comes up as a problem when family members reach out for support.

Addicts frequently resist attempts by their families to get social support. Fortunately, many family members refuse to allow the addiction to control and limit them. All the family members in the previous examples eventually asserted their rights and successfully developed their support systems.

Realizing that the addict has no right to limit your involvement in life is a critical step in recovery. First attempts by family members to assert themselves frequently are met with aggressive opposition by the addict. But, if the family refuses to cater to the addict and consistently asserts the right, say, to be with friends, the family gets stronger. In some cases, the addict accepts the rights of the family; in others, he does not. Ultimately, the family decides how far it will go in its attempts to get better as it comes to terms with the addict's stubbornness.

Other obstacles to seeking support are found in beliefs held by the family. Some of the same resistances discussed in Chapter 4, "Living a Full Life," also inhibit efforts to form relationships (see the table called "Overcoming Barriers to a Full Life" on pages 86–87). Additional obstacles are presented on page 96 in the table called "Overcoming Barriers to Developing a Support System."

Completing Exercise 4 will help you identify current, neglected and potential assets in your social world. In Part II of the exercise, we ask you to identify the experiences that are missing from your life. As you think about them, you may become aware of attitudes like those described in the table on "Overcoming Barriers to Developing a Support System" that block you from creating satisfying experiences with other people.

Exercise 5, "Relationship Sketch," offers you the opportunity to take a closer look at one specific relationship. As you complete it, your attention will be drawn to elements of relationships that influence how affection, closeness and mutual interests develop. It may seem as if relationships form in a random way and that there is nothing you can do to get closer to someone you are interested in. But relationships take shape over time and are the results of many small efforts. We do not mean to imply that a cookbook could be written offering step-by-step instructions to create friendships. However it sometimes helps to see a problem reduced to a few key concepts. By using Exercise 5, you will likely become aware of possible steps you could take to broaden or deepen your relationship with a *willing* loved one.

Overcoming Barriers to Developing a Support System

Opinions That Block Action	*Opinions That Motivate*
1. Groups (churches, clubs, etc.) are only open to families. If I went alone, people would think I was weird. I'm angry that he won't go with me, and he's in no shape to go even if he were willing. I refuse to consider going alone.	1. I am very disappointed in the way our family has turned out, but I can't stop living. There must be room for me in the community. I'll find a group that will accept me and meet my needs, even though I may have to look for a while, and even though I'll have to go without him.
2. I became part of one group—my family—and it failed. I failed. I am afraid to meet other people only to be rejected again. Other people will see in me what my family sees and treat me just as poorly—because I deserve it.	2. The family has been distorted by addiction. I have to take the chance that others will respond to me in a healthier way. I will likely run into people who treat me poorly as I try to get involved in something better, but I *will* meet some nice people if I keep looking.
3. I owe all of my time and energy to my family. Any time spent with others is a sign of disloyalty.	3. If I am getting support apart from my family, I will have more energy and purpose when I am with my family. No one owns my time. I am prepared to stand up for the way I want to spend it. I am entitled to enjoy relationships with people outside the family.

DEVELOPING SUPPORT

Part I: Current experiences. Think of one example of each of the following social situations in your life during the past six months:

Type of Situation	*Relationship* (name of person or type of relationship to the other person(s) involved in the experience)	*Description* (what happened, where, and how was it gratifying?)
Interesting experience		
Receiving acknowledgement for something good, one of my strengths, something I did well		
Discussing an interesting topic		
Discussing a personal or intimate topic		
Feeling close		
Feeling mutual attraction		
Giving or receiving help with something		
Honoring a commitment		
Meeting regularly with the same person for recreation or to participate in a group, meeting or class		
Giving or receiving emotional support or challenge		
Giving or receiving informational support or challenge		
Playing a valuable role (e.g., mother, father, friend, coworker)		
Belonging to a group and feeling accepted		

Part II: Neglected desires, standards, feelings and strengths. Go back through the list to identify social situations that once were more readily available in your life than they are now. Do you see any that could be renewed or increased? It is sometimes easier to revive a neglected habit or friendship than to start a new one.

List satisfactions that are now missing from your life but were once more important.

Type of situation or satisfaction	Relationship (who?)	Description (what, where, how?)

Part III: Potential strengths. List social satisfactions that might enrich your life.

Type of situation or satisfaction	Relationship (who?)	Description (what, where, how?)

EXERCISE 5

RELATIONSHIP SKETCH

Begin by thinking of a person with whom you have an important relationship you would like to understand better. Write his or her name here: _____
  Now complete the following items:

1. Type of relationship (e.g., wife, friend, boss): _____

2. List the activities you typically engage in together. Include leisure, work and growth-oriented activities.

3. List the content areas you typically discuss with each other. Place each topic in the appropriate column below.

Nonintimate	Moderately intimate	Highly intimate

4. Who talks most about each of the above topics? Place your answer next to each topic in item 3, above (I = I talk most; P = Person listed above; M = Mutual).

5. Describe your feelings about this relationship.
   a. General feelings and perceptions

   b. Positive feelings

   c. Irritations and other negative feelings

6. How close is your friendship? (Place an X on the scale below.)

```
├─────────────────────────┼─────────────────────────┤
```
Very distant/superficial   Cordial but not   Extremely close and
                                particularly close   intimate

7. How well do you communicate feelings about the relationship and about each other?
   a. Do you tell each other about feelings you stir up in each other?

      Positive feelings?

      Negative feelings?

   b. Do you ever touch? (Touch includes any form of contact ranging from a handshake or a backslap to intimate sexual contact.)

8. When problems develop, how confident are you that they will be resolved?

9. Invitations: Who initiates shared activities in the relationship?
   Circle one number on the scale below.

   I do exclusively   My friend does exclusively

      1   2   3   4   5

Now, turn to Appendix 8 to record memorable examples from the "Developing Support" and "Relationship Sketch" exercises. Then review Appendix 9, which describes some of the ways in which others have successfully begun the task of increasing the quality and quantity of support in their lives.

Your family will gain vitality and confidence as you learn how to increase self-care activities, live a full life and develop social support. Our focus so far has remained with family members rather than on the addicted relative: How do you increase your vitality and self-esteem? How do you weaken yourselves? Up to this point we have focused on the addict only insofar as he interfered with your efforts to recover either directly or indirectly (by sapping your energy or diverting your attention). It is time to pick up where we left off in Chapter 2 and begin a detailed examination of your relationship with the addicted family member. In so doing, you may discover the choices and actions you take in relation to him that lead you repeatedly into exasperation in Region I.

So far in this book, we have helped you define the problems directly related to the addict's drug abuse. You have studied the characteristics of your family and have discovered ways to strengthen the family and counter the damaging effects of the addiction. Now it's time to use this strong family unity to confront the addict.

Confronting the Addiction

Chapter 6

Using the Benefits of Family Membership to Support Family Health

Most support given to the addict, ranging from small favors to the continuation of relationships, is given on a voluntary basis. Yet it never seems that way. It can seem as if you have no control over your own actions. The pressure of daily life with an addict dulls awareness (and therefore freedom) of choice. Struggling to control the uncontrollable— another's drug use—creates the illusion that nothing is under control as the family's material and emotional resources are consumed by the addiction. In some families, those resources directly support the purchase of drugs; more often, however, the addiction grows because of support that is not quite as direct. This kind of support allows the addict to escape the consequences of drug use.

Gary Crosby, son of Bing Crosby and now a recovering polydrug abuser, described how his wife Barbara used her leverage first in the service of the addiction, then finally in the service of health.

Episode I: Helping the addict avoid the consequences of addiction

For the next four days I stayed loaded in my room while Barbara gathered up my music and tuxedos and negotiated with the powers that be to let me out of my contract without having to pay them a fortune. One night while she was sleeping I sneaked downstairs to the bar, then came back to the room an hour later with some total stranger, another lush I must have picked up on the street. I have no idea what was going through my drunken mind, but

103

I shook her awake and forced her to write the guy a check for a hundred dollars.

Barbara did her best to watch me every second, but I was uncontrollable. On the flight back to L.A. I conned the stewardesses into plying me with booze in the lavatory. Then an hour out of Chicago I tried to jimmy open the emergency exit and walk off the plane. Barbara grabbed me just in time. I don't think I wanted to kill myself. My Catholic upbringing said that if I did I'd go to Hell. I only wanted to drink myself to death or provoke someone else into killing me. The cops were waiting at the airport, ready to haul me off to jail. Barbara somehow talked them out of it and promised she wouldn't let me drive home. That's all I had to hear. The moment they disappeared I pushed her out of the driver's seat and tore back to the house at eighty miles an hour.

Episode II: Using leverage to withdraw support from addiction

Finally the phone rang. It was Barbara's attorney. He told me to get hold of my lawyer and bring him to his office Thursday morning at ten o'clock. Barbara was already there when I showed up, but she stayed silent and let her lawyer do all the talking. "Your wife loves you too much to see you kill yourself," he said. "So you'll either go to this place in Connecticut to dry out and never take another drink the rest of your life, or she's going to leave you. What'll it be?" Barbara was taking a chance. She knew I was not a guy to accept that kind of ultimatum kindly. Throw a challenge in my face and I'd automatically throw it right back at you just out of principle. But something clicked in my head—the same way it had that night at the Flamingo when she told me to stop beating on that stranger and get back in my seat. I may not have shown it much, but when all was said and done I loved her and I loved Steve and didn't want to lose either of them. I still didn't think I had a drinking problem, but since she did I had to go along with her. "Okay," I answered, "I'll do it. Make the reservations."

It had all been taken care of beforehand. Barbara drove me to the plane the next morning. I'd hidden a jug of vodka in my flight bag, and by the time I arrived at Silver Hill I was too drunk to see straight. But at least I was there.

In the first example, Barbara Crosby used her power to protect Gary from the consequences of his addiction. In the second, she used her freedom to continue or discontinue the relationship to promote recovery. She was determined that chaos in her life was going to stop one way or the other, married or divorced. Note that she could not control his drinking, even after the confrontation and after his decision to get into treatment. Her lawyer (a source of practical, informational support and challenge) stated the conditions (her limits) under which she would remain with her husband (a benefit of family membership to him). He could choose to meet those conditions or not.

To set realistic goals, you must first determine how much leverage you already have. How does the drug or alcohol user rely on you? The table "Benefits Controlled by the Family" on pages 106–7 illustrates some of the resources and other benefits of family membership typically controlled by family members.

When asked to list the resources under their control, family members often draw a blank. They have made so many decisions automatically! If drugs have been in charge of your family, even the idea that some family resources are under your control may be very strange to you. You may think that if you care about the addict, you cannot or should not withhold anything from him. You may feel guilty and believe that you owe him anything and everything you give. Fear may blind you to the real control you could have: "If I stop pretending, will he leave me? Kill me? Destroy my future?" Loved ones often think they are not entitled to pleasure, peace and the pursuit of happiness. We are reminded of a drinker who always grabbed his wife's purse and checkbook in the midst of a drunken fight. After scaring her and reminding her that he was "boss," he would let *her* apologize and try to win back *his* approval. The wife, in this case, believed for many years that her husband was right, that she was not entitled to challenge her husband's dictatorial control.

IDENTIFYING BENEFITS CONTROLLED BY THE FAMILY

We now address two questions: (1) Which family benefits are under your control? and (2) Which of your family's resources now support addiction? Perhaps as you read the table of "Benefits Controlled by the Family," you will begin to think of your own examples. List them now, then move on to Exercise 6 to identify others. Later on we will address the question of how to use the family's strengths, in the service of recovery, to cut off the nutrients that feed the addictive cancer in the family.

Benefits Controlled by the Family:
Examples of How Resources Can Be Used to Support Addiction

Benefit	*Clinical Example*
Material Support	
Money, shelter (a ''home''), food, luxury and maintenance items	Alcoholic twenty-seven-year-old man moves in with brother and family after losing his job, gets free room and board. He spends his unemployment check on alcohol, paying $5 a week in rent.
Effort	
Advocacy: covering, arranging; attention, problem solving, rescuing	Cocaine-dependent attorney neglects his clients. Office staff covers with clients; spouse covers with partner. Friend arranges a series of meetings with new firms. Adolescent son repeatedly drives to the office to bring dad home after two-to-three-day cocaine binges in the office.
Companionship	
Conversation, sex, emotional support, stimulation, recreation	Wife and child return home after separation when Quaalude-addicted father/husband complains that he is lonely.
Confirmation/Reassurance	
Confirmation that the relationship is OK, commitment to the addict's well-being	Valium-and-alcohol-dependent wife/mother withdraws into isolation. Family goes on as if nothing is wrong. She retains the appearance of respectability in the community. Complaints about her intoxicated rages make her aware that her family is responding to her drinking, but the fact that life goes on as usual reassures her that nothing is really wrong.

Exercise 6 will help you identify the benefits of family membership that could be under your control. Go through the items and respond to each.

BENEFITS CONTROLLED BY THE FAMILY: A SELF-RATING CHECKLIST

Material Support

1. The addicted family member depends on the family for (check all that apply):

   _____ Shelter (either by living in the home or by paying rent)

   _____ Food

   _____ Medical care

   _____ Entertainment

   _____ Clothing

   _____ Transportation

   _____ Luxury items (e.g., car, jewelry, vacations)

   _____ Educational expenses

   _____ Bail

   _____ Legal fees

2. The addict has used family money to support his addiction:

   _____ Never   _____ Sometimes   _____ Frequently   _____ All the time

3. The addict has sold family property or gifts to support his addiction:

   _____ True   _____ False

4. Family members have cosigned loans or leases for the addicted member:

   _____ True   _____ False

5. Family members have invested in the addict's business:

   _____ True   _____ False

6. Family members have paid off the addict's previous debts:

   _____ True   _____ False

7. The family has had to rescue the addict from financial problems caused by the addiction:

   _____ True   _____ False

8. List additional forms of material support your family gives the addict:

Effort and Attention

1. Family members devote time and attention to the addict's problems:

   _____ True   _____ False

2. Family members cover up when the addict fails to meet obligations (e.g., calling in excuses at the office, sending a note to school, making excuses with the family and friends):

   _____ Never   _____ Rarely   _____ Frequently

3. Without the family's help, the addict might not have been offered his job:

   _____ True   _____ False

4. Without the family's help, the addict might have lost his job or might have been expelled from school:

   _____ True   _____ False

5. Family members have had to rescue the addict when he was incapacitated by the effects of the addiction (e.g., drive him home after he passed out, take him to the hospital, bail him out of jail, pick him up from school):

   _____ True   _____ False

6. The addict's problems are discussed in your house:

   _____ Never   _____ Rarely   _____ Sometimes   _____ Frequently

7. The family must take the addiction into account when planning activities:

   _____ Never   _____ Rarely   _____ Sometimes   _____ Frequently

8. Family members have purchased alcohol or drugs for the addict:

   _____ Never   _____ Rarely   _____ Sometimes   _____ Frequently

9. Family members have arranged legal assistance for the addict:

   _____ True   _____ False

10. List additional examples of effort and attention your family gives the addict:

Companionship

1. The addict depends on the family to spend time with him:

   _____ Never   _____ Rarely   _____ Sometimes   _____ Often

   _____ Whenever he likes

2. Even when the addict is intoxicated and very unpleasant, family members spend time with him:

   _____ Never   _____ Rarely   _____ Sometimes   _____ Often

   _____ Whenever he likes

3. The family excludes the addicted family member when his behavior is inappropriate:

   _____ Not applicable   _____ Rarely   _____ Sometimes   _____ Often

   _____ Whenever his behavior warrants it

4. How satisfied are you with the *amount* of contact you have with the addicted family member in each of the following situations (we will ask about quality later):

	Not applicable	Too little contact	The right amount	Too much
Religious/civic events	_____	_____	_____	_____
Business functions	_____	_____	_____	_____
Family gatherings	_____	_____	_____	_____
Public entertainment and events	_____	_____	_____	_____
Parties	_____	_____	_____	_____
With friends	_____	_____	_____	_____
Private conversations	_____	_____	_____	_____
Sexual intimacy (to be rated privately by spouse)	_____	_____	_____	_____

109

5. How often does the addict get high and/or make you uncomfortable in each of the following situations:

	Never	Rarely	Often
Religious/civic events	___	___	___
Business functions	___	___	___
Family gatherings	___	___	___
Public entertainment and events	___	___	___
Parties	___	___	___
With friends	___	___	___
Private conversations	___	___	___
Sexual intimacy (to be rated privately by the spouse)	___	___	___

6. When you know the addict is going to be unpleasant or high, how often do you force yourself to put up with the situation in spite of your feelings?

	Never	Rarely	Often
Religious/civic events	___	___	___
Business functions	___	___	___
Family gatherings	___	___	___
Public entertainment and events	___	___	___
Parties	___	___	___
With friends	___	___	___
Private conversations	___	___	___
Sexual intimacy (to be rated privately by the spouse)	___	___	___

Confirmation/Reassurance

1. You go on as if nothing were wrong in the family, even in the midst of problems:

___ Always   ___ Sometimes   ___ Never

2. When the addict does something destructive, you confront it and tell him how you feel about it:

_____ Never   _____ Rarely   _____ Sometimes   _____ Often

_____ Whenever called for

3. You force yourself to ignore feelings about the problems in your family:

_____ Never   _____ Sometimes   _____ Frequently   _____ Always

4. How satisfied are you with the addict's performance of family roles? Listed below are examples of tasks or expectations for each member of the family. These are only examples. Select those tasks that belong to the addicted family member and rate your level of satisfaction with how he does his "job." After you respond to our examples add the other tasks the addict in your family is expected to perform.

	Not applicable	Dis-satisfied	Satisfied	Completely Satisfied
Spouse				
Confidant	_____	_____	_____	_____
Lover	_____	_____	_____	_____
Partner in recreation	_____	_____	_____	_____
Partner in life planning	_____	_____	_____	_____
Social partner	_____	_____	_____	_____
Provider	_____	_____	_____	_____
Homemaker	_____	_____	_____	_____
Companion	_____	_____	_____	_____
Parent				
Role model, teacher	_____	_____	_____	_____
Affectionate care-giver	_____	_____	_____	_____
Disciplinarian	_____	_____	_____	_____
Playmate	_____	_____	_____	_____
Creator of celebrations, parties	_____	_____	_____	_____
Confidence builder	_____	_____	_____	_____

	Not applicable	Dis-satisfied	Satisfied	Completely Satisfied
Social director	___	___	___	___
Chauffeur	___	___	___	___
Child				
Student	___	___	___	___
Follower of rules	___	___	___	___
Doer of chores	___	___	___	___
Playmate	___	___	___	___
Member of extended family (e.g., grandchild, niece)	___	___	___	___
Object of affection	___	___	___	___
Object of pride	___	___	___	___

Other tasks the addicted member is expected to perform

_____	___	___	___	___
_____	___	___	___	___
_____	___	___	___	___

5. Look back over item 4. How much of your dissatisfaction with the addicted family member is related to the addiction?

   _____ Not applicable; I am satisfied   _____ None   _____ Some

   _____ Most of it   _____ All of it

6. How open have you been in communicating your feelings about addictive behavior to the addict?

   _____ Not open. I hide my dissatisfaction and frequently pretend everything is all right.

   _____ Somewhat open. My feelings occasionally come out, but I often hold them back, hiding behind the myth that all is well.

_____ Moderately open. When something bad happens I let the addict know how I feel about it.

_____ Very open. I confront him every time the addiction causes a problem in our family. He knows that I will not be satisfied until he is on a program of recovery.

As you completed this self-rating exercise, you focused your attention on the ways you support addictive behavior and on the ways in which you set limits. When all members of the family have completed the exercise, sit down together and talk about what you have found. That will give you a complete picture of ways the family as a whole has supported addictive behavior. Then, save your answers. They will be needed when you plan specific ways to set limits and to withhold support for addictive behavior. We will refer back to them in Exercise 7.

Though it would be possible to create a numerical score and compare your family to others, this comparison would not be particularly helpful and even may be misleading. One family may contribute little support to the addiction while another provides the use of drugs the opportunity, effort and illusion of normalcy. Yet both families face the same task: to learn how to support health rather than pain. In that effort, your specific answers will be more helpful than your score.

Applying strengths to the family's recovery

Changing the family requires a deep examination of its problems and its desires, standards, strengths and feelings, followed by bold action. So far, you have defined major family problems and are now aware of ways to enhance your family in three ways: (1) increasing self-care activities, (2) living full lives and (3) developing support. The stronger you are, the better equipped you will be for the journey through recovery. In this chapter, we have returned the focus of attention to your relationship with the addict in order to contemplate using the benefits of family membership to support family health. The next stop along the way is to begin withholding those things that, by your contributing them, encourage (or at least enable) the addict to continue his addiction.

Chapter 7

Intervening: Withholding Support for the Addiction

Seeing yourself as the addict's accessory is difficult and painful. Once you are aware of the family's supportive contributions to the addiction and are discussing them with supportive people, what then? Next comes withdrawing that support. Three cases will illustrate the range of possibilities.

Case 1: the polydrug-abusing physician. Jim was a thirty-eight-year-old internist. His mother called one of the authors to see if there was anything she could do on his behalf. She reported that he had been abusing stimulants, marijuana, Quaaludes, alcohol and inhalants. She stated that his practice was suffering and that his nurse had informed her that he had treated patients while under the influence of drugs. This concerned her greatly. Jim's mother feared that he would kill someone someday. She stated over the telephone that she loved her son very much and would be willing to do anything on his behalf.

During the initial family meeting, she identified a list of people who were significantly involved with her son. These included friends, the nurse who worked in his office, parents, siblings and selected members of the extended family. After the family assessment was concluded, she developed a list of people who controlled important benefits in Jim's life. He received economic assistance from his parents. His nurse's substantial efforts were largely responsible for his continued success. Companionship came only from his parents, his nurse and his closest friend. Validation was provided by them, as well.

The family decided to bring in the entire group to a network meeting. During this fascinating meeting, each member of this group identified what he or she saw in Jim that led him or her to believe he had a problem. They all also identified subtle ways in which they helped maintain the addiction. The group was prepared *en masse* to withhold any and all support for addictive behavior.

It seemed quite possible that a small intervention was all that was needed, and that turned out to be the case. The group decided on a conservative initial plan. His friend approached Jim and leveled with him about what he saw and what he felt, and suggested that treatment would be a very good idea. The friend gave him a therapist's business card. Within two weeks, Jim called the therapist. Treatment was initiated and completed successfully.

Though it is more the exception than the rule, this case serves to illustrate the power of even a single reinforcer. Losing companionship, losing his friend's respect and losing the validation of the friendship was enough to open this man's eyes to his problem. Had it not worked, additional benefits could have been withheld.

Case 2: the adolescent. Pete was a twenty-two-year-old alcohol-, marijuana- and barbiturate-abusing unemployed man living in the home of a relative. He had abused drugs from a very early age, when he lived with other relatives, and he was sent to his uncle's home in the belief that his uncle could take him in hand.

Expectations of the young man and the uncle were very high. The uncle had taken on the task of rescuing Pete. Unable to convince his nephew to quit using drugs over a two-year period, he finally sought help. The uncle's fantasy was that he was going to drag his "broken" nephew to a therapist's office and that the therapist was going to "fix" him.

He brought Pete to the office, and the therapist talked with uncle and nephew together. It soon became clear that though Pete had very serious drug and alcohol problems, he was the last person interested in treatment. The therapist advised the uncle to continue on in treatment to figure out how to cope with his nephew and to learn to stop supporting the addiction. As he resisted the idea of setting limits for his nephew, the uncle endured much abuse from Pete. He was not convinced initially that he had a right to forbid abuse. But, after some time, he finally had had enough. He became increasingly aware of the effect the addiction was having on him and thus became less willing to tolerate all the chaos his nephew was introducing into his life.

So he began to withhold validation. He began to confront his nephew, telling him exactly how it felt to see him high. Though he continued to bail his nephew out of jail when he got into trouble, to pay legal expenses and to find his nephew jobs, he had stopped covering up his feelings about the addiction. In this case, however, withholding validation was not sufficient to motivate the addict to get into treatment.

Pete was in the habit of driving while intoxicated and had been ticketed three times. The first two arrests occurred before the uncle entered treatment. The uncle had paid court costs and fines and sought out attorneys who would help the nephew escape any consequences. The third arrest occurred after the uncle had been in treatment for a while. His response was very different; he had had enough. He told his nephew that he would pay an attorney only if Pete was willing to agree, before the judge, to go for treatment. Pete became enraged and threatened to get his own attorney. The uncle replied, "Fine, you are going to pay for it." The case went to court, was tried by the attorney selected by the uncle and resulted in court-mandated treatment. Uncle and nephew participated in the program offered by the treatment center to which the nephew had been sent. During the course of the nephew's treatment, the uncle realized that supplying a roof and food for his nephew only enabled the addiction to get worse. By the end of treatment, the uncle was able to state the conditions under which further assistance would be granted. Pete was welcome only if he was drug-free, committed to a program of recovery and participating actively in treatment. The uncle was willing to pay for the treatment but would not supply a penny if the nephew did not follow through. Pete was again enraged; he threatened to tear the house apart, then to embarrass his uncle, then to harm him. But it was to no avail; the uncle stood firm. Pete remained in treatment and the drug abuse stopped.

Case 3: the cocaine-dependent optician. Charlotte was a forty-three-year-old optician who had originally come for treatment for her drinking. She quit drinking early in the treatment and went on to work on getting her life in order. Two years into treatment, she telephoned her therapist in a panic. She requested an immediate emergency appointment. She opened the session by telling the therapist that she had been abusing cocaine for a few months and that she had fooled the therapist. She stated that she had become increasingly dependent, and was coming off of a large binge. She said that she asked for the appointment because her husband would not let her back into the house until she told the therapist about the problem. Charlotte went on to describe the cocaine problem in its entirety and, to the therapist's knowledge, never went back to using the substance. She continued on in therapy and made some major changes in her life. She increased her income dramatically, improved her relationships with other family members, and became much more involved socially with people around her and in her community.

In this third case, the patient's husband was ready to withhold everything—confirmation, the roof over her head and the relationship itself—in support of recovery. We do not know whether it was necessary to withhold everything, but it was effective. The idea of withholding support from addiction—though very appealing and sensible—may be frightening. It is a process that involves four decisions:

1. How do you decide what to withhold?
2. When do you withhold it?
3. What do you say to the addict about it?
4. What are you trying to accomplish?

DECISION 1: WHAT TO WITHHOLD

Few families can simply walk away from the addicted member. Yet walking away often appears to be the simplest solution; it amounts to withholding everything. After enduring the helplessness and disappointment that inevitably result from addiction, family members can become so angry that the only solution may seem to be to walk away. Unfortunately, initially choosing the most extreme option has its dangers. Foremost among them is that, if it does not work, there is nothing left to try. The family's determination is best demonstrated to the addict by consistent and persistent changes which can escalate over time in the face of his refusal to cooperate. Going too far, too fast may be self-defeating. Consistency and persistence may not have been practiced to date by your family. Typically, families reinforce disruptive, drug-related behaviors at some times but not at other times. Inconsistent actions by his family actually spur the addict on into increasingly chaotic behavior. So it will be very important for the family to develop a consistent, step-by-step strategy for what it can withhold and in what order.

What, exactly, is it that you can withhold from the addict? Perhaps the most obvious items are material (e.g., home, meals, money and basic necessities). The addict finds such items necessary, and having them come from the family both reduces his need to provide them for himself and increases the energy and resources he has to devote to his addiction. The son whose parents provide him with shelter and sustenance, for example, need not concern himself with providing (or even contributing to) those for himself. He can concentrate fully on his addiction.

Nonmaterial support—in the form of companionship, efforts on the addict's behalf and personal acknowledgment (confirmation)—is the other area in which families might consider withholding potential contributions to the addict's drug use.

With these general ideas in mind, do Exercise 7, "Creating a List of Things to Withhold."

EXERCISE 7

CREATING A LIST OF THINGS TO WITHHOLD

The end product of this exercise will be a list of the ways in which you currently support addictive behavior, arranged in order of the level of difficulty you expect if you withhold them. The items simplest to withhold will come first, the most severe items last. It may be possible—as in the case of Jim, the polydrug-abusing physician —to interrupt the addictive behavior without using any "big guns." Walking out may not be necessary. Confrontation may be sufficient. On the other hand, you may need to take bolder action (e.g., cut off the addict's use of the car and use of family funds). Ultimately, you may need to withhold all forms of support, as in the case of Charlotte, the cocaine-dependent optician.

The following list summarizes guidelines for creating a list of things to withhold.

1. *Consider yourself.* Try first to withhold those things that cause the least inconvenience, fear, negative feelings or danger for the family. Only later on should the family put itself through inconvenience.

2. *Consider the addict.* Arrange your list so that items at the beginning cause the least hard feelings for the addict and the items at the end are very aversive for the addict.

3. *Consider the addiction.* Items at the beginning of the list should relate most logically and directly to the addiction (e.g., giving the addict money, driving him to the liquor store).

4. *Consider what you are about to withhold.* Items at the beginning of the list should include things that simply increase the addict's comfort and sense of well-being. Later items contribute to the addict's self-esteem and confirm his sense of membership in the family. Items that are necessary for survival should not be withheld (e.g., shelter for a retarded adolescent son).

5. *Consider safety.* Evaluate the safety risks (yours and the addict's) of withholding each item. *Before you consider taking action, consult a professional.*

Now, review your answers in Exercise 6 on pages 107–13. Keeping the preceding list in mind, and on a separate piece of paper, list fifteen changes your family should consider in order to stop providing support to addictive behavior. Next, place them in order from least severe to most severe. Finally, list them on the chart below.

1. (least severe)

2.

3.

4.

5.

6.

7.

8.

9.

10.

11.

12.

13.

14.

15. (most severe)

You will use this list for creating the If-Then chart on page 132.

After you have determined how your family can stop supporting addictive patterns, you are faced with the question of timing. When do you withhold support and when do you provide it freely? What special circumstances may arise? How does one arrive at the point of knowing when to say no? It is to these questions that we now turn our attention.

DECISION 2: WHEN TO WITHHOLD

Judging when to provide or withhold support is impossible unless you understand the consequences of your actions for the addict and for the rest of the family.

1. Can you tell when support is really vital? Can you tell when it is harmful to give or withhold support?
2. What firm limits must be set in order for the family to enjoy a state of well-being? Do you know and demand respect for your limits? Or, do you voluntarily give up your desires and standards only to tumble into exasperation in Region I?

The effects on the addict of giving or withholding support depend largely on his stance toward addiction. The consequences for the family can be understood only insofar as the family defines and enforces limits to preserve its well-being. That brings us to the task of describing the addict's stance toward addiction and describing the process of setting limits. We will describe each of these considerations at some length because understanding them is crucial in deciding when to withhold support and when to be generous.

Stance Toward Addiction As a Factor in Deciding When to Withhold

Addictive disorders are progressive, deteriorating conditions that follow a complex course. The situation in your home may appear to be changing rapidly sometimes. The addict may appear to be doing well one day, then to be careening out of control the next. So, the family is left with the task of deciding when to withhold companionship, effort, material support and validation.

There is a rule of thumb for deciding when to withhold something from the addict. *Do not withhold* something if the addict's life is in danger or if he or the family is in danger of being seriously injured or disabled. Under this circumstance, your support of the addict is appropriate until the danger passes. *Withhold* something if providing it would merely increase his comfort or if it would simply produce a good feeling or the impression of normalcy or if it would keep clean a record at work, with friends, in the community or with the law.

More specifically, it is useful to think in terms of stances toward recovery. Six distinct stances are important to consider when deciding whether to withhold your effort and support from the addict. They range in severity from life-threatening to life-building. Diagram 6 places the six stances in the context of the addict's journey to recovery.

Diagram 6
**STANCES TOWARD ADDICTION AND THE JOURNEY
THROUGH THE THREE REGIONS***

Regions	Examples of Possible Actions
III Empowerment	6. Committed to abstinence from harmful drug use and to a program of recovery
II Effort	5. Committed to a plan of recovery despite occasional slips
I Exasperation	4. No plan of recovery, but drug use appears under control 3. Marginal functioning without a plan of recovery 2. Struggling and out of control 1. Life or death struggle

* Placement of the six stances in the three regions is a rough approximation. If the addict falls back to an earlier stance it is more likely that he will re-enter an earlier region in the journey. It is possible to progress fully through the stances without leaving the exasperation of Region I. However, progressing through the stances does make it more likely that the addict will progress in his journey through all three regions.

Stance 1: Life or Death Struggle

There are periods in the addictive cycle during which the addict is in danger of dying. All too often, wives or husbands find themselves in emergency rooms with their spouses after an overdose or tragic accident. It is no exaggeration to say some parents are forced to listen in horror as their children tell them that the drug dealer is going to come and kill them if they do not produce $1000 or $2000 for cocaine they bought. Although other stances toward addiction might be chronically annoying, this one can be truly terrifying for the family and dangerous for the addict.

Stance 2: Struggling and Out of Control

Here, attendance at work or school becomes irregular. Behavior is erratic. Relationships are deteriorating. Drug use appears to dominate every day. The addict is out of control.

Stance 3: Marginal Functioning Without a Plan of Recovery

In this stance, the addict is functioning marginally—perhaps attending more days of work, coming home for meals, living more or less on a regular schedule. The family begins to develop some hope that the addict may make it. However, the bad days are not eliminated. There is no plan for recovery. The addiction seems to have gone underground, and the addict seems to want everyone to ignore it.

Stance 4: No Plan for Recovery, but Drug Use Appears under Control

This is the most seductive level of functioning. The addict simply does not mention the problem and appears to be in good spirits. The family is in the bind of being with the addict and wondering what is going on but typically choosing not to ask. This is a time when the family thinks that it must walk on eggs, fearing that the most innocent question or statement may precipitate the drug use and chaos again. This is a time of great hope and fear for the family, a time when it is most important for the family to know that it cannot cause drug use.

Stance 5: Committed to a Program of Recovery in Spite of Occasional Slips

In this stance, the addict takes responsibility to do something about the fundamental problem, but he may be having some difficulty. Actual drug use may be the same as in the preceding stance, but its meaning is very different. Slips are very common in recovery. The important point is that the addict is openly taking the responsibility to do something about them.

Stance 6: Committed to Abstinence from Harmful Drug Use and to a Program of Recovery

Members of self-help groups will point out that nothing is permanent and that abstinence proceeds only one day at a time. However, it is also true that many addicts achieve long and healthy periods of drug-free living. Many addicts successfully abstain from using drugs or alcohol for a lifetime, one day at a time. During long, drug-free periods, much of the addict's energy can gradually be shifted away from the addiction and toward development of a healthy life, community involvement and other worthwhile endeavors.

Knowing the addict's stance toward addictive behavior can help the family decide whether or not to withhold resources. Providing a home for someone who is in Stance 5 is very different from providing one for someone who is in Stance 4. In Stance 5 at least the addict is taking responsibility to get better. What does it mean when you are providing a home for someone who, in Stance 4, is taking no responsibility to get better? Although providing certain things in Stance 1—life or death situation—may be very necessary, providing full support during Stances 2, 3 and 4 merely prolongs episodes of floundering, by financing them, confirming that there is nothing wrong, making it unnecessary for the addict to feel responsible and keeping him company.

With this framework in mind, let's go back to your list of increasingly severe things your family could withhold. Ask yourself which phase the addict in your family is now in. If it is not Stance 1, what might your family consider withholding from him as you apply this newfound knowledge to strengthen the family and begin to act more boldly in your own behalf? The point at which family action is appropriate is the point at which the addict violates the family's limits.

Limit Setting As a Factor in Deciding When to Withhold

We have observed that families often go through seven steps as they develop and ultimately set and maintain limits:

Step 1. Families Experience Pain, but Often Are Unable to See the Specific Problems That Perpetuate the Pain

We emphasized previously that families experience a variety of emotions. At some point, the emotions may seem overwhelming, and the family enters a crisis state. The crisis is accompanied by feelings of despair and anxiety, loss of self-esteem, panic and a frightening uncertainty about the future. Loud arguments, palpable tension, fear of destroying the children, all-night marathon discussions, panic, racing thoughts, a fear of falling apart or losing control, and a feeling of inadequacy may dominate the family's emotional life during the crisis. Family members stop believing in themselves and their strengths, and they stop doing what they do best. It can sometimes look like the family will end up with nothing, that its future, its dreams and its hopes will fall apart.

One practical problem with crises is that they diminish the family's rational observation skills. A longing to feel reunited with the addict, for example, obscures what the addict is doing that hurts so much. The family's mixed feelings about him make it difficult to pinpoint precisely what the addict does to feed the crisis. It appears impossible to comprehend how someone so important can cause so much pain and destruction. In the words of one drinker's wife, "Who is this precious enemy lying in my bed?" The parent of a twenty-two-year-old Quaalude user put it this way: "I feel like I am losing my son. We need him so badly. We want him so much to be happy. But, we don't recognize him. He's not the same person. We want our son back."

Self-blame also inhibits rational analysis of the family's predicament. Families often attribute the addict's drug use to "bad" family qualities, qualities that "understandably" push the addict to his drugs. "How else could he be happy in a rotten family like ours?" The guilt and jealousy that result make it difficult for the family to take a strong stand against the addiction itself.

In its state of crisis and exasperation, the family is unable to see what causes its pain. Early on, events appear to have no consistent meaning.

125

But with time the family begins to make sense of the pain and to end the nightmare.

Step 2. Family Members Identify What Hurts

Family members can identify what hurts by evaluating carefully the addict's behavior in the family. That is what Exercise 8 can help you do. The checklist takes off from the task outlined in Chapter 2, defining problems related to addiction.

EXERCISE 8
_____

EVALUATING FAMILY PAIN

Listed below are examples of harmful behaviors and attitudes frequently associated with addiction. Try to remember the last time you were concerned about each one. How much distress and worry did you feel? Rate every one below. Try not to be distracted by how often a problem occurs. Try instead to zero in on how the behavior affects your family when it occurs, not how often it occurs. Rate a behavior "not applicable" if it does not occur in your family.

Addict Behavior or Attitude	How Intense is the Pain and Worry for the Family Regarding Each Problem?					
	Not applicable	None	Mild	Moderate	Severe	Unbearable
1. Intoxication at home	____	____	____	____	____	____
2. Intoxication away from home	____	____	____	____	____	____
3. Any alcohol or drug use at all	____	____	____	____	____	____
4. Arguments about drugs and alcohol	____	____	____	____	____	____
5. Illnesses caused by drugs or alcohol	____	____	____	____	____	____

Intervening: Withholding Support for the Addiction

Addict Behavior or Attitude	How Intense is the Pain and Worry for the Family Regarding Each Problem?					
	Not applicable	None	Mild	Moderate	Severe	Unbearable
6. Broken promises to quit using drugs or alcohol	____	____	____	____	____	____
7. Loud yelling and name calling	____	____	____	____	____	____
8. Physical abuse, actual violence	____	____	____	____	____	____
9. Sexual abuse of children	____	____	____	____	____	____
10. General un-reliability: broken promises about things other than drinking or drug use (e.g., not coming home on time)	____	____	____	____	____	____
11. Job problems related to ad-diction	____	____	____	____	____	____
12. Money spent on drugs or alcohol	____	____	____	____	____	____
13. Jeopardizing family safety (e.g., drunk driving)	____	____	____	____	____	____

Confronting the Addiction

Addict Behavior or Attitude	\ How Intense is the Pain and Worry for the Family Regarding Each Problem?					
	Not applicable	None	Mild	Moderate	Severe	Unbearable
14. Arrests, violations of the law	——	——	——	——	——	——
15. Bringing intoxicated friends home	——	——	——	——	——	——
16. Waking the family up during sleep time	——	——	——	——	——	——
17. Shirking responsibilities in the family	——	——	——	——	——	——
18. Selling drugs	——	——	——	——	——	——
19. Avoiding responsibilities to work toward recovery	——	——	——	——	——	——
20. Uncaring attitude	——	——	——	——	——	——
21. Failing to express affection, respect and understanding for other family members	——	——	——	——	——	——
22. Spending too much time away from home	——	——	——	——	——	——

128

Addict Behavior or Attitude	*How Intense is the Pain and Worry for the Family Regarding Each Problem?*					
	Not applicable	*None*	*Mild*	*Moderate*	*Severe*	*Unbearable*
23. Sneaking drinks or drugs	___	___	___	___	___	___
24. Associating with un-savory peo-ple in the drug world	___	___	___	___	___	___
25. Failing to carry out family re-sponsibilities	___	___	___	___	___	___

Others: Add and rate items not listed above.

26. _____	___	___	___	___	___	___
27. _____	___	___	___	___	___	___
28. _____	___	___	___	___	___	___
29. _____	___	___	___	___	___	___
30. _____	___	___	___	___	___	___

Your answers to each item of this exercise will serve as the basis for setting limits. We will refer to them as we go through Step 3.

Step 3. Family Members Formulate Limits to Prevent the Repetition of Pain

As the sources of its pain become clear, a family can set limits on what behavior it will tolerate in the future. After defining limits, the family is ready to design a course of action.

Each hurt, each assault can be translated into a restriction or limit. The process of identifying limits can be very reassuring, it can relieve anxiety, and it can provide a channel for the expression of anger. Defining the experiences you are determined to avoid gives you more power.

Step 3 typically begins when family members take a look at the results of the "Evaluation of Family Pain" exercise (Exercise 8). They often notice that rage gradually has crept up on the pain. One teenage daughter spoke of "turning ugly" when she thought of her mother's Valium drunkenness. A drinker's wife reported, "I'm starting to hope that he'll load up and get behind the wheel and kill himself."

Rage can motivate action. Most people are familiar with the destructive actions that are triggered by rage: violence, breakdowns of communication, and emotional abuse, among others. The constructive effects of rage may be less familiar. When filled with anger, people are better equipped to "draw the line" for others and to resolve to stop others from crossing it.

Anger helps families leave behind the belief that they can control the addiction, and it fuels their determination to interrupt their cycle of recurring pain. For many family members, this is a bitter-sweet triumph. In the words of the mother of a twenty-eight-year-old Quaalude-abusing woman:

I'd thought about what I had learned in Families Anonymous and in therapy. I knew for the first time that I'd reached my limits, that I'd have to walk away. I love my daughter. I am there for her when she needs me to help her get healthy. But I'm not there for her if she needs me to help her to get sick. I knew exactly what I had to do. It hurt, but it felt good to know for the first time what direction to take to escape the confusion.

Defining limits is a relatively simple task at this point. One family took a look at the results of its pain evaluation exercise. The limits were there. Family members decided what level of pain they were willing to endure. Each item rated at or above that level was a limit. They decided that they would tolerate nothing more than mildly painful experiences in the future. They took every item they had rated from moderately to unbearably painful and added it to the "If" column of the If-Then chart in Exercise 9. "If's" are limits; "then's" are family responses to violations of each limit.

EXERCISE 9

IF-THEN CHART

The end product of this exercise will be your family's *tentative* If-Then chart. Developing and implementing a plan from this exercise will require professional and self-help group support. We will provide a general orientation to the steps involved in setting limits, but we will not be able to provide sufficient guidelines to create a complete plan for your family. Again, we are the travel consultants for your journey, but not the tour guides.

There are an infinite number of circumstances that could be included on the chart. We recommend that you list no more than fifteen as you go through the four-task process of creating your chart. An If-Then chart, which you can fill in with your family's information, is set up on page 132.

Task 1. Define the limits of your tolerance; which behaviors on the part of the addict disturb you enough to be unacceptable? Review the six stances toward addiction on pages 122–24 and Exercise 8, "Evaluating Family Pain." Identify up to fifteen behaviors that are disturbing enough to prompt you to withdraw from the addict. Select items that are as different from each other as possible. Write them in the space on the If-Then chart in the form of rules or standards (e.g., transform "Intoxication at home" from Exercise 8 into "Remain drug-free and work on a program of recovery"). Your rules should be stated concisely.

Task 2. Identify benefits from family membership that could potentially be withheld when rules are violated. Review the escalating list of benefits to be withheld that you developed in Exercise 7. Make a list of the fifteen most important ones.

Task 3. For each rule in Task 1, identify related benefits from the list in Task 2. For example, "If she is not drug-free, she will not use the car." Ideal pairings are logically connected, practical (though they may require effort), safe and simple. Chances are that you will soon recognize logical patterns; several benefits may relate well to several of your rules. For example, living at home, eating with the family, using the family car, being invited to family parties and receiving loving reassurance may be appropriate only if the addict is sober and actively pursuing a program of recovery. In terms of the If-Then exercise, this example translates to: "If [the addict] follows rules 1 and 2, then benefits 1, 2, 3, 4, and 5 will happily remain a part of his life." Other benefits may appear either unrelated to any of the rules or too difficult to control. Such items may be dropped from the list. Write the appropriate benefit(s) to be withheld next to the matching rule, so it serves as the corresponding "then" in the If-Then chart.

The goal here is to communicate that you are serious about your intent to eliminate the effects of alcohol and drug abuse from family life. The most effective If-Then pairings are based on the idea that you refuse to go on with business as usual until the addiction is squarely addressed. We are not advocating that you attempt to control the addict's behavior by using rewards and punishment. You are *not* in control of the addict's behavior. He will make his own choices. Our belief is that you will feel better and stronger if you stop supporting the addiction and instead start supporting health. If the addicted family member behaves in a way that makes the family feel whole, then the benefits can be given freely.

We recognize that the ideas provided here are very general. You may not be able to apply them to your situation. Task 3 varies considerably from family to family. The specifics of the task are best worked out with a therapist.

Task 4. Add the consequences of complying with each rule. This task will be completed after reading Step 6, regarding communicating limits to the addict, on pages 135–36.

For now, hold on to your chart. Step 6 will help you identify the consequences of complying with each rule developed in tasks 1, 2, and 3.

The If-Then Chart

If		*Then*
Family rule (from Task 1)	Consequences for addict of violating family rule (from Tasks 2 and 3)	Expected benefit for addict and his family of complying with family rule (to be added as Task 4 after completing Step 6)

1.

2.

3.

4.

5.

6.

7.

8.

9.

10.

11.

12.

13.

14.

15.

Step 4. Family Members See Themselves and Their Futures as Separate from the Addict

To move any farther in setting limits, family members must be able to visualize themselves flourishing without the addict. If family members believe their future happiness depends on maintaining close ties to the addict, they cannot risk alienating him. In this situation, any time a limit is stated, the future will appear to be crumbling, and the family will experience unbearable anxiety fearing the loss of the addict and of its hope for the future. All the steps described previously as methods of identifying and building strengths are methods of seeing oneself and one's future as separate from the addict: answering the four questions defined in Chapter 1, taking care of yourself, getting support and living a full life.

The need to develop an independent vision of success away from the addict was graphically illustrated by Bob Woodward, as he described the deterioration of John Belushi, in his book *Wired*. In this case, Judy, John's wife, unsuccessfully battled John's business associates who purposely fostered his addiction out of their own dependency on the "star."

For some time, [Judy had] been wondering about the extent to which the movie industry people—agents, managers, studio executives—had a hand in John's drug use. Were they orchestrating it? Assisting? . . .

Briskin [assistant to John's agent] explained it was a $40,000 looping session, and John had to be there. It was the only way to make sure he'd stay awake. There were only a few pills.

Let him fall asleep, Judy said. We've got to quit postponing the moment when the drugs cause a big fuck up. *Let him fuck up.* Don't you see? That's the only way he will learn. We've got to stop being his custodians. She walked out abruptly.

Briskin disagreed. Too much was at stake: not just one looping session but the whole movie. And if the movie got derailed, then John—whose reputation in the business was awful to begin with—could place his entire career in jeopardy. Then there would be no more million-dollar-plus contracts; no vacation houses, first-class travel, expensive dinners, accountants, lawyers, agents and *managers.* John—all of them—needed success. . . .

Judy didn't care about the reason. She wanted them to stop feeding John speed under any name. She argued and begged: *Let John fuck up.*

Briskin said they couldn't. Not this time.

The value of psychological independence is clearly illustrated in the example of the Critch family. Jack Critch was a thirty-three-year-old factory worker who sought help in coping with his thirty-eight-year-old cocaine- and alcohol-addicted wife. Beverly worked as an accountant. Her income, aggressiveness and prestige left Jack feeling chronically inadequate. He had been raised in a middle-class family and had consistently shrugged off challenges. When Beverly's addiction became evident, Jack was panic-stricken. In the passage below, Jack explains some of the keys to his family's recovery, emphasizing his development of a vision of himself and his son flourishing separately from Bev.

Our bills were already getting out of hand. Today, I know that Bev's $700-per-week cocaine habit was responsible for burying us financially. Back then, I just thought that we were poor. I reached my limit with her many times: the first time she stayed out all night and each of the twenty times that she did it thereafter, her two affairs, forgetting to pick up our son at the baby-sitter while I was at work, and so forth. But, I didn't have the guts to confront her because I thought that I couldn't live without her. So I put up with it, driving myself deeper and deeper into despair and helplessness.

One day, after jogging with my friend Josh, I started opening up. I told him how desperate my family had become, that I was trapped. Josh asked me why I couldn't leave her. I stammered something about loving her, needing her help in raising our son and in paying the bills, and feeling that I couldn't desert her. While we were talking, I realized that Bev was not really helping me in any practical way. I began to wonder whether any other woman would want me.

As the addiction progressed, I fantasized more and more about raising our son alone. I took over more of the responsibility and began to separate our financial affairs. I knew that I was testing myself. I started taking better care of my appearance, just to see whether I could get any attention from women.

Then I started thinking about the type of life I wanted to have. Somehow, I got the idea that I was determined to provide a sane, loving atmosphere for my son and myself . . . with or without Bev. I thought through all of the practical details and could even imagine some good times: Little League games, barbecues, hugs, maybe changing jobs, music in the house, family get-togethers . . . good things.

Only then did I really feel ready to confront Bev. I felt stronger. I felt ready to insist on a good life no matter what Bev chose to do.

After a stormy three-month period, Bev moved out of the house. She took an apartment downtown. We separated our finances. Bev continued using cocaine and alcohol for another two months, until [her employer] threatened to fire her and offered her the option of seeking treatment. Once she entered the outpatient program, Bev started her recovery.

Three months into recovery, Bev invited me to start marriage counseling. I felt so much stronger by then that I was ready to fight it out with her. I told her what I needed from her in order to be happy and found her to be very receptive. Standing up for myself and feeling independent somehow made it possible for me to fall in love with her again. I am more attracted to her than I ever was.

Step 5. Family Members Get Support for Becoming Independent of the Addict and for Setting Limits

Developing sources of support for the family is important here. Setting an independent course for the family—one that may not include the addicted member—is clearly stressful. To the outside, uninformed world, it may appear that the family is abandoning the addict at a time, in the words of one parent, "when she needs us more than ever." Whether or not outsiders actually say it, many families fear recrimination, perhaps because of the newness of their actions or a sense of guilt. The support of others who understand the need for bold action is crucial at this point.

Those who understand what the family is doing can help members recall, for example, that setting limits is very important for the health of the family. Caring friends would be in a position to challenge guilt feelings by saying that, if the family did not set limits, it would risk disintegration and would then be of no use whatsoever to its addicted member. In Step 5, families gather support from others. Support will make Step 6 much easier.

Step 6. Family Members Communicate the Limits to the Addict

Once the limits are well understood, it is time to tell the addict about them. For many, this can be a genuinely frightening task. Families often fear the worst as they imagine what will happen when they tell the addict about the limits they have formulated. Some are concerned that the addict will break off contact altogether, others that he will be violent toward either family members or himself. Because of the complexity and possible danger in communicating limits to the addict, we recommend seeking the assistance of a therapist. We will address the question of what to say to the addict on pages 138–39.

When limits are formulated well, they include at least three components: the rule, the consequence of violating the rule and the implications for the addict and his family of following the rule. These are illustrated in the "Examples of Limits" table. It is a working synthesis of the If-Then chart.

A well-stated rule is brief and to the point. The consequences are logically related to the violation of the rule and to complying with it. Now return to the If-Then chart you prepared in Exercise 9, and complete Task 4. These are the positive consequences of complying with each rule. Your family may feel more comfortable seeing the limits in black and white before approaching your addicted relative.

Having finished these tasks, your chart will be complete. It will contain the things you want to tell the addict. Two key points relate to the task of communicating limits. First, presenting the limits to the addict is a *process*, not an event. It takes place over time and is reinforced by your consistency. That is why a written chart may be a helpful reminder as you proceed. Second, the task of communicating limits is a task of expression, not of manipulation. The purpose is to let the addict know what you are going to do. It is not to get the addict to do (or stop doing) something. If you approach this task from the standpoint of controlling the addiction, you will fail. You cannot control the addict's behavior; you can control only your level of support.

Step 7: Family Members Recognize They Must Stick to the Limits or the Nightmare Will Continue

Above almost everything else the family may have done, the process of setting limits requires a radical and visible change in the family's behavior toward the addict. It can seem at first that limits do not solve anything and instead create new tension and friction. Families often report that, in the face of the new tension, the impulse arises to give in to the addict —to violate their own limits—just to restore the appearance of sanity and peace. One family member said, "Maybe life is better the old way. Our home wasn't a battleground and didn't seem to be falling apart."

Giving in to the addict sometimes buys time, creates the appearance

Examples of Limits

Rule	Consequences for addict of violating rule	Consequences for addict and his family of complying with rule
1. Enter treatment and stay until you can maintain sobriety	Leave the family	The family can again become a safe, happy, supportive environment
2. No drinking when driving	Cannot use the family car	Safety
3. No drug use or intoxication in the house	Live someplace else	House will be drug-free; family members won't have to cope with intoxicated relative
4. Seek, find and hold a job; pay room and board	Find someplace else to live	Family gains financial stability and stops supporting addiction. If addict is in late adolescence, this rule helps him successfully launch into adulthood as a more responsible person
5. No more infidelity	Divorce	Rebuilt trust, intimacy and harmony
6. No more fondling of the children	Call police again and press charges	With great effort and much treatment, help the children rebuild their shattered world
7. Come home for dinner at time agreed upon; call if unavoidably late	Confrontation; make own dinner	Rebuild harmony and structure family life

of normalcy and seems to reduce anxiety. Addicts typically try to exploit concessions made by their families. They see them as evidence that the family's resolve can be broken. Gradually the insanity returns with the drugs and alcohol. Drug use typically inches (and sometimes leaps) back to previous levels as the family tolerates more and more use.

Maintaining the limits will be a struggle. In the words of the husband of one addict:

It felt like she was ripping away my skin. The rejection was unbearable. As she drifted away, I became aware of my passionate involvement with her and I was really torn. I *struggled* to remember that our relationship could not continue while she shot heroin. I could forget so easily. Heroin would ultimately destroy me, it would destroy our children and it would sap our vitality and strength. I could not be the man I wanted to be if I stayed with her. Our children could not grow up to be the people we want them to be. I fought through my passion like a bad dream. The insanity had to end, simply had to end. I had to then remember myself without her. I had to remember my goals, the things that are important in my life. The force of her personality, my fascination with her, her sexuality, the tantilizing hope of maintaining our intimacy drew me back in repeatedly. Thank God I remembered my pain.

Having placed your family in a position to act, how then do you talk to the addict about your decisions?

DECISION 3: WHAT TO SAY TO THE ADDICT

Saying no can be so intensely uncomfortable that families sometimes come right out and ask us to tell them what to say to the addict. But we cannot tell our clients what to say. We encourage them to say what is on their minds and in their hearts. Having said this, we can suggest three guidelines: (1) Simple statements of facts, derived from your If-Then chart, are best; (2) telling the addict one thing at a time is most effective; (3) being brief and to the point is crucial.

Families who withhold *material support* commonly stress to the addict that they will not continue to participate in the addict's destruction by making it easier on him. One mother told her son, "As long as I give you bed and board and as long as you can steal from us, we are helping you self-destruct. We feel terrible about that, and we've decided we will not continue to do that. You'll have to pack up and move out."

Families intent on withholding *confirmation* stress their implicit role in a charade that seems to excuse the chaos. "I will no longer go on pretending we are the ideal couple when you come home at night and shoot up. From now on, I will speak up when people ask about us," was the way one husband put it to his wife.

A family that decided to withhold *companionship* told its addicted child, "It's no fun to be with you when you're high. We've decided to go on without you today so we can enjoy ourselves."

Finally, a family that had determined to *redirect its energies* away from what it saw as wasted effort on its addicted member explained, "It's your bed, sleep in it. You insisted upon using those drugs, and now you are paying the price. We won't have the family paying the price anymore."

Use May Continue

Some families hope that, if they withhold support for the addict's behavior, he will come around and rejoin the family for a healthy life. And no wonder; the chaos in the family begs for some resolution, some peace of mind.

But it is important for the family to realize that their actions may have little impact on the addict. He may continue to use his drugs even after the family withdraws its support.

The family's goal at this point is to disengage itself from complicity—intended or not—in the addictive process so it (the family), not the addict, can get better. The family must pull out of its possible partnership in the addiction, and it may need to go forward without the addict.

While the family is not abandoning the addict forever, in the event he stops using drugs, it *is* putting a distance between him and family members. It may be difficult, therefore, to adapt to the addict's continued and chronic use of drugs. This is when the family's independent strengths and values are important to press into service. They will chart the family's course and help bolster its resolve that the decision to withdraw from the addiction was the correct one.

Even so, one additional factor may come into play. What is the addict going to do?

The Addict's Reaction

By now you may be wondering, "Do they think the addict in our family is going to let us get away with it?" "Won't he do something horrendous?" In some cases, the answer to that second question is yes. Safety is often a concern around an addict. Any attempt to withhold support from the addict, or any attempt to deprive him of anything, must be orchestrated carefully and take adequate account of safety. The extremes of homicide, suicide, sexual abuse and other terrifying, violent acts are relatively rare but much too common in addictive families.

If any of these are possibilities in your family, you have one additional and very strong reason to seek professional help. There is a real danger in underestimating the risk. Because you may feel disloyal, frightened, ashamed or uncomfortable in some other way when you begin to grasp the extent of the problem, you may continue fooling yourselves about the severity of the problem as you begin to try to solve it. This is all the more reason to engage a professional in helping estimate the risk. It is often the case that families can set limits safely, and the risk may not be so extreme in your family. But, it is essential to make an honest and thorough appraisal.

Even if the addict does not become violent or self-destructive, it is likely that he will become angry when the family confronts him. There may be no way to avoid this. He is entitled to his feelings. All the family can do is to continue to stress its caring for the addict, its awareness of the addict's strengths when he is not using drugs, and the family's goals. Holding firm is essential. The family that lets itself be bullied by the addict is in for a much longer bout.

DECISION 4: WHAT ARE YOU TRYING TO ACCOMPLISH?

The journey now proceeds to defining the ends to which your family's strengths can be applied. If you could radically improve family life, how would you change it? How would it be different from what it is now? Much of what we have presented so far is geared to help identify problems and current strengths. It is equally important to develop a picture of family life that is worth fighting for. Dr. Nicholas Cummings wrote that one of the first tasks in treating an addict is to understand—and help him understand—his far-off dreams. We find the same to be true for families; families need to recognize what their goals are.

Though complaining can be invaluable, complaints rarely provide direction on their own. For this reason, industrial consultants have long been teaching managers to define problems in a goal-oriented way. Dr. Robert Mark invented a convenient linguistic device to help managers get into the habit of reaching creative solutions to problems: A problem statement always begins with the words "How to." If we apply this rule to family life, then rather than define a problem as "There's too much screaming in this house!" it might be more productive to define the problem as "How to get along better," "How to keep our voices down when people are trying to sleep," "How to resolve our conflicts" or "How to show more understanding for each other." Problems can be restated in many different ways, each restatement giving form to some aspect of the ideal you are approaching. As the family discusses its ideals, it will be useful to rephrase them in "how to" format.

After you have defined your problems, strengthened yourselves, and defined goals and limits, you will have set the stage for the planned attempt to change. What are you to expect? These are difficult problems. Solutions do not come quickly. However, our own clinical experiences and those of our colleagues make us very hopeful; many families do recover and go on to achieve high levels of intimacy, comfort and harmony. In Chapter 8, we alert you to some of the hidden passageways to Region III and illuminate some of the pits through which you could fall back below the surface. In Chapter 9 we will describe several families in some depth at a point two or three years after they confronted the addiction. In Chapters 10 and 11, we will present various types of assistance available to you from professionals and self-help groups.

When a family is in the midst of a crisis, a year or two may seem to be an eternity. Each day seems to merge with the next. Holidays seem to come up by surprise. They do not seem much different from other days. Crisis seems constant. Setting accurate expectations will be very difficult. That is why we strongly support the position of self-help groups: Start a program of recovery and take it one day at a time. We have stressed in great depth the earlier steps in recovery. We will now move on to some of the processes that unfold over longer periods of time.

PART IV

Thriving as a Family

Chapter 8

Moving Forward and Getting Better

The process of getting better involves changing both your own behavior and some aspects of the environment in which the addict lives. That environment involves not only you and the addict, but all the people and circumstances surrounding the addict. In this section we talk about the ways in which family members interact during the process of getting better. We will describe how families can get on with their lives by first letting go of the trauma they have suffered, and how they can overcome some of the most common obstacles to progress. We'll begin with the Three R's.

THE THREE R'S

The term *Three R's* refers to a three-step process through which most families pass as they try to reconstruct a relationship with an addicted relative. The Three R's are *retribution, restitution* and *refuge*. The process begins even before—and whether or not—the addict stops using drugs. It continues when the addictive behavior ceases and the addict attempts to reestablish his relationships with family members and friends.

Retribution

When the addict is using drugs, he does and says many things, and he behaves in such a way that he alienates and hurts many people around him. It is usually the ones closest to him who are hurt the most. Mere acquaintances can easily break off their relationships with him. Those in his family, however, usually care more about their relationships with him and consequently suffer a greater impact.

Those people who have been hurt get angry and become resentful. One way this resentment manifests itself is that they begin to think about ways in which they might get back at the addict for the pain he has inflicted on them. These thoughts of retribution arise whether or not the addict stops using drugs.

Now, it may be difficult to imagine yourself wishing to seek some sort of revenge on the addict, for two reasons. First, sometimes people don't realize how angry they are when so much of their attention is riveted on the addict's day-to-day hurtful behavior. A lot of the family's energy is consumed by trying to cope with the various problems the addict presents and by trying to survive each day. Second, it may be difficult to recognize this feeling of vengeance because most of us have learned that feeling vengeful is not nice. Consequently, we seek to avoid the recognition of it in ourselves. The desire for retribution, however, is a normal outgrowth of a normal reaction to the infliction of long-term pain.

In confronting and dealing with vengefulness, it's important to reduce this issue to two concrete implications. First, think about whether it is indeed possible to get back at the addict in a way that would make up for the suffering which his drug use inflicted on the family. Consider what form the revenge would have to take to be satisfying and how it could be accomplished. The second step is to decide whether getting back is desirable, especially if you conclude that it could have a further destructive impact on family life.

At some point, you may decide that retribution is undesirable or impossible, or both. It may also be that different family members have different reactions to the addict and, therefore, experience vengefulness to different degrees. By talking about family members' reactions to the addict, and by discussing specifically the anger and vengefulness that family members may feel, the potency of this issue may be reduced for the family. Venting anger helps you let go of the need for revenge. Discussions with the addicted family member can help, particularly if he shows he understands your feelings. Supportive discussions with friends, other family members, self-help groups or a therapist are also helpful. You can only let go of the need for revenge once you have fully understood and described—aloud—the chaos that led to the anger in the first place. Without getting perspective on your suffering, you may feel as if you are reliving it, even after your circumstances have improved. Open discussion allows you to determine whether your life has really changed.

One very insightful recovering alcoholic expressed his view of this problem by using the metaphor of a broken slide projector. He said his wife refused to confront him with the pain he had caused during his drinking days; he felt she was punishing him all the time. It was as if she were viewing two slides simultaneously. The image of the patient during his active drinking phase was always stuck in the projector. Images of the couple's present life together were never visible alone; they were always superimposed over the old painful images from the drunken past. He complained that she was unable or unwilling to see and touch his sober self. She appeared locked in the past. Ultimately, through marriage counseling his wife was able to vent her anger, "dislodge the drunken old slide" and develop a loving intimacy with her now recovering husband.

There is great comfort in talking to fellow sufferers. It might be tempting to believe that wishing will eliminate the need and desire for revenge. It probably won't. But, in our opinion, discussion is indispensable.

While thoughts of retribution arise and are important for the family to face—whether or not the addict stops using drugs—the family can progress to the second of the Three R's only if the addictive behavior ceases, if the addict shows interest in working with his family once again, and if he shows understanding and respect for the feelings expressed by the family. Under these circumstances, it is time to confront the second of the Three R's.

Restitution

After letting go of the need for revenge, addicts' families usually discover a need for restitution, repayment by the addict for sufferings he inflicted while he used drugs. You may find that hope for repayment is easier to recognize than revenge, since, for one thing, it is easier to justify. The manner in which such restitution can be made, however, is usually not so clear, and you might be unable to express what you want in concrete terms. As a result, if you approach the addict in your family, he may become frustrated by his inability to meet the ill-defined expectation. One son described his parents' expectations this way: "What do you want from me? Tell me what you want. OK, we've established that I went back and used the junk again, and I know that you got real upset, but I don't know what you want from me now. It's like you want me to make it up to you, but you haven't told me how."

Ultimately, this family worked out an agreement that described how the son and his parents would spend a specific amount of time together each week in order to talk about things affecting the family, including the way each felt about what was going on with other members. The parents were satisfied because spending the time with their son gave them hope that things could improve in the family. Furthermore, they could settle on this agreement for improved communications as a way of being repaid for their sufferings. Note that the act of restitution in this case did not literally make up for past losses. To do that would have been impossible. How could one provide so much pleasure that it erases ten years of hell? In fact, what helped this family get past the need for restitution was relatively simple: the son included himself in the family as a caring, communicative, responsible person, working toward a happier family life. He made the family situation whole by taking responsibility for contributing to the family's happiness *now*, in the present.

Refuge

An important consideration, after the first two R's have been addressed, is that there are no guarantees. As much as we might like, and as much as we might try, we cannot predict perfectly what will happen in the future. We can, however, allay some of our fears about the future by preparing for some of the possibilities. The third R addresses this point. It is the desire for refuge: protection against future disruption of the family and protection against the addict's return to his addictive behavior. Seeking refuge is seeking assurance that the family's future will be relatively secure. In many families this is not an idle concern; the addict has suffered lapses in the past.

But finding refuge as such is not entirely possible. After all is said and done, the addict cannot offer you a binding promise that he will not go back to using drugs. In many families promises by the addict have not counted for much. A Catch-22 situation usually arises. On the one hand, you are seeking a guarantee from the addict. On the other hand, you cannot trust any guarantee he offers. Given his past behavior, it is natural and justifiable to be suspicious of any promise he makes. This means that the family must be willing to live with some uncertainty.

If solemn promises and the benefit of the doubt aren't enough to meet the family's need for refuge, what can help? The family gains comfort from open communication about sobriety and from a secure belief in the limits it has set.

Trust grows quite naturally as the newly sober person talks with his family about his support program and about feeling urges to use drugs. Seeing the recovery process in action and learning about it from the recovering addict can be very reassuring. If words and actions are consistent, the family can relax its guard and can accept some uncertainty, because the addict is no longer hiding, no longer as irresponsible, no longer conning. He no longer keeps the family in the dark. If relapse is imminent, the family will likely have some warning. Communication and/or the addict's support program usually decline before a relapse.

Once you have formulated limits and have communicated them to the addict, you will be in a better position to deal with your need for refuge. You will have decided how to react should he begin to use drugs again. This has three advantages. First, you can draw strength from the knowledge that you will never again permit the kind of suffering that once permeated your life. Second, the decision about what the family will do is best made during a time when there is not a lot of chaos in the family. At times when the addict resumes using drugs, the family may be quite upset and distracted, and it may be very difficult to reach firm conclusions and reasonable decisions. Third, by deciding ahead of time both what the family will do and when the family will institute its actions, the family is spared the ordeal of formulating those decisions at a time when the addict may claim some compelling extenuating circumstances to explain his behavior. The family will be prepared and it will be ready to act firmly. Knowing of its resolve, the family experiences less of a need for iron-clad promises from the addicted family member.

Some addicts become so frustrated by the time it takes their families to move through and past the Three R's that the process may seem to bring about its own demise. In such cases, it often turns out that the family mistakenly views the addicted member as the problem, neglecting the needs of other family members for support and emotional growth. These families remain stuck in the first of the Three R's—retribution—and prevent themselves from growing with the addicted family member. Though it may seem unthinkable, many recovering addicts in such families are told, "I liked you better when you were drinking." A return to substance abuse, the tragic breakup of the family or frigid emotional isolation may result when a family gets bogged down in its movement through the Three R's. Self-help groups and therapists should be consulted to help it regain momentum.

LEARNING TO COMMENT ON THE OBVIOUS

There are other aspects of the process of getting better to which the family must begin to pay direct attention. The first is learning to comment on the obvious. We distinguished earlier between facts and opinions arising from our observations of facts. Learning to comment on the obvious makes direct use of this distinction.

One of the pitfalls of responding to an addict is that the family very easily can offer him an out. This is particularly so when the family voices opinions the addict can contradict. At best, arguing about opinions reduces itself to an agreement to disagree; the addict merely can insist that he interprets things in a different way. Case closed. At worst, the argument deteriorates into a battle that freezes communications. The family must therefore strive to avoid this pitfall by learning to give free information to the addict based solely on the facts that the family observes. Facts are not as easily dismissed by the addict. A nonjudgmental comment is more likely to be heard than a damning one.

Learning to comment on the obvious is important because, while it is often ignored, it is the most persuasive element in confronting an addict with his behavior and the effect of that behavior on the family. Families often end up directing their attention and energies to the day-to-day annoyances the addict produces. And understandably so. But focusing on these details means that the family may be missing the more important and obvious points that transcend his day-to-day behaviors.

Consider this analogy. Imagine that someone places an automobile in the middle of your living room. Clearly this will present family members with many obstacles. Some may take it upon themselves to rearrange

150

the furniture, others may complain about the inconvenience of having to be so careful in walking through the living room. But, unless the family notices and comes to grips with the obvious—in our home there is a car, which needs to be dismantled and carried out—the family's day-to-day aggravation will continue unabated. Without making that first observation, the task of coming to grips with the obvious cannot begin, and the family won't make headway on resolving the problem.

Earlier, we emphasized the importance of identifying and remembering two kinds of hard facts in family life: observations and feelings. Now, we ask you to consider the importance of discussing the facts openly. The single most important change a family can make is to adopt rules that will encourage and protect the sharing of free information.

This change has two components. *Confrontation* is the process of telling someone your observations of his behavior. Simple, specific, nonjudgmental statements are actually easiest to hear. *Leveling* is the process of revealing the feelings that were stirred by the behavior. Recall the fact/emotion lists you made as you proceeded through the material in Chapter 2.

Confrontation and leveling are two active ingredients in a commonly used and very powerful procedure called "family intervention." The procedure was developed by family therapists in Minnesota and adopted by treatment centers around the country. Many families use it effectively, with the help of a therapist experienced in this technique. Facts are very powerful motivators. As family members start commenting on the obvious, major changes become both necessary and achievable.

The power of free information is illustrated in the following vignette, based on case material and the facts we discussed in Chapter 2. The following discussion took place in a therapist's office. We join the family after they have completed two months of preparation and therapy.

Doctor: John, Jr., you have begun telling your Dad about some of the things you noticed while he was drinking. John, Sr., would you like to hear more?

John, Sr.: Not particularly. This makes me very uncomfortable, like I'm an awful person. But, I guess if John, Jr., had to live through it, I can listen to him talk about it.

Doctor: John, Sr., I want to be sure before we begin that you really agree to this and that John is safe in telling you his feelings.

John, Sr.: Yes. Of course. Go on already!

John, Jr.: Dad, remember last year's party at Uncle Oscar's house? You and Uncle Oscar were yelling at each other. You threw your empty pint bottle against the fireplace. I was really scared and embarrassed. Then you ran out without your coat. Mom grabbed it and told us kids to get ready to go. We chased you to the car. Tim, Mom and Susan got into the car. But the doors were still wide open and I was still getting in when you sped off. The door slammed and nearly caught my foot. Everyone was screaming. Boy, was I scared, ashamed and angry. I felt lost, like the world might explode.

(John, Sr., listened but turned away, staring at the floor. His face was white.)

Doctor: John, Sr., what did you hear your son say?

John, Sr.: His dad nearly killed him.

As you can see from this example, nothing was exchanged except direct observations and reactions. They are undeniable. There was no retort to John, Jr., when he told his Dad about the broken whiskey bottle or that he was scared. Once John, Sr., agreed to listen, what he heard were observations about which there could be no argument. His only choices were to accept or ignore them.

LEARNING IT IS OK TO HAVE DIFFERENT FEELINGS

Another important step along the way to getting better is to realize that absolute agreement among family members is not necessary and rarely desirable. It is OK to react in different ways to the incidents that arise concerning the addict. It is OK to disagree.

This is not to minimize the importance of reaching a consensus. Clearly it is important. Without a consensus, the family will not be able to act as a unit. But along the way it's good to recognize that different family members have different feelings and reactions to the addict and to each other. Getting to the point where the family can identify and accept these variations among its members is an important milestone to getting better. Without this step, family members will not be able to come together to solve their problems.

For example, Mike and Laurie were faced with a choice about how to spend their Saturday. Mike felt an obligation to meet with members of a church committee on which both he and Laurie served. That particular weekend, their newly married daughter and son-in-law were visiting from out of town. Laurie wanted to spend time alone with the kids, but

152

she was afraid that Mike would disapprove. She could imagine him saying, ''After all, we did make the commitment to the church. I don't like your spending time with the kids without including me. There I'd be at the church doing *our* work while you're off having fun and probably talking about me.''

Despite her fears, Laurie did not abandon her plans. She exercised her newly discovered right to have her own feelings and preferences and to take them into account when planning her day. For her, the church work was less important than spending a day with the kids. When she told Mike, he was disappointed, but he knew clearly that this was something she wanted to do, and he did not interfere. Mike went alone to the church meeting, and the day worked out well for both of them. They were able to respect each other's reactions. Had they pleased each other by abandoning their true feelings, both would have felt miserable. Laurie would have been sullen and withdrawn at the church meeting or Mike would have felt guilty and distant spending time with the kids.

In this example, acknowledging different feelings meant taking independent action. In other cases, acknowledging different feelings may lead to a compromise in which the parties act together.

PROBLEMS ALONG THE WAY

As you begin to work together on the task of coping with the addict's behavior, you may find that the road is strewn with a number of problems and hurdles. We will describe eight problems that families typically face along the way to empowerment in Region III. Unless you are prepared to deal with them, you may get lost in your journey and find yourselves sliding backwards into a state of exasperation in Region I.

1. Fear of uncertainty, change and emptiness
2. Getting over the hump
3. Losing sight of the goal
4. Getting hung up on details
5. Embarrassment
6. Counterproductive, or dysfunctional, communication
7. Blaming
8. Inertia

Which of them may arise in your family's efforts to get better?

Fear of Uncertainty, Change and Emptiness

As you start the process of getting better, you cannot know how your efforts will turn out. Your hopes and your actions, of course, are directed toward getting better. Nevertheless, fear of the unknown is often a formidable obstacle. Often, the unknown may seem more treacherous than the familiar, even though the familiar is painful.

It is often frightening to shake up an already chaotic situation by attempting to change. This is not to say that you want to hold on to painful ways of living. But each unfamiliar step, each change may feel risky or foolish, as if it will blow up in your face. It is natural to fear that you will fail to turn the family around *and* that by changing you will destroy the few redeeming aspects of the old way of doing things. Letting go of old methods of solving problems means that there will be many times that you will not know what to do next. Consequently, you may find yourself lacking direction, focus and hope, feeling empty. Emptiness is a feeling that means you are taking a pause; it comes when there is a break in the flow of action. Emptiness gives you the opportunity to let your feelings come to the surface. Sorting out your feelings will allow you to identify what to do next, to find a new focus of attention and action.

Family members associate a fear of change with concerns that take many forms. Claire, the wife of one recovering cocaine- and alcohol-dependent man, expressed several common fears and concerns.

Before Bobby stopped using, I did whatever I wanted whenever I wanted to do it. There was no accountability. I never had to consult him when I bought something, when I went somewhere, or when I decided how to spend time with or how to take care of our son. In short, I was the boss. Bobby was completely dependent on me. Now that he is sober, I have to deal with him. He has ideas about how we can save money, how we can spend our time together and how we should raise our son. He has needs I don't know how to respond to. Sometimes I get crazy enough to think that I liked it better the old way. It was easier to be myself when I didn't have to please him. Sometimes I feel like a wife playing a goody-goody role on a comedy show, instead of being me. I used to be the hero and was able to get some of what I wanted quietly, behind the scenes. Now, I'm sometimes the goat and still miss out on what I want. I went for years feeling that I did no wrong. Now there are times that my weaknesses are on center stage and it feels like I've lost my job in the family. When I feel like I'm failing, I feel like *I'm* not good enough for

154

him! What a switch! But, down deep I think I was afraid that if Bobby stopped using drugs he would conclude—as I feared myself—that he was superior to me somehow. No wonder I was afraid to change things.

Fears of uncertainty, change and emptiness can take many other forms. But to overcome the fear barrier, you will need to learn to take charge of yourself and make choices. Learning to answer the four questions is an excellent way to overcome these fears. It is much easier to face an uncertain future knowing what you want, what you admire, what you feel and what personal strengths you can count on. A positive vision of yourself in the future gives you a direction to hold on to at times of uncertainty. In Claire's words,

During the difficult months of panic and uncertainty, I held on to several facts. I wanted to live in a home that was free of drugs. I wanted to be close to a man who would treat me with love and respect, who would pull his share of family responsibility and who would be gentle, sexy and understanding. I wanted to finish my degree and excel as an engineer. I wanted my son to grow up in a loving home. I wanted to have normal friends and share them with my partner. And I was determined to succeed with or without Bobby.

Before I could recite this list, the fear and emptiness were unbearable. Even after I knew what I wanted, it took me a while to be able to learn how to go after what I wanted in a specific situation. There were many times when I sat at the kitchen table with the emptiest feeling in my stomach. It wasn't hunger for food. I had to learn how to figure out how to read my feelings so that I'd know what I hungered for. Once I learned how to do that, I knew I was ready to face the unknown.

Getting over the Hump

The process of getting better involves learning to observe unpleasant behavior in the family more accurately. In this process, people discover many things of which they previously were unaware. Things may look like they are getting worse. It may seem that family problems are multiplying, even though what the family is really looking at are previously stashed problems and experiences. They are not new. Remember the analogy to the family's psychological closet.

As the family works on its problems, it may incorrectly attribute the *seemingly* increased number of problems to deficits in the family rather than to the family's positive efforts to discover problems that have not been recognized. This may make it more difficult to believe that things really will improve. But, like the things in the closet, your discoveries are really nothing new; you have seen them all before and they have not multiplied.

In addition, it may be difficult to see progress, because changes other family members make may upset the delicate balance in the family. Consider the graph depicting "An Addict's Behavior in Relation to Change in the Family." It illustrates that, as change occurs, the addict initially may act more disruptively more often as he seeks to reestablish the old (and unpleasant) pattern of relationships in the family. In other words, as you change, the addict becomes more involved in his counterproductive behavior. By doing so, he hopes to reverse the change and force the family back to point 1.

In the midst of this rather complicated series of developments, it may seem that the addict is getting worse. Be assured, however, that at this point your consistent, productive behavior as a family unit will be what gets you over the hump (point 3 on the graph). After a period of time and a trial of your patience, the addict will recognize that he will not be able to change you back to the way you were before. From then on, his efforts will begin to diminish (point 4 on the graph), and the family will be less and less influenced by his counterproductive behavior.

An Addict's Behavior in Relation to Family Change

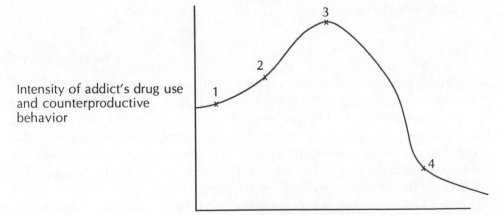

Intensity of addict's drug use and counterproductive behavior

Family change over time

Losing Sight of the Goal

Establishing the family's destination and sticking to a course of action are often difficult. Some families may lose sight of their goals because they lack experience, confidence and support. In other families, the addict redirects attention and diverts it from its originally established goal. Regular attendance at self-help groups or therapy can help bring the family's attention back where it belongs. With or without help, a return to the original process of thinking through the problem and the family's reactions to the problem may be in order.

Getting Hung Up on Details

We've discussed the need to recognize the family's goal, to set reasonable expectations and objectives, and to learn to comment on the obvious. The first problem as families work toward their goals is that they get hung up on details. This is especially a problem if the addict's day-to-day activities vary. Sometimes the variations in the addict's behavior lead to false hopes, fruitless attempts to manipulate the addict, disappointments and resentments.

For example, one couple described a situation few of us would envy. Their heroin-addicted daughter came to the house looking better than she had in months. She was drug-free, well dressed, articulate, and—best of all—witty. The couple enjoyed her visit. Near the end of the evening, their daughter asked for a loan to support her new business. This put the parents in a terrible bind. Their daughter was still using drugs regularly and had not committed herself to a program of recovery. They rightly feared supporting a lifestyle that was doomed to fail. On the other hand, they wanted terribly to believe that everything was going to be OK and to see this request as the first glimpse of a hopeful future. How could they ruin it by withholding the loan? Maybe refusal itself would "force" their daughter to increase her use of drugs. How should they position themselves to stop their daughter from using heroin?

This couple thought their daughter's drug use was contingent on their behavior; one false move and into the garbage she would go. Every detail, every word, every decision assumed a false importance. In the end, refusal to support the unsound plan was the only decision that made sense. You cannot buy recovery with money, with kind words or by hiding from the truth. Nor can you allow yourselves to be sidetracked by seductive but unproductive and inappropriate details. You must not lose sight of the forest by focusing only on a few trees, either the wilted ones or those that are beautifully green.

Embarrassment

Change often means facing things with family members, friends and acquaintances that the family may have chosen not to reveal in the past. For many families, this may be embarrassing.

Embarrassment takes many forms. For some family members, it may be embarrassing to admit that they went along with a harmful, deteriorating lifestyle for so long, that they are not perfect, that they sometimes feel lost and that they need help. Others may find it embarrassing to confront and express feelings that went unexpressed before. They may feel particularly embarrassed about expressing their troubles and efforts to people outside the family, as if others will decide they are no longer worthy of respect.

In some families, the fear of shame is a large obstacle to getting better. We aren't suggesting that people prefer the problematic aspects of the family, but potential embarrassment may be enough to slow down the recovery process and encourage more caution than is necessary.

Counterproductive, or Dysfunctional, Communication

We can view communication patterns in the family along two dimensions. First, are they abrasive or harmonious? Continually getting into arguments with the addict or other family members probably isn't satisfactory for you. Reducing abrasiveness is clearly an important step to finding some measure of peace.

The second dimension, however, is the more significant of the two. It concerns the productivity of communication in the family. Here are some other pitfalls to avoid as you redirect your communication efforts toward greater productivity.

158

Interrupting

Each of us can seriously consider only one thought at a time. This has an important bearing on the success of our communication. For our views to be considered, they must first be heard. And to be heard, the other person must be ready to listen. When others are talking, their minds are occupied with their own thoughts, and they are unlikely to hear what we say. Interrupting, therefore, usually prevents communication. The views we want to express never make it into other people's minds.

Jumping to conclusions is an internal interruption of the process of hearing another person out. If we listen only to part of what others say, then cut off our attention by reaching premature conclusions, we fail to gather enough information to formulate our ideas adequately. Even though we may not interrupt others physically, something is still lost; we do not hear fully the ideas other people want to tell us. So we are less informed than we need to be to make good decisions.

When communications are interrupted, nothing gets settled. The same topics are rehashed endlessly. Participants in the conversation don't feel satisfied that their points have been heard, understood and respected. To reverse this process, you have to make a painstaking effort to listen, to understand, to empathize with and to restate each point made in important discussions. This process feels awkward at first, but it is well worth the effort.

Diversions to Unresolvable Matters

Communication efforts cannot meet their goals if they are diverted to unresolvable issues that consume large amounts of our energy. For example, trying to *fix blame* on someone else focuses communication on the opinions that assign fault. "I'm suffering because you did the following things" is a familiar refrain. The usual response is an attempt by the other person to reassign fault. "That's not the way it happened. You're focusing on irrelevant things." Fixing blame is unproductive if the person being faulted is an unwilling recipient. It usually degenerates into an argument about the accuracy of the opinions each person has constructed.

Attempts to *establish the truth* (''What *really* happened was . . .'') consumes large amounts of energy to define the undefinable. Truth in human relations frequently depends on our opinions, and not everyone will agree with what we think. Attempts to establish the truth are, therefore, unproductive.

Trying to *make others feel guilty* similarly reduces the productivity of our communications because it diverts the communicator's goal from a fair hearing of his views to a tangential, unrelated objective. Attempts to make others feel guilty convert potentially useful communication to weapons for imagined gains over another person. Productivity is lost. Frustration is the outcome.

Calling other people names is another time-consuming diversion. Name-calling is labeling. Labels are conclusions, our opinions on which categories we think people fit into. Opinions invite arguments about their merits, or outright denial. ''You're a jerk'' can easily be denied both by ''I'm not a jerk'' and by an argument about the truth of the original opinions. Name-calling also may invite counter-calling: ''Oh, yeah! Well, you're a bum,'' and so forth. Neither comment can be productive because both focus on discussion of whether the label is acceptable and divert attention from the discussion of observations. This can drain people's energy and spirits.

Trying to Read the Other Person's Mind—Making Assumptions

I know you believe you understand what you think I said, but I am not sure you realize that what you heard is not what I meant.

Confusing, right? But not uncommon. Many times we fall into the trap of believing we know what is on another person's mind without checking it out. Family communication suffers because members make assumptions either about what other people are thinking or that other people know what *they* are thinking. In order to deal with this problem, we suggest a rule of thumb for the family's communication patterns: Nothing is understood unless it is spoken.

Family members can't assume that they understand what other family members mean. And they can't assume others share *their* interpretations of things that happen in the family. It requires an extra effort on the part of each person to be absolutely clear in communications. We can be sure others will know what we think only if we tell them. We can know what is on their minds only if they tell us. Deviations from open, direct and frank communication patterns invite chaos to sneak back into the family's life.

Mind-reading is attractive but unreliable. Recall our rule of thumb: Nothing is understood unless it is spoken. If we respond to other people on the basis of what we guess they are thinking, we clearly run the risk of acting on an inaccurate assumption. When you make silent adjustments, you compound misunderstandings. Although it is true that you can learn to read *some* of other people's consistent reactions, particularly when you communicate intimately with them, you will be wrong much of the time. In distressed families mind-reading does not work. Mind-reading can be dangerous to your family's health.

Predicting Futility

It is natural to estimate the effect of one's communications on other people and then use those predictions to shape what you say. Negative predictions can squelch the desire to commmunicate: "I know that if I say it, nothing will happen (or change, or be different). He's just a creep."

While such predictions may be based on your experiences, deciding against saying what is on your mind may be self-defeating. Not only can we not predict whether things will change, but also we run the risk actually of preventing change. If communication patterns in your family have been unproductive, they cannot change if members prejudge the potential for change and, on the basis of that judgment, kill their own incentives to talk to one another differently. Predicting futility increases the probability of failure. When it comes to your family, you cannot afford to keep quiet. If you do not assert yourself, you *will* be unhappy.

Seeming Extreme

When we include words like "every," "none," "never," "always" and "all" in our communication, we open ourselves up for responses that focus on the all-inclusive nature of these words rather than on the substance of our views. To the family member who complains, "You have never acknowledged my feelings," for example, comes a reply that fo-

161

cuses on disproving the extreme nature of that claim (i.e., "never"). The extreme can be refuted by one or two examples to the contrary, and it invites a debate on the all-inclusive (and therefore seemingly exaggerated) aspect of someone's views. In the process, the substance gets lost. Avoiding extremes will help you avoid this pitfall.

Being Vague

Vagueness is an important impediment to effective communication because it doesn't allow the other person to see clearly what is being stated. As an example, consider the word "enough." When someone says of us that we do not do enough, or that what we do is not good enough, that person has drawn attention to a deficit. But, the standard is undefined —or at least underdefined—and its vagueness gives us no clue as to how we might change our behavior to correct the deficit. Vagueness breeds frustration, and frustration obscures effective communication.

Turning Statements into Questions

The seventh mangler of communication is asking questions when you ought to be making statements. The former is for getting information, the latter for giving it. If you ask others questions when you should be telling them something, you confuse the issue and leave doubts in your listeners' minds as to your motives.

This is particularly true when you communicate with your addicted relative. Take limit setting, for example. If you approach him and ask, "What would you think if we no longer allowed you to shoot up at home?" you invite discussion. If you say, "We will no longer allow you to use drugs here. If you do, you will have to move out," you make clear not only your decision but also your resolve. Try not to hobble your well-developed family cohesiveness by introducing your resolve tentatively with decisions posed as questions.

Tackling Too Much at Once

"One thing at a time" is a cardinal tenet of productive communication. We sometimes go astray if we try to tackle too many problems at one time. Communication is most productive when we break down our com-

162

plex problems into their manageable components and then work on those components one at a time.

Some families define their problems in overwhelming terms, as if to say, "We can't possibly handle this." As they describe one problem, their attention quickly shifts to an even more overwhelming problem, only to shift again to another. For example, one family described their predicament in these terms:

> We've just set those limits on John's cocaine use and he's surly, the plumbing is leaking, Mom has those time-consuming projects for work, the collection agency keeps calling, we haven't been to the health club in a month, the kids are screaming at each other, the car is on the fritz again and the kids still don't have clothes for school.

The problem for this family was that whenever they talked about any one of these problems, all the problems would be dredged up. By focusing on all the problems at once, they never had the energy to solve any single problem. This family had not yet reached the point at which complaining stopped so that problem solving could begin. By being so ambitious and trying to tackle all the problems at once, they got nothing done.

Blaming

Blaming interferes with progress toward the family's goals by diverting attention, blocking communication and undermining hope. Two types of thinking lead families to assign blame. The first occurs when the family becomes embroiled in attempts to figure out how they got into the uncomfortable position in the first place. This may involve trying to assess blame for the addict's behavior and its cause, and it may involve assessing blame for reactions to the addict's behavior.

The second type of thinking that frequently diverts the family's attention into assessing blame has to do with wondering why the family is not moving faster in its attempt to get better. This kind of thinking is especially harmful. It arises from a sincere desire on the part of family members to resolve long-standing and painful problems in the most expeditious manner possible. Things previously seen as hopeless now seem possible to resolve. Consequently a feeling of impatience among family members occurs as they think about the family's problems. "Let's get on with it," may be their thought. And when getting on with it does not go fast enough, families sometimes begin to focus on who is to "blame" for the delay.

While it is important to recognize the desirability of solving the family's problems as quickly as possible, it is also important that the family's attention not be diverted from this task by trying to force others to go too fast or by trying to assess blame for what is perceived as slow progress.

Inertia

Inertia is a concept from physics that holds that, unless outside force is applied to it, an object at rest will remain at rest and a body in motion will move in its current direction.

We can speak of inertia in a family. Distorted by the addictive process, some families head in unproductive directions. For those families inertia governs, and they tend to continue in that unproductive direction.

Other families are stuck, like an object at rest. A force is required to establish the motion and direction in which the family will head. But what is that force? In our experience, the force that motivates change is unleashed by confronting the four questions outlined in Chapter 1 and by defining the problem as described in Chapter 2. By differentiating desirable experiences from detestable ones, by differentiating admirable decisions and actions from shameful ones, by differentiating strengths from weaknesses and by identifying feelings, you expose yourself to powerful internal sources of direction.

As we mentioned previously, getting better involves changing the environment in which the addict functions and the roles of family members who are part of that environment. Change, in other words, involves actively doing something, and doing it differently. Otherwise, the family's efforts are paralyzed. Nothing changes and inertia governs.

The process of moving forward and getting better is one of accomplishment and anticipation. As with other phases of your journey to recovery, it is helpful to have the outline of major tasks and normal obstacles to serve as your map. The Three R's help you understand the intensity, duration and course of the feelings you have about the addict.

Learning to comment on the obvious and acknowledging family members may have different feelings encourages you to forge ahead, despite what may seem to be roadblocks. Anticipating problems along the way prepares you for obstacles that otherwise might halt your progress. As an informed traveler, you now can be alert to the potential hazards of your journey.

Pause for a moment and consider where you are in the journey. So far, we have emphasized the most difficult aspects of recovery: moving out of a state of exasperation in Region I and exerting a Herculean effort to move through Region II. In defining the problem, we discussed one method of evaluating patterns that destroy family morale, identifying the details of Region I living. In the next three chapters, we focused on specific ways in which individual family members might strengthen themselves—taking better care of themselves, living full lives and getting social support—focusing on how to feel empowered as separate individuals; that is, on learning how to enter Region III. We reasoned that, with increased vitality, individual family members are then able to be more effective and energetic in addressing family problems.

The next three chapters dealt with how family members learn new ways to work together and leave exasperation behind. Members learned how to identify the ways in which the family supports addiction, how to withhold support from addictive behavior and how to work together to support positive changes. In this chapter, we focused mainly on the nature of the family's efforts in Region II; specific efforts that are required to maintain progress. We are now ready to turn our attention to the destination of this long and difficult journey: Region III, a state of empowerment.

Chapter 9

Flourishing

How will you know when you have succeeded in your recovery? One client put it very well when he said, "I'll know I'm on the right track when there are moments when I like being me." Such moments can grow into hours, the hours into days, and the days into a lifetime.

When we refer to success, we are not implying lasting and uninterrupted happiness. Success in recovery means that family members have learned enough about themselves to feel a sense of purpose in their lives. In other words, they find their way into Region III of their journey and spend increasing amounts of time there. Life has meaning, family members are involved in valuable pursuits and they experience excitement, pride, warmth, comfort and other emotions they associate with success.

The rewards of successful recovery can vary widely among family members. However, there are certain kinds of experiences most people find valuable: intimacy, sexual fulfillment, love, warmth and closeness, friendship, recognition for excellent achievement, challenging work, athletics, enjoyable play, good health, self-esteem and confidence, smooth functioning, a "good name," financial security and involvement with others in the community. We can make no comprehensive list of such experiences—no catalogue of the joys of living. In order to feel fulfilled each individual must pursue his own special satisfactions and set his own priorities.

Family members are better able to shift their attention to more productive and rewarding matters when they are no longer preoccupied with a shameful secret and when they are free of chaotic behavior. For example, at a critical stage in her family's recovery, one teenage girl chose to let herself get excited about her upcoming date. She explained that she could look forward to the date because she knew that she would no longer have to baby-sit for her alcoholic mother. She knew also that she would not have to fear that her mom would humiliate her again by seductively fawning over her boyfriend. She was free to invest her attention and energy in living and growing, not in rescuing or in scheming to avoid humiliation.

As they move forward in recovery, family members gain confidence in their ability to take risks and to make and honor commitments to others. As in the case of the teenager, confidence grows more rapidly after chaos is eliminated. Yet the effort to build a full life must begin before the chaos is eliminated.

In some families, the focus of attention and effort shifts to health as the addicted members become sober. In others, the family must separate itself from its addicted members in order to escape the chaos of Region I.

Without the draining, frightening and sometimes exciting war zone atmosphere of Region I, family members are free to confront themselves with the four questions that lead from exasperation to empowerment. It is time to return to the four questions and examine how answers to them can help you flourish.

1. What experiences do I want?
2. Which choices and actions would I admire in myself?
3. What strengths do I have and what skills can I develop?
4. What do I feel?

1. *What experiences do I want?* In Region II, in your unrelenting effort, you may be guided by vague ideas about what others think you should have rather than by knowledge of your own wants. When you lack information about your needs, feel that you are too undeserving or simply feel too timid to assert yourself, you give up the opportunity to live fully. If so, you may often experience needless confusion, anxiety and resentment. As family members plod along in Region II without a clear direction, it is normal to feel the weight of unrewarded effort. It is as if they are climbing toward the surface but cannot be sure their efforts will get them there. They may feel lost and possibly trapped underground.

Those who persist will gradually come to understand their wants and learn how to get more from life. By pursuing what you want, you will find paths to Region III.

Trusting your own assessment of what you want can help you break through to the surface and lead you into Region III. Knowing what kind of experience you want, pursuing it and being successful is empowering. Our clients often find their first experiences in Region III to be memorable. For example, Ben viewed one special afternoon with his sons as a turning point in his recovery. For years he had related to his sons out of a sense of slavish obligation. One morning before picking them up for his weekend visitation, he began to think about the ways he could enjoy himself with the boys. Instead of groping for ways to please them, he focused on himself *with* them. The ideas kept coming: riding the fast rides at the amusement park, hitting pitched balls at the batting cage and seeing an adventure movie, among others. When the boys got into the car, he told them about his ideas, asked them if they had any to add, then chose to take them to the amusement park. This was a real step forward for Ben. Previously, he would leave the planning and the choosing to his sons. The boys had been used to having more power. Upon hearing their father's list of choices, they initially made a fuss but quickly got swept up in his excitement. On the way to the amusement park, Ben noticed that he felt free, and he was filled with a new affection for his boys. He had found a way to feel happy with his sons for that day, and no longer felt like a doormat.

2. *Which choices and actions would I admire in myself?* Rather than get lost in fixing blame for past actions or problems, the best thing you can do at any moment is "the next right thing." After leaving Region I, most family members will need to learn how to earn their own respect in a range of situations. During the inevitable period of uncertainty and exploration in Region II, it is normal to wonder if you are doing anything quite right and to feel particularly dependent upon the approval of others. But, after taking the risk of choosing "the next right thing" over and over again, you will learn to rely on your values as a guide for action. Clear values evolve through reflection, discussion and practice. You will not feel lost when you know how to get what you really want in a way you respect.

By taking good care of himself, Ben—in the example above—felt more enthusiasm and energy to share with his sons. When they asked appropriately for lunch, snacks or soft drinks, he felt more generous. When their spirits began to sink, he let them rest, rather than pressing them on. He could afford to be flexible. Instead of stumbling passively and resentfully through the afternoon, he thought about what he would admire in himself. He made choices based on his values: spontaneity, humor, flexibility and nurturance. In looking back on the afternoon, Ben reported feeling buoyant. He felt more lovable, more effective as a father. The day had not gone perfectly, but perfection was not required. In retrospect, Ben knew that he ended up keeping the boys out too late on a school night. But he did not let one error ruin a beautiful time together.

3. *What strengths do I have and what skills can I develop?* Another source of self-esteem and direction is an awareness of personal strengths and skills. When facing a challenging task, like a job interview, you are probably aware that you examine yourself to be sure that you are ready to handle it. In ordinary situations, however, the process of checking yourself is probably unconscious. If you perceive yourself as inadequate, you may feel anxious, fearful, depressed, inferior or angry. If you see yourself as competent, you may feel buoyant, elated or quietly confident.

Knowing what you do well will equip you to make better choices and to find your way into Region III. By describing your strengths and good points in your own words, you will be in a better position to make use of them. Consider the example of Sherry. After one year of sobriety, Sherry felt that life without alcohol was drudgery. Sobriety was definitely not enough. Prompted by her therapist, Sherry reflected on some of her strengths and assets. She described herself: "I am capable of learning trivia from books and lectures, I can be affable with strangers, I can be very persistent, and I like to be kind to less fortunate people and to animals." She thought about the places where her strengths would be valuable. In a flash, she thought about becoming a volunteer at the zoo: guiding tours, caring for the baby animals, and lending a hand where it was needed. Sherry's first sustained sober moments of joy happened at the zoo. While riding her bike through the zoo, she noticed the trees changing color, the beauty of the animals, the crispness of the air and, most importantly, that she was on her way to do something valuable and to do it well. The zoo was a place where Sherry felt alive, involved and competent. Without focusing her attention on her strengths and without taking them seriously, Sherry never would have discovered this whole new world in Region III.

4. *What do I feel?* In a confusing situation, the single most important thing to do is to focus your attention inward, on your feelings. Feelings will alert you to important elements of the situation you are dealing with and will equip you to identify your wants, values and strengths in the situation at hand.

The answers to these four questions provide direction in specific situations. Early in recovery there are few clear answers. Each family member may have little understanding of what he or she wants. Wants may conflict with values. Family members may have little experience identifying strengths, and feelings may remain unconscious because they have been ignored. But with persistent attention and discussion, each family member can bring his personal vision of recovery into sharp focus.

It is difficult for families in the early stages of recovery to be able to envision what lies ahead. In the midst of chaos, family members often find their perspectives narrowed, and it is hard to summon and sustain a vision of where the family's efforts could lead. For this reason, in the pages that follow, we will describe four families, focusing most of our attention on examples of success in recovery. These vignettes offer images of what families may find when they enter Region III and stand atop the three-layered world through which they journeyed to recovery.

We'll take a look at the Klaus family, which succeeded in including the addicted member in the recovery process from the beginning. The Williams family twice reached the point of breaking up but emerged intact and sober. The Greenberg family was unable to remain together, but all the members ultimately achieved a stable and rewarding recovery. The Chase family broke apart, and only a portion recovered.

In our experience, families seeking treatment prefer the first outcome to the second, the second to the third, and the third to the fourth. It may

The Varieties of Recovery

Who recovered?	Family remained intact	Family came close to separating	Family separated
All	Klaus	Williams	Greenberg
All but one			Chase

be reassuring to learn that families completing treatment achieve the more desirable outcomes more frequently than the less desirable ones.

Two other outcomes occur all too often but will not be explored below. It is sometimes the case that while the addicted family member succeeds beautifully in getting better, other family members remain stuck in their own emotional traps, blaming an addiction that no longer exists. In such families, it is not uncommon for the addiction to be taken up by a previously nonaddicted family member in the next generation. Finally, there are cases in which nobody gets better; everyone remains miserable, and the addict dies of his addiction. While success is within the reach of every family, it is not assured and it is not easy.

THE KLAUS FAMILY

The Klaus family consisted of Karl (thirty-five-year-old father and husband), Susan (thirty-four-year-old wife and mother) and Inge (five-year-old daughter). Karl sought treatment for his wife, who was dependent on cocaine, alcohol and marijuana at the time she entered treatment. Karl worked full time as a middle manager, took care of most of the household chores and was the primary parent for Inge. Susan had lost a series of jobs, because she failed to come to work during cocaine binges. She always succeeded in finding new jobs quickly, and she knew that employers viewed her as attractive, articulate, engaging and bright. Susan described herself as a great con artist. At the time she entered treatment, she had managed to accumulate drug debts totaling $40,000. Karl professed deep love for Susan and expressed the hope that he could experience drug-free family life with her. Susan had been an abuser since the beginning of their courtship, and Karl had served as an able rescuer.

Karl contacted one of the authors, stating that his wife was depressed and that she had abused drugs for many years. Susan agreed to an assessment of her drug use, consisting of a mixture of individual and marital sessions. In the treatment environment, Susan appeared receptive to Karl's loving but frank confrontation. Although she voiced her pessimism about her chances for recovery, she expressed a kind of amused interest in individual treatment.

Throughout the first five months of treatment, Susan had occasional slips but worked actively to shorten them and to prevent future occurrences. She grudgingly attended Narcotics Anonymous (NA) meetings. One bittersweet moment of awareness came when Susan chose not to steal some money given to her daughter by grandparents. The fact that she considered stealing from Inge crushed her, yet Susan expressed the hope that by talking about such impulses she would equip herself to deal with them. This was a significant moment in treatment, a moment when Susan stood at the boundary between Region I (exasperation) and Region II (effort) and consciously chose to resist the pull into shame and chaos, back into a world we envision as buried deep below the ground.

During the first five months of treatment, Susan occasionally used drugs. Karl maintained sporadic contact with the therapist. He responded with hope and pleasure to Susan's initial successes, while trying to keep in mind the therapist's warnings that slips are commonplace. After one particularly dramatic relapse in which Susan disappeared for two days and again lost her job, Karl sought consultation. It was at this point that he acquired the motivation to set limits, to cut off support for drug use and to start living his own life without relying on Susan. Karl completed the exercises in Chapters 2 through 7, revealed his problem to friends for the first time, solved the practical problems that made divorce appear impossible (child care and financial arrangements, for example) and began to get more involved with his friends. Karl's new sense of power and detachment helped create an atmosphere in which Susan could see herself more clearly than ever. For the first time, Susan knew she was in danger of losing everything. She felt shame and anxiety, knowing she was the only person who could salvage the remains of her life. From that point in treatment, Susan exhibited a new sense of responsibility. Karl's change in behavior (taking care of himself and quietly planning for separation) and attitude (letting go of the rescuer role) appeared to have a sobering effect on Susan. The vignettes below are specific experiences as Susan and Karl described them in treatment. Each clearly belongs in Region III. Each is a moment when the speaker liked being himself and when Karl and Susan valued their relationship. Karl speaks first:

> We got up together to get ready for work. While I was showering, I knew that Susan was helping Inge pick out a dress and that breakfast would be waiting for me in the kitchen. The shower felt great. I felt so normal. At breakfast, Susan reminded me about our evening plans. We had invited some

friends to join us at an outdoor concert. *Susan* was reminding *me* to be home on time. What a switch! How unfamiliar it felt, how wonderful, how normal. Inge looked so comfortable at the breakfast table. It seemed as if she was consciously enjoying the new harmony between her mom and dad. Susan kissed me before we left the house, and Inge hugged us together, a regular three-person hug. It was great! Instead of feeling that Susan was conning me, I felt reasonably secure—for that moment anyway—in her love. Her lips were very soft, very warm and responsive.

The idea that Susan might use cocaine that day did not cross my mind. A relapse would have been tragic, not only for Inge and me but also for Susan. You see, Susan now cared about us, about her job and about our friends. I was no longer the bad parent, no longer responsible to keep Susan from using the magic potions she craved.

We left the house together and took Inge to school. I felt proud of my family. I felt free to throw myself into my work and began to consider shooting for a promotion I never would have been able to take on before. I looked forward to the concert that evening. Susan is a gas when she's straight!

This is what Susan had to say:

Karl and I have been spending more time with our friends, couples we've recently gotten close to. When Karl and I are out on the town, we can look pretty sharp. Karl was always pretty friendly; and since I've been straight I can be pretty charming, articulate and cute. Getting attention isn't difficult for me. Last Saturday night, we went to a party with friends. Karl kept ragging me. I had no idea what was bugging him. Rather than do what I used to do (either cause a scene or quietly burn and feel sorry for myself), I waited till the end of the party to talk to him about his behavior.

Now I must admit that I was no model of maturity when I started the discussion. I asked him what rodent had crawled up his --- and told him to get off my ------- case. But by the time we got home I was able to ask him what could be bothering him enough to make him want to keep zinging his loving, attractive and nearly perfect wife. When he just sat there without saying anything, it occurred to me that he might not know what was bothering him. If I approached him more gently, we both might figure out what was going on. But I asked myself whether I was mature enough to do a 180-degree turn midfight, decided that I wasn't and got in one or two more good licks.

The next morning, however, I awakened Karl by taking him in my arms and asking him what had gotten him so angry. I showed so much love, patience and humor that it was easy for Karl to talk to me. We both seemed to know that we would be able to work our way through any problem that came between us. It turned out that Karl had felt a little insecure at the party. He said that I seemed so healthy to him that he began to wonder whether I'd leave him. The more attention I got and the less we talked at the party, the lonelier he felt. He needed some reassurance from me. The problem seemed very easy to resolve once we understood it.

The Klaus family did not live happily ever after. Susan's final slip to date occurred two months after the "normal morning" described by Karl. The company she worked for fell upon hard financial times and Susan was laid off. Her first day of unemployment stirred up overwhelming feelings of self-pity, boredom, emptiness, guilt and hopelessness. In her words, "See, I got straight and look at what happened! Why bother? I might as well use coke." Rather than call her husband, a friend or her therapist, and rather than go to an NA meeting, work on her resume, go jogging or escape at a movie, Susan called her old drug connection and brought half a gram of cocaine. After snorting the cocaine, she was able to stop herself from following her usual pattern; she did not go out to get more. She stopped herself by confronting herself with what she was doing. She felt awful.

Susan phoned Karl to tell him about her slip and to ask him to meet her for lunch. She was not asking to be rescued and would no longer be high when they met; she wanted Karl's support so that she could get back on track. Karl was flooded with anxiety and rage, but he agreed to meet her. He commented later that Susan's attitude appeared different this time. She was asking directly for support. She was not creating a chaotic situation for him to straighten out. Despite this awareness, Karl reflexively took on his old enabler role. He felt responsible for the slip and felt he had to manipulate Susan so that she would not return to drugs. He felt angry with her, superior to her and downright contemptuous of her.

However, Karl was able to overcome these reactions, because he was aware that they were part of a counterproductive pattern. By the end of the discussion at lunch, he had restored his sense of himself. He recognized that Susan's drug use was not his responsibility and that he could not control it. He was then able to express his rage and disappointment. He asked Susan what she planned to do about her problem and was relieved to find out that she had already contacted her therapist to arrange an extra session. She expressed the hope that she could learn as much as possible from this slip, and she went on to enjoy many years of drug-free life.

THE WILLIAMS FAMILY

Wendell was a forty-five-year-old retailer who lived with his wife Betty and two sons, Ralph, age nineteen, and Michael, age seventeen. Wendell described himself as a trim, silver-haired talker. Betty described herself as "an outgoing blond who is a little plump." In Wendell's words, she was "a real dresser. She looks really good in those expensive clothes." Ralph and Mike impressed the therapist initially as spoiled kids. They came late to family sessions, put their feet on the table, and were overly familiar in calling the therapist by his first name without asking permission. Wendell and Betty were concerned that the boys were trying to buy friends in their suburban community, as if they were unsure how to make and maintain relationships.

Wendell introduced himself to the therapist by saying, "I'm the addict in my family." He and Betty had suspected the boys of using marijuana and were concerned that they might be developing an addiction, but they could find no solid evidence to support their concerns, and the boys denied using any drugs.

Wendell began abusing alcohol when he was seven years old. Initially, he began to sneak drinks from his father's liquor cabinet with his older brother and his brother's friends. Wendell was particularly proud that he got along well with older kids. His drinking increased progressively through high school. By that time in his life, Wendell based his identity with his classmates on his high tolerance for alcohol and on his ability to obtain alcohol, despite his age. Soon older kids sought Wendell out as their alcohol source.

By age sixteen, Wendell was drinking heavily four or five days each week. He wondered in treatment if his parents had known about the extent of his drinking, even though they gave no hint of it in his high-school years. In college, Wendell's drinking got out of hand. Despite his talent and because of his drinking, he managed to graduate with the lowest possible average only after considerable cheating and manipulation of his teachers. In the ten years after graduation, Wendell tried a number of businesses. Almost all his ventures ended in bankruptcy.

Wendell met Betty when he was twenty-six, and they were married one month after their initial date. She had been pressured by her family to get married and said she had been drawn to Wendell immediately. After fifteen years of marriage, Betty reached the end of her rope. Wendell was out every night until 3:00 or 4:00 A.M. Most nights he drove home drunk and passed out on the bed next to her. They never talked, their sex life had died, they had no mutual friends and Betty had no help raising the boys.

Betty bitterly confronted Wendell with her misery and demanded either that he enter treatment or that he move out. She reflected that at that time she did not know what his problem was and that she did not suspect that alcoholism could be involved. She viewed him as a "miserable person"; he was miserable himself and made others miserable as well.

Wendell did not want to leave home. But he did not want to enter treatment, either. He resolved this dilemma by appearing for his first therapy session drunk and challenged the therapist to help him. He told the therapist that he was not really interested in therapy and that he had come just to placate his wife. He explained that he came for therapy following "an argument with Betty, but I don't expect to get anything out of it." A thorough history revealed the extent of Wendell's drinking problem. The therapist diagnosed Wendell's alcoholism, confronted him with the diagnosis and provided him with education about alcohol problems. He also recommended that Wendell stop drinking immediately.

Wendell stayed sober for three months, during which he saw the therapist individually. He agreed somewhat reluctantly to the therapist's suggestion that Betty and the boys be included in treatment. He had resisted bringing the family in from the start and later demonstrated his ambivalence by starting to drink again after the first family session. He stopped drinking quickly and thereafter did not take another drink. He did, however, begin surreptitiously using cocaine nine months after the start of treatment. It took him a full year to reveal this new addiction to his therapist, and he did so then only after Betty refused to let him back in the house. "She told me that telling you was my ticket of admission," he told the therapist. From that point on, recovery accelerated.

As he discussed the course of treatment with his therapist sometime later, he was able to identify two ultimatums that

> helped motivate me along the way. The first was when Betty told me it was therapy or divorce. That got me here. The second was when she told me I couldn't come home until I told you about the cocaine. That was the point at which I finally came clean with you and got superserious about getting well. After that, there was no more horsing around.

As recovery progressed, some striking changes took place in the family. Economically, the family moved from debt to prosperity, in part because Wendell stopped using cocaine and in part because his productivity increased. His store moved solidly into profitability, and he began to expand his business ventures. Emotionally, there was a climactic change in Wendell's relationships with the boys. They had been neglected and frightened during Wendell's drinking days. He had been a sloppy and aggressive drunk, and the boys revealed later that they had often pretended to be asleep when he came home so he would not bother them. Betty had coped by losing herself in her friendships and was emotionally unavailable to the boys. When Wendell stopped drinking and using cocaine, he spent much more (and more productive) time at home, and family members began to talk to each other. Only then did the boys' problems come into focus.

Ralph and Mike had been below-average performers in school, and both were isolated from their peers. Kids their age, in Mike's words, "got turned off by us. Even if I didn't know a kid in school, when he found out I was Ralph's brother, that was enough. I never saw him again. And the same type of thing would happen to Ralph because of my reputation."

When Wendell learned of the boys' problems, he was shocked and felt hurt for them. He and Betty began to devote a great deal of energy to the boys' education and to their social development. The boys improved their school performances, and they developed more friendships. As they felt their home base become more solid and predictable, they felt more secure exploring new social activities. For Wendell it was as if the boys had popped into view for the first time. For Ralph and Mike, it was as if they suddenly had parents.

Early in treatment, Wendell had guessed the boys hardly noticed his drinking. Now they were able to tell him in painstaking detail of their terror, embarrassment and revulsion. They spontaneously began to review specific experiences with him.

Betty had described herself early on as someone who was generally inadequate but who might have the potential to do more with her life. She was dependent on Wendell for income and direction, which effectively meant that she had no direction. Over the course of recovery, she discovered strengths she did not realize she had, got a job, made a rapid advance through her corporation to a managerial position and found she was a talented sales manager. She dieted, changed her appearance with clothing and cosmetics and developed relationships with the friends who were really valuable to her. The following exchange captures a few of the changes they had made three years after therapy began. Wendell began:

I was sitting in my office after a long day. I had cleaned up all the odds and ends and thought about the business plan that I had avoided writing for the last nine years. I took out a piece of paper and a pen, and I began to write. I felt inspired, and the words kept coming. After six pages I stopped. I couldn't believe what I had written.

All those little thoughts about how I could improve my business had been floating around in my head all those years. They came together in a very exciting form. I read over what I had written, and I just couldn't believe it. I was so excited, I had to call Betty. When I told her about my plans to shape and direct my business, I don't think she could grasp what I was talking about. It seemed so foreign to us for me to be excited about the future.

The next day I contacted my banker and a couple of outside investors. We arranged to meet at the bank the following week. I painstakingly made flip charts, putting my ideas in slick graphic form. I bought a new suit for the presentation and when I appeared at the bank I appeared dignified and polished. For the first time my silver hair made me look experienced rather than just old. I had prepared a fifteen-minute presentation. Rather than ramble on and on, I actually stuck to my outline and finished talking in fifteen minutes. Questions went on for another hour. At the end of the meeting the banker and other investors offered me exactly what I had asked for and told me that there was more if I needed it. The investors were enthralled with me and my idea. I knew that I was off and running.

After the meeting, I treated myself and a friend (one of the investors) to a nice victory lunch—with no drinks I might add—and then returned to my store. I sat in my office and I was struck by the fact that I had underestimated my ability in all areas, not only in business. I could do a lot more than I had ever dreamed of. I had spent all these years without friends for no good reason! I could have friends, too. I saw the reactions of the people at the meeting, and I knew other people could like me in a social situation as well. I started thinking about those acquaintances who had expressed an interest in getting together to do one thing or another. I made a list. I thought about what I might want to do with them. Ideas popped up. There were interests that I had ignored for years. I had an interest in hot-air ballooning, sailing, handball and hunting. So I made a few calls, and to what would have been my surprise at another time, people agreed to go with me to places I suggested. This was an extraordinary day!

Then Betty spoke:

Wendell, I've just got to interrupt you here. The excitement that you're showing is just great. It's only been during the past few months that I've seen you get this excited, and I just love it. These feelings remind me of what's been happening in my own life.

The promotions I've gotten since I went back to work have been as exciting for me as the new turn in your business has been for you. My first promotion hit me like lightning. I was sitting at my desk and I was called into a meeting with all the division heads. I looked around and thought that I was in the wrong place. I asked my boss sheepishly, "Am I supposed to be here?" He said, "Of course you're supposed to be here. You're the new local sales manager." I was absolutely stunned! As I looked around there were a lot of smiling, friendly faces. I could barely contain my excitement, but I sat there and followed through with the meeting. Afterwards I went over to my boss and said, "How could you have promoted *me* to this position? I've been here only six months. I haven't had a chance to prove myself." He said, "You proved yourself the first week on the job." And I knew then that my work really did speak for itself. I was a highly valuable employee in the company.

Months later when I was promoted to regional sales manager, success came more naturally for me. I knew I had been gunning for that position, and when the regional sales manager was promoted I hoped my efforts would be rewarded. I got it. The money's been great. The recognition's been great. And the new challenge has been both anxiety-provoking and exciting.

But, you know, all of this talk about jobs reminds me that there's a frontier that, Wendell, you and I have yet to take on. I wonder what would happen if we made something like a business plan for our marriage? I wonder what we'd want to invest our time and energy in. What would be exciting for us to do together? It's this area that I'd like to devote a lot of time and attention to.

Shortly after this discussion in the therapist's office, Wendell reported that he and Betty had decided that they not only needed a plan for their marriage but that they also needed to take another look at their relationship with the kids and develop a plan for the family. It has now been two years since Wendell and Betty completed treatment, and the family has stayed in periodic contact with the therapist. They report that the whole family remains sober and that Wendell has succeeded in achieving business goals he outlined in his plan. Wendell and Betty have begun jogging together, have developed a lively interest in the arts and have begun to do some traveling together. Ralph has completed college and Mike is in his senior year. Wendell and Betty and their family continue to encounter problems and to experience moments of indecision. But they have succeeded in living most of these last two years in Region III, involved in pursuits they find rewarding. They are proud of themselves, and they have been able to solve most problems quickly and effectively.

THE GREENBERG FAMILY

The Greenberg family consisted of Ursula (forty-two-year-old wife and mother), Maury (forty-five-year-old husband and father), Robert (fourteen-year-old son and brother) and Jennifer (twelve-year-old daughter and sister). Ursula sought help for her family, stating that she saw so many problems she did not know what to talk about first. She feared for the children. Robert appeared to be bright and talented but exhibited "impossible" behavior problems. He was disruptive at home, at school and any place he went. Jennifer was becoming a social outcast at school and appeared to be an underachiever. And Maury was becoming a domineering drunk. He drank every day, often to the extent of passing out on the living room floor. Before he passed out, he was frequently very aggressive. He often insulted family members. He derisively called Robert "the Neanderthal" ever since Robert entered puberty. Maury regularly telephoned members of the extended family to provoke arguments. Ursula felt that whenever Maury was drinking, the whole family had to "walk on eggs"; one false move or misstatement could lead to a cascade of insults. Ursula described herself as an incompetent parent and an awful wife. She blamed herself for all of the discomfort in her children's lives. She felt responsible for Maury's drinking, saying, "If only I were a good enough wife for him, he wouldn't need to drink." Ursula was proud of herself in only one area of her life. She had confidence in herself as a computer systems analyst. She had been offered several promotions at work, only to turn each down. She feared that if she entered a managerial position, her employees would walk all over her.

Ursula contacted the therapist out of desperation. Her level of helplessness was so high that the therapist briefly doubted his ability to assist this family. After the initial assessment, Urusla summoned up the courage to tell Maury what she had been trying to do and to invite him to a session. Maury refused vehemently. He tore up the literature the therapist had recommended and threatened a lawsuit.

Ursula persisted in her effort to get well, despite her husband's resistance. She continued in therapy, made a concerted effort to set limits with the kids, talked openly about her feelings with her friends and continued going regularly to self-help group meetings. After several weeks, she decided that she could tolerate the chaos in her home no longer. She confronted her husband, set her limits and was dismayed when he called her bluff and moved out. Maury told her, "This is what I've been waiting for, you witch! I've never loved you! Good riddance!"

Stunned by her husband's assault and by the prospect of divorce, Ursula became depressed and endured six miserable months. After Maury moved out of the house, he began drinking early each day, he allowed his business to slide and he filed for divorce. Ursula was panic-stricken every time the kids visited their father at his apartment. Should she let them go? Should she let Maury drive the kids home? Should she discuss these issues openly with the kids?

In treatment, Ursula focused on regaining control of her life and establishing her authority with the kids. Both children attended most of the therapy sessions. She built up her circle of friends and became involved with her synagogue. As her confidence grew, Maury deteriorated. His business partner, a long-time family friend, phoned Ursula to inform her that he was being forced to consider buying Maury out to stop him from destroying the business. One awful day Maury drunkenly stumbled into the school to pick the kids up.

When the kids told the therapist how humiliated they had felt that day, he asked them if they would invite their dad to a session. Perhaps because he was in greater pain by that time, Maury accepted their invitation. He was closer to his "bottom." At this post-divorce session, the kids were able to share their "fact–feeling" lists (as presented in Chapter 2) with their father. At that session, Maury committed himself to enter treatment with another therapist and promised further to do whatever it took to stay away from alcohol. Though such promises are rarely trustworthy alone, Maury proved to be committed to sobriety and to his children.

Over the course of treatment, Robert became much more considerate of others, learned to channel his energy into appropriate athletic and social involvements, and became much more cooperative and loving at home. Jennifer went through a period of depression and gradually grew much closer to both her parents. Ursula gained confidence in herself as a parent and learned to provide her own firm, loving and enriching brand of parenting for her kids. Maury started a new business, remained sober and maintained a high level of attentiveness to his children while he remained firm in his determination to stay distant from Ursula. He expressed the view that marrying Ursula had been a mistake from the beginning. Maury did, however, overcome his tendency to enlist the kids in an alliance against Ursula. He learned eventually to support her authority as a parent.

The following vignettes were described by Ursula, Robert and Jennifer in different sessions, several months after Maury stopped drinking and well after the divorce was final. First, Ursula:

We returned from our vacation, and the house was a mess. Instead of helping me straighten up, the kids went immediately for the TV and started picking on each other. I knew that I felt sad that the vacation was ending. I was not looking forward to going back to work. And I felt sorry for the kids because I assumed that they were raw about going back to school. But instead of catering to my self-pity and my pity for the kids, I thought about ways of salvaging the evening. What would make the evening a great one? My answer came to me quickly. I'd feel better if the house were cleaned up and we all felt prepared for the next day. If we could do all of that, then I would feel good about relaxing. Then instead of doubting my authority, I turned the TV off and told the kids what I had in mind. I wanted their cooperation in cleaning up and getting ready for the next day. If we finished in time, we could rent a movie and watch it together. The kids resisted at first but gave up when they saw how serious I was. I felt strong and I felt that I was in charge. The kids really pitched in. The house was clean in no time, and we were soon curled up on the couch together laughing at Bill Murray. I felt a warm, close, maternal feeling toward both kids.

Now, Robert:

Dad and I went to our first football game ever. Need I say more?

This is what Jennifer had to say:

For a long time I thought that my mom and I were both weird, that nobody would ever like either of us. I certainly didn't. In fact, I hated both of us.

The best thing that happened to me was that I learned that I could be smart and that I could be pretty and fashionable if I just tried. For a long time I just didn't care about homework and I didn't care about clothes. To be honest, I don't know why I changed my attitude. One day, I went shopping with a friend (Charice was my only friend at the time) and tried on some great clothes. I liked the way I looked. So did everyone there. I decided to get my mom to buy me the clothes. She loved them. I started getting a lot of attention from boys, not so much at school but more at gymnastics. My mom had forced me to sign up for this class because there were others kids in it.

The other important good thing happened in school. I started trying to get A's. Why? I still don't know and I'm still threatening to stop trying. But, I have been getting A's and a few B's and I know I can do it if I want to.

As for my mom and I, we still have our problems, but I know I love her. She doesn't seem so weird to me anymore. We've had some nice times together. She doesn't seem to bug me as much as she used to.

The Greenbergs had a rough time of it but were very successful in their approach to recovery. Ursula mourned the loss of her marriage for a long time but ultimately met another man, with whom she became very happy. Maury's success in his abstinence program, in his relationships with the kids and in his business were so stunning that Ursula had to get over a deep jealousy along the way to her recovery. Robert, the older child, had always shown exceptional promise as a student and as an athlete. Once he was able to get his behavior under control, he performed beyond already-high expectations. During the therapy, Robert had been able to link his own obnoxious behavior to the chaos in the family. He literally asked for Ursula to set down some rules. Even more surprising was the fact that he followed them after his mom responded. Jennifer had a difficult time at first. Of the four Greenbergs, her pain appeared to be the most severe and her confidence the weakest. Yet once she began to realize that she could succeed, she made rapid progress.

THE CHASE FAMILY

Chris was a fifty-six-year-old electrician who worked for a contractor. He had been a good employee for seventeen years, and his work record and community reputation were impeccable. People always thought of Chris as an exceptionally nice and sensitive guy. Lilah was Chris's fifty-year-old wife. She had become addicted to diet pills (amphetamines) and to Valium to calm herself down. She had lots of acquaintances, but people found her abrasive and demanding, and they resented her need to be the center of attention. One friend had told Chris, "She wants to be liked, but she doesn't know how." Lilah later explained that she chose to be so arrogant in order to avoid being seen as inferior.

Chris and Lilah had two daughters. Diana, age twenty-nine, was just like her father, to hear Lilah describe her. She was steady and stable and had worked hard to become an electrical engineer. She was strong-willed, although she had a great deal of compassion. Georgette, at age twenty-five, was generally regarded as more attractive than her older sister and quite vain. She always had been able to find the soft spot in her father, and she used that talent to manipulate him. She was allowed to live at home without working and to flunk out of school, and Chris gave her money for clothes and make-up. Her self-esteem was low, despite her appearance, and she needed a lot of reassurance from others to bolster her feeling of worth. She had begun to use drugs in high school.

Lilah started using diet pills after struggling with her weight through her adolescence and early adulthood. She had been ecstatic when she discovered amphetamines. Initially, she got prescriptions for them from her doctor, but later she had to purchase pills surreptitiously. She used Valium to calm herself down at the end of the day when Chris came home. She became progressively more depressed and anxious until she was hospitalized with a "nervous breakdown." She did not tell the doctors in the hospital about her abuse of Valium, and they prescribed it for her when she left the hospital. She later succeeded in getting off the amphetamines. Chris brought her to treatment when she reached a deep level of despair.

Chris initially viewed Lilah's suffering as the result of Georgette's drug problem and her failure to assume adult responsibilities. The therapist diagnosed Lilah's addiction and proposed treating it along with her depression. When it became apparent that Georgette had a serious drug problem, the therapist proposed that the family be treated as a whole.

Georgette joined treatment reluctantly and denied Diana's descriptions of her cocaine and alcohol problems by repeating, "It's not that bad. You're just out to get me." As treatment progressed, Diana stuck to her guns in her evaluation of her mother's and sister's drug use. Chris developed a clear picture of the family's problems and set limits. He made clear to both Lilah and Georgette that he was interested in staying involved with them only to the extent that they would commit themselves to getting better. Though he loved them dearly, he could not stay close to them and watch them destroy themselves. Chris warned them firmly that he simply would walk away if they continued their destructive drug use.

Georgette continued to deny the extent of her drug use and to attack other members of the family. Lilah was relieved that her problem finally was out in the open and astonished by the extent of Chris's and Diana's devotion. Under her doctor's care, she tapered off and ended her use of Valium and started attending self-help group meetings on her own. Georgette continued using drugs and flaunted her use in front of the family. She was unemployed, staying out all night, sleeping all day, did not clean up at home or pay rent and appeared ill and disheveled at times, despite her efforts to maintain her appearance. The several jobs she got through her father and sister ended in disaster when she failed to show up for long periods of time.

Chris and Lilah strengthened themselves over a six-month period. Lilah remained abstinent and developed a commitment to her relationships with Chris and Diana. Together, Chris and Lilah were able to arrive at an accurate picture of Georgette's condition and the chaotic effect she had on family life. Chris, in particular, saw for the first time how he made it possible for Georgette to remain addicted. Difficult as it was for them, Chris and Lilah insisted Georgette stop using drugs and get a job if she wished to remain under their roof. Georgette pretended to go along with them, but soon it became apparent that her drug use continued unabated. At that point, they imposed the consequence and set a moving date. They were horrified when Georgette's scraggly, drug-addicted friend pulled up to take her to his house. Though they were filled with anxiety, self-doubt and guilt, they did not waver; they let her go. Thereafter, they did not hear from Georgette often. They struggled daily with the question of whether to call her. Instead, they wrote her a letter stressing their love for her and their eagerness to help her get well. In therapy, they learned to support each other through the disappointment that she did not call them. At this point, all agreed that the real focus of therapy was the marriage, and Diana withdrew.

Chris and Lilah focused their treatment efforts on their own communication, development of intimacy and sexual fulfillment, their social lives and recreational activities, and on financial planning. They were able to reflect on the progress they had made. Lilah said:

We had been in treatment for six or seven months when Chris and I began to address our sexual relationship. Before treatment, we never talked about sex. I never felt that talking about sex was OK. One or two months after opening up to each other about our sexual feelings, Chris and I went out for a very nice dinner. At the table, Chris handed me a gift. I opened it. In the box was a key to a hotel room. Chris had packed a bag for us and had bought an attractive nightgown for me. When we went up to the hotel room I saw he had arranged for flowers. I just couldn't believe that Chris was capable of being so romantic. I felt very excited, but a little bit scared. I had been aware for several months that I loved Chris dearly, and I felt vulnerable. To be frank, I had not felt love for him for many years, certainly since the addiction began. It took a while after I had stopped using Valium to feel any romantic feeling at all. That night I was just full of sexual and romantic feelings. The teenager in me was alive and scared. How could Chris love me after all I had put him through? I looked at Chris as the kind of man I would really like to be involved with. He looked very attractive; he was both gentle and passionate. During our lovemaking, I was able to tell Chris what felt good and what didn't. He listened and he really liked knowing. I got very involved and I became pretty aggressive with him. I surprised myself, but I shocked Chris! We had a very fulfilling experience. It will always stand out in my mind as a new beginning for our marriage.

186

This is what Chris said:

The thing that stands out most for me about recovery in our family is that my wife is alive. I thought she was dead for a long time. I have an alive, attractive, exciting, interesting woman living with me in the house, and I didn't for a long time. It just didn't seem like anything was happening in our relationship. I always cared, but I never knew how she would react. She was so unpredictable.

I feel funny saying this but one of the things that stands out is that I have been eating a whole lot better. Lilah is a great cook, though she hadn't been cooking for a long time. Since all this started, we eat beautifully. She makes it nice for me to come home for dinner and she seems interested in talking about things and maybe we go someplace after dinner.

I really wish that Georgette would let us help her get better but I realize, and I think Lilah knows, too, now, that we can't do anything to force her to get better. Lilah chose to get better and I'm very happy about that and I'm very sad that Georgette chose to leave our home. But maybe someday she will let us help her. We still do get phone calls from her but usually she just wants money. We've gotten used to saying no because we know that giving in to her would only be destructive for her.

The images of recovery presented above are imbedded in complex lives, lives that continue to unfold and develop. As you read this paragraph, Georgette may have begun her recovery, she may have died of an overdose. No outcome is final until life itself is over; only then can we really know how it turned out.

To develop your own personal vision of a meaningful life, free of the effects of addictive behavior, you will need support, sustained concentration and challenge. We have stressed the importance of professional therapy, education and self-help groups. Now let's turn our attention to the many well-organized resources that are available to help you on your journey.

Chapter 10

How to Get Treatment

In this chapter, we have listed a number of sources of information to help you understand—and get help for—addictive problems. The listings here are certainly not exhaustive, but these resources will get you started on your search for information and help.

Treatment for addictive problems is available to addicts in residential and nonresidential settings.

RESIDENTIAL SETTINGS

Residential programs are those to which addicts go to live and be treated for some length of time. They come in four general varieties: detoxification centers, inpatient programs, therapeutic communities and halfway houses.

Detoxification Centers

Detoxification is the process of "drying out," that is, giving the body a chance to get rid of the drug the addict has put into it in such large quantities. The patient's primary job during the detoxification phase is to abstain from taking any more drugs in spite of the discomfort and craving he may experience.

Although detoxification—or withdrawal—is a complicated chemical process, it is generally more uncomfortable than it is dangerous. In many cases it is best accomplished under medical observation, though only a minority of people actually face life-threatening complications when they dry out. The most severe complications occur among drinkers who also abuse other drugs, because they must adapt to falling levels of several different drugs simultaneously. Of all of the drug families, alcohol and other sedatives produce the most dangerous withdrawal complications.

Many communities provide services to "street alcoholics" and other "street addicts" in detoxification centers, often located in facilities that are not hospitals. Treatment always begins with some form of health evaluation and observation. Hospital-based centers can provide medical care, and "social-setting" (or non–hospital-based) centers have arrangements with local hospitals for such care should it be required.

In most cases, the best detoxification tool is time. The body needs time to rid itself of the drugs and to adapt to the drug-free state. Medications can help with the discomfort and prevent complications during withdrawal. More intensive treatment may be required in cases that present medical dangers, particularly when the patient is in poor health, has a history of severe withdrawal symptoms or appears dangerous to himself or others.

Inpatient and Intermediate-care Programs

The next level of care is inpatient treatment. By "inpatient," we mean in an institution, such as a hospital or other treatment center. Programs in nonhospital settings may be referred to as "intermediate care" and are typically less costly because they require less medical equipment and fewer medical personnel. In either case, the addict lives at the center for the length of the rehabilitation program, often running between ten and twenty-eight days but occasionally lasting as long as twenty-four weeks. Often the addict detoxifies in the same center before the process of rehabilitation begins.

Inpatient rehabilitation programs frequently involve several treatment experiences. Typically, each patient is assigned to an individual counselor who meets with him regularly to provide support, gather important information, explain the program and gain insight into the patient's perspective on his treatment. In addition, the addict meets with other addicts in educational seminars and in group therapy sessions, and he is introduced to the appropriate self-help groups. In treatment centers that emphasize "milieu therapy," patients assume responsibility for maintaining shared living spaces, resolving disputes, setting the proper tone for the environment and planning holiday and weekend social events. In programs that emphasize communication and support, close bonds develop among patients, as they often do among classmates, army buddies and important companions in other formative experiences.

Treatment centers vary widely in their commitment to serve the family. At one extreme are those centers that exclude the family entirely. At the other are those centers that require family participation as a prerequisite for admission. A small number of treatment centers have developed residential programs for the entire family; spouse and children literally move in for one to four weeks of intensive treatment and education. Many treatment centers offer family night or intensive family weekend workshops. Some provide outpatient counseling following the intensive treatment phase.

How much treatment and education should be provided to the individuals in the family? In our view, family involvement in treatment can be extremely valuable for all concerned. All too often, family members feel cut off from their addicted loved one and are left alone with their fears and uncertainties. During the assessment and treatment-planning discussions, it is important to evaluate the needs of the whole family and to establish goals. At a minimum, every family should be offered an assessment, a thorough education about the problems they face, preparation for the next steps in their journey and referrals for additional support (e.g., self-help groups, therapy).

Regardless of how motivated the family is, some of the addict's counseling must be private—that is, it excludes the rest of the family. The addicted family member must have a confidential forum in which to vent his feelings, form his own opinions about his addictive behaviors and set his own goals for the future. Ultimately the decision to work for sobriety is a very personal one. Treatment must support the development of individual freedom and autonomy. Too much togetherness can be a bad thing. Some individuals are not equipped to benefit from therapy in which the whole family participates.

Therapeutic Communities

The therapeutic community is far more intensive than detoxification centers and inpatient and intermediate-care programs. Its chief goal is helping addicts develop new, more functional lifestyles, a process referred to as *resocialization*. The addict is removed from his usual environment and immersed in an alternative culture for a substantial period of time, ranging from six months to three years. Addicts progress through a series of steps, or phases, as they demonstrate the ability to function responsibly and move away from drug-related patterns of behaving and thinking. During the initial phases of treatment, contact with the outside world—mail, telephone and visiting privileges—is severely restricted. Family and friends are purposely excluded. As the addict makes progress, he is granted increasing amounts of contact with loved ones.

At advanced stages of treatment, careful attention is paid to preparing recovering addicts for successful involvement in the community at large. Before moving out of the residential program, patients must be gainfully employed and participate regularly in self-help groups. After discharge, patients often continue in aftercare counseling. Sometimes after completing treatment the recovering addict maintains contact with the therapeutic community in the role of counselor, volunteer or board member.

Halfway Houses

Halfway houses are what their name implies. They are places where several addicts live together, and they are "halfway" between a structured treatment center and life independent of an institution. Each halfway house expects residents to participate in certain required activities. These may include individual contact with a staff member, self-help group meetings and various chores around the house.

Unlike therapeutic communities, halfway houses typically expect residents to begin more quickly to become involved in activities outside of the house. The goal is not one of comprehensive resocialization. Recovering addicts are usually required to attend self-help group meetings outside the house, find (or resume) a job, pay for room and board and reestablish contacts with friends and family. Although halfway house treatment typically is of longer duration than inpatient rehabilitation programs, it is also less intensive. The addict assumes ever greater responsibility for his life as he moves from institution to halfway house and eventually back to the community.

NONRESIDENTIAL SETTINGS

Most treatment received by addicts or their families takes place at a clinic or office to which they come while living at home. For some, nonresidential treatment follows the completion of inpatient rehabilitation programs. For others it follows graduation from a halfway house. Some undergo nonresidential treatment without having been in any form of residential program. There are also situations in which a patient continues seeing the same therapist before, during, and after admission to a treatment center.

Ambulatory Detoxification

For those addicts who do not need medical supervision of their detoxification from drugs, some centers offer detoxification on an outpatient basis. This is frequently called *ambulatory detoxification*.

Most frequently, ambulatory detoxification begins with a medical evaluation. A physician estimates the likelihood that the addict will experience serious medical problems during detoxification. For those addicts not likely to have such problems, detoxification at home may work.

During the ambulatory detoxification process, the addict is given instructions to take home. Those instructions govern the addict's diet and level of activity during the detoxification period. They also usually list the most common signs and symptoms of serious complications, which should be brought to the attention of the physician.

Acute withdrawal is often very stressful, both for the addict and for his loved ones. Physical stressors are compounded by many emotional ones, such as fear of change, ambivalent feelings about drug use, fear of failure, blaming and conflicts among irritable family members. The addict and his family benefit greatly from support during this family crisis. Unfortunately, many treatment centers do not routinely offer such support during ambulatory detoxification. However, when the family makes its needs known, most centers are very responsive and will provide counseling sessions or telephone contact during periods of uncertainty. They also will encourage self-help group attendance.

Ambulatory detoxificaton programs typically focus on the patient who is addicted to only one drug. Most frequently, such programs specialize in one particular drug family: either opiates like heroin and codeine, or sedatives like Valium and alcohol. Detoxification from multiple sub-stances is usually accomplished in a residential setting. In the case of some drugs, like marijuana, detoxificaton may require little or no medical supervision.

The need for supplementary drugs to help the addict through the detoxification process varies from addict to addict and depends substan-tially on the drug or drugs the addict has been using. The process of detoxification often involves the introduction of a new drug from the same drug family, followed by the gradual elimination of drugs. For example, methadone is used as a substitute for heroin, and phenobarbi-tol and other sedatives are used as substitutes for alcohol.

Typically, alcohol-dependent patients are instructed to visit, daily, the treatment center or the office of the private physician supervising the detoxification. At each visit, the nurse or physician evaluates the pa-tient's blood pressure and other vital medical signs and reviews prescrip-tions for any medication given to treat the complications of withdrawal. Doses of medication typically are reduced daily, until the addict is free of all substances related to his drug of choice.

Sometimes detoxification is completed very quickly: three to nine days in the case of alcohol or heroin. In sharp contrast, methadone mainte-nance programs are based on the idea that, for many opiate addicts, detoxification should proceed very slowly. In a long-term detoxification, dosages are adjusted depending upon the patient's condition. When the patient is emotionally, socially and medically stable, he may elect to reduce his dosage of methadone. During periods of discomfort, he may request an increase in medication. The hope—not always fulfilled—is to achieve gradual reductions in dosage until the patient is completely drug-free.

Intensive Outpatient Psychosocial Rehabilitation Programs

Following detoxification, and sometimes following inpatient treatment, some addicts enter evening programs, or intensive outpatient rehabili-tation treatment. The services they then receive are similar to those of-fered in inpatient programs, but patients remain on the job and continue to live at home.

For the patient who does not require a twenty-four-hour residential structure, intensive outpatient programs have many advantages. They are far less costly, less restrictive and less disruptive of daily life than are inpatient programs. Family members often feel more involved in the process of getting better. In outpatient care, the addict has the opportunity to use treatment to learn how to cope with immediate problems without having to use his drug of choice. Recent studies have demonstrated that, for selected groups of patients, intensive outpatient programs match or exceed inpatient programs in effectiveness.

PSYCHOTHERAPEUTIC TREATMENT

A key goal of treatment is to help addicts and their families leave drug-oriented lifestyles and establish new patterns of personal and family life. Although this cannot be accomplished unless an addict comes to grips with his drug use, focusing merely on drug use usually is not enough to formulate and maintain meaningful change. Psychotherapy—the process of self-examination and change assisted by a qualified therapist—is the ingredient of treatment that helps addicts and families forge resilient new life patterns.

The goals and methods of psychotherapy are often misunderstood, particularly as they apply to problems of addicts and their families. What issues do therapists and patients address? What do patients learn in therapy that is of any use in solving real-life problems? Is therapy just a demoralizing, painful and misdirected search through old experiences, or do the patient's efforts lead to new understandings that help him improve his self-esteem and his relationships with others?

This is not the place for a primer on the theory and practice of psychotherapy, but we will describe briefly what we believe you are entitled to expect in psychotherapy. Please bear in mind that we are simplifying some important and complex issues about which much more could be said. For our purposes here, though, brevity and simplicity are appropriate.

There is a wide variety of psychotherapeutic methods available, each with strengths and weaknesses. The following several pages apply to many forms of therapy but not to all of them. Specific questions about your own needs can be answered only by a professional who is aware of your family situation. Nonetheless, reading the material below will equip you both to ask better questions and to better evaluate the answers you get.

Therapy presents you with opportunities to focus your attention deeply on whatever is emotionally most important for you at the time. If you have difficulty recognizing your feelings and emotions, a therapist should be an expert at helping you learn to discover them. If you have difficulty deciding what is important, a therapist can help you discover how to distinguish the truly important from the distracting but less important.

The agenda of therapy varies from person to person. Although some people lead relatively comfortable, financially secure lives, others are forced by their circumstances to attend to problems that jeopardize health and safety, or to struggle to establish a stable, practical base from which to work on ending the emotional chaos in their lives (e.g., securing food, shelter, finances, a job). Thus, practical issues may dominate the therapeutic agenda at the beginning of treatment for some families and never require much attention in therapy for others, leaving them free at an earlier stage to confront the issues outlined in the preceding chapters. Once the chaos is over, the emphasis of therapy often shifts to solving the problem of how to maintain the newfound comfort and peace, how to sustain the effort during the long and often boring period in Region II.

There comes a point in most therapies when the patient becomes aware that the chaos is well behind him, that the strengths he has developed are reliable and effective in preventing a fall back into Region I. It is at this point that there is a great opportunity to discover Region III and to develop it. The patient attends therapy in order to discover enough about himself to develop the kind of life he can feel great about. Rather than feel that he must continue to talk about the problem that brought him to therapy, he can move and explore as yet unknown wants, standards, strengths, feelings and reactions to the challenges of love, friendship and work. This period in therapy is often very exciting. When the patient feels confident that he has established purpose and meaning in his life and that he can both maintain his progress and move ahead on his own, then it is time to end therapy.

With the help of an active, involved therapist, it becomes possible to achieve and sustain a high level of concentration and a clarity of focus. Therapy should enable you to:

a. Overcome the problems that originally brought you to therapy
b. See alternatives that would otherwise be obscure
c. Identify ways to have more influence in your life
d. Learn about your areas of strength and how to exercise them
e. Take credit for effective action
f. Recognize and interpret your feelings
g. Improve your self-esteem and relationships with others
h. Learn important skills in communication, problem-solving and negotiation

Therapy is most of all a place to learn important things about yourself and your family.

The four most common ways in which psychotherapy takes place are with an individual and a single counselor (individual therapy), with a group of addicts and one or two counselors (group therapy), with the addict and his family in conjunction with one or two counselors (family therapy) and with several families led in discussion by one or two counselors (multiple family therapy). Each form offers useful growth experiences. The forms differ in the extent to which they emphasize the many "active ingredients" of growth.

Individual Therapy

The focus of individual psychotherapy is on the individual: his perspective, his feelings, his relationships and his development. Several members of the same family may become involved in their own individual therapies concurrently, each with his own therapist. It is seldom advisable for the same therapist to treat more than one member of the family in individual therapy at the same time. The advantages of this form derive from the fact that the patient receives more undivided attention and has the opportunity to develop a strong helping relationship with the therapist. The therapist helps the patient attend to the most pertinent issues and develop the strengths necessary to take charge of his life.

In intensive therapy, the therapist and patient form a strong and rewarding partnership devoted to helping the patient articulate and achieve his goals. Difficulties that arise in the process of forming the relationship are often examined. In doing so the patient learns many valuable lessons: how to improve his relationships with others, how to

196

communicate more openly and confidently, how to evaluate his impact on others, how to identify needs in a relationship and how to avoid reenacting old destructive patterns. Indirectly, the benefits of therapy can spread from the patient to his family and friends.

Sometimes, family members feel threatened when loved ones enter therapy: "What is he saying about me? Is the therapist going to let him blame me for his problems? Will the therapist judge me?" A competent therapist will encourage the expression of all feelings, including anger. However, it is equally important to help the patient get past his initial feelings and take responsibility to improve his life, rather than blame others for his plight indefinitely or wait for others to change his life for him. Typically, the benefits for the patient's family are well worth the initial anxiety and conflict that accompany the therapy.

Group Therapy

Group therapy adds another dimension to psychotherapeutic treatment. In group treatment, the individual has the opportunity to understand the impact he makes, not on a single individual but on a group of his peers. The number of perspectives on his own problems increases, and he has the opportunity, and perhaps the obligation, to offer other group members his perspective on their problems. Group therapists focus on assisting group members in helping each other and on helping individuals benefit from belonging to the group. They offer the group feedback on how it is functioning and give individual group members assistance if they get stuck in their attempt to understand themselves.

Group therapists tend not to intervene directly in helping individual group members solve their life problems—group therapy is rarely individual therapy in public. Treatment centers frequently conduct groups for addicts and separate groups for family members.

Family Therapy

Family therapy involves both the addict and members of his family. It is included in many treatment programs because the family becomes distressed, unfocused and unproductive when one of its members becomes addicted. The distressed family provides a poor climate for recovery and sometimes even helps perpetuate the addict's destructive behavior.

Family therapists aim to help family members work together productively to accomplish three basic goals of family life:

1. To create a harmonious and nurturing environment that encourages love, intimacy and serenity
2. To raise children in such a way that they develop high self-esteem, competence and the ability to be happy, and to prepare them to be launched into independent adult life
3. To find meaningful ways of being together and healthy ways of being apart

Family treatment tends to be very pragmatic. Attention is focused on immediate problems faced by the family. Many of the steps described in previous chapters are addressed in different forms of family therapy with families of addicts. Success in dealing with an addiction builds confidence and promotes success in achieving other goals. The unique advantages of family therapy are the opportunity to receive guidance during family conversations and to reach a consensus about directions for change. Shared family understandings are powerful in either supporting or undermining change. One disadvantage of family treatment for family members who feel very insecure is that the action may proceed at an intimidating pace, so fast that sessions are too traumatic. The therapist in such cases must either work with the family to slow the action or suggest an alternative to family therapy.

Multiple-family Therapy

Multiple-family therapy combines some of the strengths and weaknesses of family therapy with those of group therapy. Participants learn a great deal about the universal elements of family problems. Observing other families solve their problems can inspire confidence, suggest new solutions for difficult problems and dramatically increase members' sense of determination. One common fear about this form of therapy is of overexposure, embarrassment and "airing dirty laundry in public." Skilled therapists take this concern into account as they structure the experience. Leaders encourage group members to open up gradually, first discussing less personal material. Later, as trust and mutual understanding develop, members find it natural to discuss their own family problems and to help each other.

EMPLOYEE ASSISTANCE PROGRAMS

Employee assistance programs (EAPs) have been increasing in number in recent years. They aim to recognize and deal with employee substance abuse and other personal problems. Personal problems become a direct liability for employers when they reduce the productivity and impair the health of the workforce, thus increasing turnover, absenteeism and the use of health and hospitalization benefits. Employee assistance programs are designed to help employees overcome those problems and function more safely and effectively on the job.

Typically, employee assistance programs are sponsored by employers or unions or both. Either these programs are set up within the organization, or outside professional organizations are engaged to provide confidential evaluation and referral services for distressed employees. In some cases, employees contact the programs themselves and request assistance. In other cases, supervisors refer troubled employees to EAPs either out of personal concern or when they notice the performance of an employee has become impaired.

The EAP offers a distressed employee an opportunity to identify and find help for personal problems. Counselors who work for the employee assistance program seldom offer therapy themselves. In most programs, EAP counselors perform an assessment and then refer the employee to treatment centers or private practitioners.

Employee assistance programs can be particularly useful for addicts who seek help for their problems voluntarily and freely. As we have mentioned before, many addicts believe their addictions go unnoticed by those around them, including their supervisors at work. In most cases this is not true. The employer who offers an employee assistance program is, therefore, usually supportive when an addicted employee chooses on his own to take advantage of the program. If the addict you know works for an employer who sponsors an employee assistance program, the addict may want to turn to this program if and when he decides to seek help. EAPs maintain strict confidentiality. Unless the referral is imposed by a supervisor, common ethical practice among EAP counselors is not to provide employers with personal information, including the fact that the employee sought assistance. When the referral is based on poor job performance, policies on release of information vary among companies.

Be careful, though. While an increasing number of companies are amenable to employee assistance programs, not all companies subscribe to this approach. Consequently, it is best that an addict be cautious in discussing personal problems like addiction with a supervisor. There is little or no risk in asking whether the company offers confidential employee counseling for personal problems. If the supervisor asks about the nature of the problem, he can be told that the problem is private. In the event that the supervisor does not know if the employer sponsors an EAP, contacting the company's personnel department may be the next logical step.

CHOOSING A THERAPIST OR TREATMENT CENTER

Now that we have described the array of treatment services available for getting help with an addiction-related problem, we can consider how to find the best help available to you. Our objective is to help you create a mental bridge to cross the gulf between deciding to get help and actually becoming involved in treatment. We will begin by examining some of the common barriers that prevent families from getting onto the bridge. We will then provide advice on how to cross the bridge: how to choose a therapist or treatment center, how to solve problems that arise in treatment, and how if necessary to cope with an unsatisfying treatment experience.

Removing Barriers to Treatment

Some barriers to getting started are practical, while others are emotional or attitudinal. Finances, conflicting commitments and the limited availability of time, child-care, and transportation may appear to block the way to getting help. Hidden attitudes and fears about treatment may foster the illusion that such practical problems are unsolvable. However, people often find practical solutions once they understand their underlying feelings.

To identify your personal reservations about treatment, start some sentences with, "I don't want to get help because _____." Write down your answers. Think about them, and then continue reading. The "Attitudes and Emotions" table on pages 202–3 lists several common examples of feelings that may interfere with your attempts to get help. If you decide to consider professional consultation, it would be very useful to discuss your reservations with the therapist who performs the assessment. After identifying your personal list of reservations about getting help, it may be easier to grapple with practical obstacles.

There is one concern everyone must consider: finances. Treatment costs, over the course of recovery, range from zero to hundreds of thousands of dollars. At the catastrophic end of the continuum are those alcoholics who develop serious medical and psychological complications requiring long periods of hospitalization. At the other end of the continuum are those families who rely heavily on self-help groups and who receive inexpensive treatment in programs subsidized by government or philanthropic agencies.

Financially strapped individuals need not give up in the search for quality care. Federal, state and local government agencies subsidize treatment centers throughout the country. Catholic, Protestant, Jewish and community philanthropies subsidize treatment centers in many locations. Health insurance companies are required by law in many states to provide reimbursement for addiction-related services. Community mental health centers and even many private therapists employ sliding scales in setting fees for many outpatient services. Halfway houses and therapeutic communities typically defer requests for payment until after the patient has secured employment. Although there are discouraging gaps in the health care safety net, funding problems often prove to be solvable when approached creatively.

Delaying treatment can be very expensive. Addictions tend to get worse over time and pass from one generation to the next. A good rule of thumb is: The longer you wait the more it will cost. If the intervention begins before the addict becomes physically dependent on his substance, he will likely be able to avoid a costly hospital stay. If the children are assessed and helped before they sustain severe academic, social or emo-

Attitudes and Emotions That May Block Treatment

Barrier	*Attitudes That Circumvent Barriers*
Avoiding dependency	
"Getting help means that I'm weak. I'm tough. I can handle all of my problems." "You can't depend on anybody."	"The most powerful people depend on many others for expert counsel, for help, for support. I gain strength from learning from and relying on others. Isolation makes me weak. With help, I can learn to be interdependent and to manage more of my life independently."
Low self-esteem	
"I don't deserve help. Therapy is too self-indulgent." "I'm really OK [denying distress signals, ignoring needs in decision making]." "My therapist won't like me. He'll laugh at, be disgusted by, or look down on me." "I'm a lost cause."	"I want to feel better, and I must decide I'm worth it. Not getting help is the same as choosing to hold on to my misery. I have to take the risk that I deserve happiness and respect even if I don't know exactly how or why. If my therapist doesn't understand me, I'll find one who will."
Enmeshed family members	
"Talking to a therapist about my real feelings would be disloyal. I can't betray my family." "My family will feel threatened." "If I get started on my anger, I'll never stop. I'll have to run away or yell at someone." "I might be tempted to confront everyone and say how I feel. That will only make them angry."	"I can no longer cater to our destructive ways of being together. Unless I take the risk of finding out what I think, there is no way to make things better. My honesty may help all of us. If we really are best off together, we will find out how to be comfortable together."

Barrier	Attitudes That Circumvent Barriers
Misconceptions about treatment	
"The therapist will blame me or members of my family and tell us we are crazy. Maybe we *are* crazy."	"The therapist's job is to understand my perspective and to help *me* get stronger, to help *me* choose my own direction, and to provide expert consultation when I ask for it. I can end therapy whenever I like: when it is successful or if progress seems too slow. If my therapist is weird, I'll go to someone else."
"The therapist will tell me to do things and will interfere in ways that are none of his business. I'll be trapped."	
"Therapy will go on forever and nothing will change."	
"All therapists are crazy anyway. A therapist will just make me crazy like him."	

tional damage, normal development resumes and a long course of therapy may be unnecessary; they may find ways of coping without relying on substances. Our advice is to get an expert assessment, then nip any problem in the bud.

If you decide to get help, you will be faced with the question of how to find effective professionals and self-help groups to work with. How can you tell a good one from a bad one?

Quality

Not all treatment centers and practitioners are equally qualified. Many are excellent; a few are harmful; and there are many levels of quality in between. Experts in mental health and addictions have not yet arrived at a consensus on a definition of excellence. We offer our frank opinions below. First, we'll describe characteristics that equip a therapist to guide and support you on your journey. Then we'll address the issue of quality in treatment centers.

If the material below seems discouraging, because we describe deficiencies that you may find in a therapist, please remember that many therapists are very helpful and well qualified to help you. We will equip you to recognize excellence. Later in this chapter, we will explain how to find a list of competent therapists to choose from.

To be helpful, a therapist must combine a high level of technical competence with several desirable personal qualities. Therapists who do not specialize in addiction treatment sometimes do their addicted patients a disservice by providing inappropriate treatment. Research our colleagues and we have conducted has demonstrated that many health care professionals (psychiatrists, social workers, nurses) receive little or no academic preparation to diagnose or treat addictive disorders. Furthermore, when addicts or their families present their symptoms in psychiatric clinics, they are often misdiagnosed. Addicts may receive therapy and tranquilizers for years, without addressing chemical use as an issue. Family members may receive supportive therapy that enables them to remain in damaging situations without directly confronting chaos-producing addictive behaviors. When it comes to helping families who are affected by chemical dependence, there is no substitute for a detailed understanding of addictive disorders and their treatment. In addition to specializing in the treatment of addiction, we believe that a therapist must have a solid academic foundation in theories of personality change, supervised experience in each form of treatment he provides and supervised experience with each age group of patients he sets out to treat.

How can the patient find out whether a prospective therapist has specialized skills in addiction and solid technical skills? We advise you to get a referral from someone you trust and to ask specific questions of any therapist you consider hiring to help your family. "Where and when did you develop your specialty in addictions? What supervised experience have you had in treating people (or families) like me (us)? Please tell me about your training in therapy." Questions like these, when asked politely, can result either in uncertainty or in greater confidence in your therapist. If you feel unsure whether the first therapist you consult has the skills to be of service to you, we advise you to shop around. Talk to another therapist. Compare. Choose the one you feel best about.

The personal qualities that make for good therapy are virtues in other contexts as well, but they are even more important in a therapeutic setting. As teachers of psychotherapy, we attempt to help trainees develop empathy, warmth, genuineness, a down-to-earth manner, alertness to themselves and their patients and acceptance, as well as the ability to take good care of themselves. Coldness, arrogance, dogmatism, phoniness, dishonesty, harshness, stupidity and lack of interest are incompatible with the goals of therapy.

Therapists are human beings, and like members of all other professions suffer from a full range of human maladies and misfortunes. You may go to a therapist and detect alcohol on his breath, he may seem strange, or he may make you feel uncomfortable in some other way. *Do not ignore these danger signs.* Listen to your feelings. If you are displeased with your therapist, confront him with your feelings if at all possible. Therapists should be expert at listening to such feelings and responding to them productively. If the therapist dismisses your feelings or insults you somehow, you should probably change therapists. Skilled therapists understand the benefits of discussing problems in the therapeutic relationship.

Helping professionals receive training in many different disciplines (including psychology, psychiatry, nursing, social work, counseling or educational psychology, addiction counseling) and at different levels (certificate, associate degree, bachelor's degree, master's, and doctorate). Some counselors have no formal training at all and feel that they need none, having learned "on the street." There are many professionals with modest formal training who are equipped to be helpful in a range of situations, in limited roles.

The issue of which type of professional to choose under what circumstances is a subject of bitter debate. The question is too complex for us to be able to advise you here on how to choose one discipline or level of training over another.

The problem of choosing a treatment center is somewhat different. Differences between programs may appear subtle. If you have the luxury of shopping around for a treatment center, you might consider looking into five variables that are important in thinking about quality.

1. *Multiple levels of care.* When a treatment center offers only one level of care (e.g., inpatient) the pressures of the market may create a bias in favor of that level of care. Unnecessary treatment may be provided in order to fill beds. Having multiple levels of care under one roof reduces this conflict of interest and makes it easier to move the patient from one program to the other when the patient needs it.

2. *Comfortable atmosphere.* Do you feel comfortable in the treatment environment? Do the staff members and other patients seem comfortable? Is there an active alumni group? A treatment center with a strong

sense of purpose and effectiveness feels more comfortable than one in which staff and patients are confused.

3. *Wide range of services, presented creatively.* Excellent treatment centers encourage their professional staff members to identify and respond to patient needs by developing helpful programs. Many centers offer family programs, vocational counseling, recreational therapy, fitness classes, relaxation training, milieu therapy, extensive exposure to volunteers from self-help groups, specific skill-related groups, psychological testing when needed and medical services and treatment when needed. Others provide none of the above services, regardless of the need.

4. *Cost and location.* Much of the cost of inpatient care is determined by the room rate in the institution that houses the program rather than the actual cost of the program. Some of the best care is provided relatively inexpensively. Convenience is an important factor in choosing a center because of the large time commitment.

5. *The staff.* In addition to the individual characteristics and levels of training and expertise of each individual staff member, it is important to consider the way professionals on the staff work together. Staff members who feel threatened and burned out do not take care of patients as well as staff members who feel supported. The ideal treatment center invests consistently in training its staff, hires highly dedicated individuals, maintains low rates of turnover in staff and administration and actively communicates its approach within the professional and general community.

We caution you against delaying action to wait to find the ideal treatment environment. The best way to get to the right place is to take a step, even if the first step takes you in the wrong direction. Most treatment centers offer valuable experiences. One way of checking to be sure that a program has met minimum standards is to see whether it is accredited by the Joint Commission on Accreditation of Health Care Organizations (JCAHCO). Only the poorest of centers will have lost their JCAHCO approval. More detailed information about treatment centers in your area may be obtained by talking with addiction specialists in your community, by meeting program graduates in self-help groups or by calling the intake coordinator(s) at the treatment center(s) in your hometown.

Finding Treatment in Your Area

In the event that the addict or other family members decide they want to get help, there are several ways to start the search for a treatment center in your area. The first step is to look for an agency, hospital, health or mental health center or private practitioner who can evaluate the family. A good diagnostic evaluation will examine a full range of family strengths and problems, including addiction, and will help identify the objectives for improvement. After the first session, the diagnostician should offer you an opinion about the type of treatment necessary, recommending a specific level of care to accomplish specific objectives. In some cases, additional outpatient diagnostic sessions will be required before a final disposition can be made.

But how does one find a competent practitioner or treatment center? Consult a family physician, clergyman, friends, relatives, neighbors or anyone else you trust who may know of treatment programs. If available, ask a counselor at your company's employee assistance program. EAP counselors may be the single best-qualified sources of information about treatment in the community. Evaluating treatment resources is one of their principal responsibilities. Other excellent sources include school psychologists and school social workers, teachers who coordinate school drug abuse education curricula, your attorney and members of self-help groups. If you run out of leads, you might try contacting addiction experts at a local hospital, college or medical school. Just call the departmental secretary in psychology or psychiatry to get the names of faculty members who might be familiar with local resources.

Hospital and professional organization referral services are additional sources of prospective therapists. Hospitals and local and state psychological and medical associations, as well as professional organizations for social workers, nurses and counselors, frequently offer referral services to interested callers. These organizations will refer you to therapists who have asked to be included in the referral service. Although this does not mean necessarily that these therapists can*not* treat your problem, it is also no assurance that they *can*. Names of interested therapists are usually given out, three at each inquiry, in rotation, as requests are made for referrals. Call the main number and ask if the organization maintains a referral service. If it does, ask the person giving you the names if he knows these people and can vouch for them.

When all else fails, check the phone book yellow pages under "Alcoholism" or "Drug Abuse" for listings of treatment programs. However, the yellow pages will mention only those programs that have paid for advertisements. There may be other programs in your area that do not advertise in the yellow pages. If you are a veteran of the U.S. Armed Services, you can contact the nearest Veterans Administration hospital or clinic.

You can also contact the office of your state government that specializes in alcoholism and drug abuse services. Appendix 3 is a listing of those offices for each of the fifty states and Washington, D.C.

With these general guidelines in mind, you can begin the task of securing for your family the best and most appropriate professional help for your problems. Remember that the ideas, exercises and suggestions in this book are not intended as a substitute for professional psychological help. All matters regarding your family's health require the attention of a competent psychologist, physician or other health care professional.

IF YOU ARE DISSATISFIED WITH A THERAPIST OR TREATMENT CENTER

The best therapists will occasionally make an error. None is perfect. Even if the therapist does nothing wrong, the personal chemistry between the two of you may not be right. If a prospective therapist or even one you have been working with for some time disappoints you, what should you do? As a consumer of services, you have at least three options. In most cases, we would advise you to confront the therapist with your feelings and give him or her the opportunity to be responsive to you. Just as it is a mistake to assume that loved ones should know what you need from them, so, too, is it a mistake to assume that a therapist should be able to read your mind. In rare cases, specifically those in which the therapist says or does something so troublesome that he destroys your confidence in his judgment, we would advise you to find a new therapist. Finally, there are situations in which it would be wise to get a second opinion to help you evaluate your options. The second professional can help prepare you to confront your therapist or to terminate the first relationship with greater confidence.

We urge you not to ignore your dissatisfaction. Blaming yourself will not help. Getting stuck in another unsatisfying relationship merely perpetuates your problem. We believe from our experience and that of our many colleagues and students that therapy can and should be extremely beneficial. But, as in all personal relationships, you cannot have a satisfying experience unless you stand up for what you need.

Coping with dissatisfaction in a treatment center is usually somewhat more complicated, but it is usually well worth the effort to assert your needs in the appropriate context. There are three channels of communication to work with: your counselor, patient groups (e.g., therapy groups, treatment center community meetings) and formal administrative channels. Most treatment centers have formal quality assurance systems including grievance procedures or managers whose job it is to maintain the quality of care. Don't settle for a less-than-satisfactory experience.

Chapter 11

Self-help Groups

Self-help groups are organized by recovering abusers or by loved ones of abusers, and their functions reflect the needs of those who organized them. The best known and the prototype is Alcoholics Anonymous (AA). In this final chapter of the book, we will shift our emphasis from the family to focus directly on AA and its role in recovery from alcoholism. There are many similarities between AA and its family-oriented offspring (e.g., Al-Anon, Adult Children of Alcoholics [ACOA], Nar-Anon, Families Anonymous, Gam-Anon, Alateen and Alatot), though their foci differ. This chapter will explain the structure of such groups, how to join them and how to see through common misunderstandings that scare people away from joining. When you understand the philosophies and practices of AA, you will grasp those of other self-help groups more rapidly. But the best way to find out whether self-help groups are for you is to try them. Without actually going to meetings, you will not be able to see how such groups really work.

ALCOHOLICS ANONYMOUS

AA has been in existence for more than fifty years. Its founders began their organizational efforts in the mid-1930's, and by 1938 AA was a functioning entity. AA groups exist all over the United States and in some 114 countries abroad. Estimated membership is 1½ million; 800,000 members live in the U.S. and Canada.

210

For many years AA and alcoholism treatment were nearly synonymous in the U.S. AA remains a major form of treatment, and is the oldest and largest group of its kind. A great many people over the years have found AA to be extremely helpful. Some have found it to be the only effective form of treatment for them. Other AA members combine participation in AA with the other forms of treatment.

Program Description

The AA program mirrors the population of problem drinkers in its diversity. Just as it is difficult to describe the typical problem drinker, it is also difficult to describe a typical self-help group meeting. Members gather in churches, synagogues, schools, hospitals, private homes, restaurants, corporate boardrooms and other meeting places. Professional societies, such as the American Medical, Dental, Bar and Psychological Associations, have long provided facilities for self-help group meetings at their annual meetings. At most meetings you will find a very broad cross-section of the community. For example, one popular meeting in Chicago is attended by working people, professionals, street people, members of all racial and ethnic groups and traveling business people. Meetings can also be very specialized. Alcoholic nonsmokers, atheists, homosexuals, Jews, doctors and other groups have organized special meetings to address their particular needs within the AA structure. We even know of one meeting for nonsmoking atheist attorneys with more than one year of sobriety. To find groups that enrich your life, you will need to attend several different meetings, get to know people and ask questions. Members of AA and other self-help groups are extraordinarily open to newcomers and will be happy to help you find what you are looking for.

The traditions of AA explicitly discourage any form of activity that might distract members from their primary goals: to remain sober and to provide a supportive environment in which to achieve and maintain sobriety. An informal structure handles functions such as the maintenance of facilities and the distribution of publications. But, as a matter of principle, its organization is given little emphasis.

The general guidelines under which AA operates are known as the Twelve Steps and Twelve Traditions. The major components of the AA program remain the same around the world. Nevertheless, the AA pro-

211

gram is adapted to meet the needs of each group. Each member contributes to the atmosphere, to the discussion and to the direction taken in the meeting.

Entering the Program

Joining AA is very simple. In its official words, "The only requirement for membership is a desire to stop drinking." The way you join AA is to attend meetings. Period. There are no formal membership criteria, application procedures, referral forms or review boards, and there are no fees. Twelve-step programs are the only organized groups we know of that truly welcome strangers *unconditionally and at no cost*. A traveler can get off an airplane in most of the world's cities, call the central number of AA and quickly find people who will talk with him, take him to a meeting and share a common interest. AA views itself as a caring community; it lives up to its philosophy.

Meetings

Many people have a notion that AA meetings are huge affairs with formal agendas and rigid formats. Actually, though, AA meetings are quite flexible in both content and format.

Beginners' meetings are usually much smaller than general AA meetings. Beginners' meetings occur either prior to a general meeting or as a subsection of a general meeting. In these meetings, experienced AA members describe the program to new members and answer any questions. Beginners are usually considered to be those who feel like beginners.

In schedules of AA meetings, programs are designated as "open" or "closed." Anyone may attend an *open* AA meeting, whether he thinks he has an alcohol problem or not. Family members are welcome to attend with or without their alcoholic loved one, whether or not he has quit drinking or joined AA. Commonly, an experienced member presents a "lead," which is a series of opening remarks. Then those who wish to comment can do so, and those who do not can say "pass." A lead may consist of personal reflections on an element of program philosophy as it relates to the life of the speaker, or it may consist of a short account of the speaker's life or "story." Although there is no rigid format for a story, speakers often cover their early use of alcohol, how alcohol came to interfere with their lives, their introduction to the AA program and the positive steps they have taken since joining AA.

Open meetings are quite useful to a new AA member in helping him find people with whom he can identify before labeling himself alcoholic. In the words of one individual who began attending AA years after getting sober in therapy, "You diagnosed me alcoholic and it never sank in. I went to AA and discovered so many people like myself that it was inescapable. I finally knew deeply what was wrong and that millions of people had found a way to do something about it together. It was like drawing deeply from the well at an oasis."

Closed meetings are restricted to those who know they have a drinking problem. While one member may start by telling his story, closed meetings may follow a different format. They may be discussion meetings with an open agenda, large "drunkalogue" meetings (in which members tell about their drinking experiences) or meetings that focus on a particular topic, like trust, humility or resentment. They may also be step meetings, devoted to discussion of one or more of the Twelve Steps (see pages 216), perhaps rotating through the Steps in order, focusing on one Step per week; in some places, subgroups form to focus on different Steps.

Very often a member of the group will share some recent triumph or tragedy in a closed meeting. Other members then provide support and relate how similar experiences have affected them. The primary focus of these discussions is sobriety, and many helpful techniques are shared.

It should be noted that a steady diet of only one kind of meeting is usually not sufficient. Participation limited to speaker meetings, for example, can enable the drinker to remain uninvolved. In particular, it does not provide a format for examining one's own sobriety and discussing new coping strategies. Attending only discussion meetings that feature the same group of regulars may lead the drinker to look at his drinking behavior through rose-colored glasses. How convenient it is for all of us to forget our past mistakes. Mixed speaker meetings attended by new members are helpful to older members because such meetings help prevent them from becoming complacent. One AA publication states, "The reminders you get of the miseries of active alcoholism can help extinguish any lurking desire to take a drink." Many drinkers say,

"What do I want to listen to that guy for? I did all those things myself."
Precisely. An AA slogan is "Remember when."

Veterans of AA have often said that it is uncanny how often discussions in meetings touch upon whatever they were thinking, worrying about or celebrating that day. One can enter a meeting without clear direction and find some new insight or strength.

Literature

Reading AA literature offers several benefits to the AA member. First, in privacy, literature can inspire you to develop a deeper and more personal understanding of the program than is available from meetings. Second, there is a wide variety of literature and at least part of each publication addresses some special interest or concern that may not be addressed directly at meetings. Third, the literature can be taken home and reviewed in a crisis.

Some members refer to AA literature as a meeting in print, and this seems an apt description. Take one example. The concept of a higher power is central to successful participation in AA, yet it is often difficult to grasp. None of the members at a particular AA chapter may have an interpretation of the higher power that makes sense to a particular individual. One pamphlet contains seventy-five interpretations of the concept. The variety of viewpoints increases the likelihood that a member will find one to his liking.

Variety

AA World Services, Inc., prints a selection of books about alcoholism and AA. Probably the best known is *Alcoholics Anonymous*, also known as "The Big Book." While a number of early members contributed to the book, the first portion of it was written by Bill W., a cofounder of AA. The basic precepts of AA are presented in this book, and it is regarded as the primary sourcebook by most AA members. It was AA's first publication.

A more recent publicaton is *Living Sober*, which is subtitled "Some methods AA members have used for not drinking." This relatively short book (eighty-seven pages) lives up to its subtitle. It focuses primarily on practical tips on how to stay sober. It is not the kind of book to read in one sitting. Its best use is similar to that of Dr. Spock's *Baby and Child Care;* that is, as a resource book for solutions to particular problems.

Another book that is best digested piecemeal is *Twenty-Four Hours a Day.* Each page is devoted to a different day of the year and contains a short essay. The topics vary, but the tone is generally inspirational. Some AA members start their day by reading the appropriate page from this book. By doing so, they begin the day with a positive mental attitude and with greater serenity, so that they are not as easily disturbed by events.

AA also prints a number of pamphlets. Some of these address particular subgroups (the military, industry, drug abusers), while others concern more general issues. Excellent introductory works include "This is A.A.," "'Is A.A. for You?" and "The Jack Alexander Article." These pamphlets can help the prospective member learn what to expect from AA meetings. Beginner packets are available through the AA central office in your area.

Use in a Crisis

There are times when an AA member cannot attend a meeting just when it is needed most, perhaps upon awakening or retiring, during physical illness or while at work. AA literature can be most useful during those critical times that are most likely to lead to a relapse.

Many AA publications present short, inspiring messages to focus attention on successful guidelines for recovery. The Serenity Prayer, for example, states, "God, grant me the serenity to accept the things I cannot change, the courage to change the things I can, and the wisdom to know the difference." While this prayer did not originate with AA, it is well-suited to its members' uses. Many drinkers have reported that reciting it has given them the moment's pause they needed to reevaluate a situation before returning to drinking.

In AA, "Remember when" is called a slogan. Other AA slogans are:

Easy does it.
Just for today.
Live and let live.
First things first.
Do the next right thing.

As with the Serenity Prayer, some of these sayings have been around for years and certainly did not originate with AA. However, as used by AA, they represent a shorthand version of various aspects of the AA program.

The Twelve Steps

The core of the AA program is the Twelve Steps, which were devised by the early members of AA. All meetings revolve around the Twelve Steps, and all writings are based on them.

1. We admitted we were powerless over alcohol—that our lives had become unmanageable.
2. Came to believe that a power greater than ourselves could restore us to sanity.
3. Made a decision to turn our will and our lives over to the care of God *as we understood Him.*
4. Made a searching and fearless moral inventory of ourselves.
5. Admitted to God, to ourselves, and to another human being the exact nature of our wrongs.
6. Were entirely ready to have God remove all these defects of character.
7. Humbly asked Him to remove our shortcomings.
8. Made a list of all persons we had harmed, and became willing to make amends to them all.
9. Made direct amends to such people wherever possible, except when to do so would injure them or others.
10. Continued to take personal inventory, and when we were wrong, promptly admitted it.
11. Sought through prayer and meditation to improve our conscious contact with God *as we understood Him,* praying only for knowledge of His will for us and the power to carry that out.
12. Having had a spiritual awakening as the result of these steps, we tried to carry this message to alcoholics, and to practice these principles in all our affairs.

The concept of the Twelve Steps is an important contribution made by recovering alcoholics to the culture as a whole. Applications can be found in everyday life, even for nonalcoholics.

While there are many ways to analyze the Steps, they represent four stages of the recovery process—surrender, assessment, making amends, carrying the message.

Surrender

The first three Steps involve the surrender process. In this process, the drinker gives up his resistance to important facts about his life. He gives up the illusion that he can go on drinking without harm. He learns that many things in his life are not under his control but do follow some order and do have meaning. The religious AA member looks to God to understand that order and meaning. The atheist will look to nature and to other people as he tries to understand the sources of power and influence that shape his life. The drinker surrenders his lonely and desperate struggle to drink away the emotional consequences of problems in living. He learns that "there is no problem a good drink can't make worse." He opens up to forces in the world that can help, exchanging alcohol for group support and for caring. When things do not go his way, he "turns it over." Rather than let disappointment shake his belief in himself and in others, he learns to take losses in stride, to understand that some tragedies are inevitable.

During the process of surrender, many drinkers come to realize that they are not able to moderate their drinking. A popular AA slogan is, "One drink is too many, a thousand aren't enough." This process is not easy for most drinkers. Many relapses result when the drinker thinks, "I've been sober six months now. I can handle just one or two drinks." In the AA framework, this kind of thinking serves as evidence that this person has not yet "taken the first Step," that he does not yet see himself as truly powerless to control the effects of alcohol.

It is often difficult for the new AA member to accept the idea of the "power greater than ourselves" and to ask that power for help. Many new members are not actively religious and do not believe in a God. What is often helpful at this stage is to emphasize that even if the drinker cannot yet believe in a power, at least he can recognize that he has not managed his life well up to this point. As a result, he may give up his need for control and instead be open to the possibility that the caring and advice given by others have value. Some members eventually come to see the spirit of fellowship in AA as their greater power. In other words, they believe that with the help of other members they can accomplish feats that previously had exceeded their grasp.

Assessment

The fourth through seventh Steps involve:

- Making an honest, fearless assessment of one's flaws
- Sharing the results of this assessment with another person
- Letting the higher power remove these character defects
- Asking the power to do so

Many people who relapse despite participation in AA have ignored one or more components of the assessment sequence.

Most of us are willing to admit to superficial flaws. However, the key word in the fourth Step is "fearless." In a fearless moral inventory we probe all those areas we do not usually let ourselves think about—for example, that we have failed our children, ruined our health or destroyed our marriage. These assessments seem to have more impact if they are done in writing. Hazelden Educational Services has published two excellent pamphlets that serve as guides to completing the assessment. Hazelden's address is in Appendix 2. Another popular guide for the fourth Step appears in the "Big Book," *Alcoholics Anonymous*.

If the assessment is done well, it will undoubtedly bring a lot of painful memories to light. During the assessment, the member cannot help but become aware of certain weaknesses or flaws in himself. AA calls these flaws "character defects," and the process of exploring them is called "taking inventory." Some of these character defects may seem so shameful or embarrassing that the member cannot picture ever sharing that material with anyone. But through participation in AA, the material is often gradually revealed. As other AA members share their stories, the new member can identify with various aspects and therefore share his material. After some time in AA, most members find someone with whom they feel particularly comfortable and to whom they reveal the rest of their inventory. This sharing need not be done with an AA member, merely with another human being. Clergymen, counselors, close friends and relatives have all been partners in this sharing process.

The sixth and seventh Steps are sometimes difficult for drinkers who do not have a sense of God. Once a drinker has honestly looked at his flaws and discussed them with someone else, he is usually ready—even eager—to change. And so he looks for the strength, understanding, courage and good judgment to alter his behavior. For the devout AA member, prayer is a natural way of focusing himself on the task of changing and asking for the strength to change. He asks God to remove his flaws. On the other hand, an atheist must create another focus in his yearning to change. He may focus on the group, humanism, health or self-actualization. He wishes for the strength and circumstances to allow him to grow. This procedure does not imply that he does not need to work hard on improving himself, but merely that he leaves himself open for assistance.

The key word in Step seven may well be "humbly." It is hard not to let your pride get in the way when asking for help with your flaws. The discipline called for in Steps four and five requires the drinker to take an honest look at himself, to see both the weaknesses and the strengths. If, out of guilt, he is unable to acknowledge strengths, it will be even more difficult to acknowledge weaknesses, particularly when revealing self-perceptions to another person. Balance is necessary; a negatively biased picture of oneself is of little use. The AA program encourages honest and fearless self-evaluation. It does not value masochism. The moral inventory is not an exercise in dragging oneself through the mud.

During the assessment process, the drinker often comes to recognize the ways he has hurt others. The eighth and ninth Steps involve having this recognition and beginning to make amends. These Steps can be quite satisfying in that they involve concrete action. There are often a number of tangible amends that need to be made—financial debts to be repaid, "borrowed" belongings to be returned, damaged property to be restored and long-neglected chores to be completed. In addition, there are usually a lot of apologies owed to others—employers, neighbors, friends, relatives, spouses and children. The apologies need not be overly flowery or excessively humble—acknowledgment of past wrongs, expression of regret, and the beginning of actual change is all that is required for most. In some cases the wronged people may be so annoyed with the drinker that the apology is better done by letter than in person. It is also important to remember the second half of the ninth Step, that drinkers should make amends "except when to do so would injure them or others." For example, if the drinker has pilfered money from his daughter's piggy bank without her knowledge, and has already replaced it, it might be best not to tell her.

Carrying the Message

Understanding the Twelfth Step is central to correct stereotypes of AA. In the positive stereotype, selfless AA members will appear any time of the day or night to provide any form of help to a drunk. In the negative stereotype, AA fanatics go about preaching the AA gospel, badgering those with no significant drinking problems. As with all stereotypes, both are inaccurate.

Spirituality is distinct from religion in AA. Members practice many different faiths, and some are atheists and agnostics. AA is not a religion. It does not promote beliefs about God and does not focus on the nature of the relationship between man and God. AA is a spiritual community whose members share some specific values and agree that certain types of behavior are admirable. For example, AA stresses the importance of caring, support and love. It emphasizes that it is important to structure your life to include giving and receiving support. Similarly there is value in taking good care of yourself. Getting worse through neglect is viewed as bad; doing what it takes to get healthy is good. It is good to find your place in the world, a base from which you can be involved assertively and comfortably with other people. Isolation is viewed as dangerous. Passively giving in to other people to seek their approval is termed "people pleasing" and is also viewed as dangerous.

Many new members report being impressed with how much the members genuinely care for each other, with no thought of repayment. The experience of such caring can certainly be referred to as spiritual, and it is this message that AA wants its members to carry to others; there is help available from people who genuinely care. The literature emphasizes that this message should be carried willingly and unselfishly. In particular, those doing Twelfth Step work should not expect any additional reward if their message is effective, nor let their lives be disrupted if the message is rejected.

Twelfth Step work is only done with those who request it. All types of aid will be offered to help the person get sober. However, this help need not include, for example, becoming a taxi service or bodyguard. Only the help that will aid someone in beginning a program of sobriety need be offered.

The negative stereotype has some kernels of truth. Some members who do Twelfth Step work are quite dogmatic and insistent. However, every collection of human beings has a certain percentage of fanatics, and AA undoubtedly has its share. Some may be new members of AA. Like all people who have found something new they enjoy, their enthusiasm may override their common sense. However, these people are in the minority in AA. And since Twelfth Step work is done in pairs, it is highly unlikely that both members would be equally dogmatic. One usually balances the other.

It is important to emphasize that the Twelve Steps constitute a circular, not a linear, process. In other words, the Twelve Steps are not a recipe for sobriety with which you start at Step one, go through to Step twelve and then expect sobriety to bloom. Instead, they are a process of continuing reappraisal and growth. For example, in doing Twelfth Step work, you can discover things about yourself that you did not know when you initially passed through the fourth Step. None of the Steps is ever irrevocably completed.

Also, not all AA members go through all the Steps, and many do not go through them in order. Some prefer to begin making amends before they have completed their assessment. The important thing is not to dismiss any of the Steps totally, while remembering that the program does not obligate anyone to do anything that appears foreign or senseless.

Sponsors

Another important aspect of the AA program is the sponsor relationship. A sponsor is an experienced AA member who becomes a less experienced member's teacher, guide, big brother, mentor. As one AA member has said, "Choosing a sponsor is like buying shoes—choose what you can be comfortable with over a long period of time."

Sponsors have varying degrees of responsibility for the newer members. At the very least, the sponsor is supposed to guide the participation of the newer member, offering helpful pamphlets, describing good meetings, introducing him to other members who might be helpful. The sponsor also may accompany his "sponsee" to meetings if necessary. Sponsors usually confer with the new members to help assess their progress in the program. The conferences may be at the newer member's house, by telephone or over coffee or a meal after a meeting.

At the next level of responsibility, the sponsor is a major resource for the member in crisis. It is the sponsor who is called by a member who becomes jittery at night or feels the urge to drink. As warranted, the sponsor can invite the member to his house or travel to the member's home.

Finally, a sponsor may help a member get professional assistance, as necessary. The sponsor also may assume responsibility for seeing that a hospitalized member has visitors.

The sponsor relationship is definitely an important part of the AA program, but it is also an aspect that can be easily misunderstood. Some members never select a sponsor. They fear that a sponsor will take over their lives and judge them harshly. Others choose sponsors too quickly —some to get immediate relief from the pain of not having someone to rely on, others because they think they must quickly have a sponsor in order to be full-fledged AA members.

No member is required to keep the same sponsor forever. Some sponsors are better for particular stages of sobriety—the very active sponsor may be best for the initial stages of sobriety, a less directive one later on. Also, since both the sponsor and the member are improving and growing, they may grow away from each other. Traits they shared or enjoyed in each other at first may change over time. If any of these conditions occurs, there is no reason not to replace the sponsor or even to have two sponsors. One caution is that sometimes one is tempted to replace a sponsor who tells the unpleasant truth. Self-help groups encourage people not to replace a sponsor casually. Many members wisely choose temporary sponsors until they are more aware of their needs, smoothly setting the stage for a change later on if it becomes necessary.

AA in Perspective

As we said at the beginning of the chapter, some people equate Alcoholics Anonymous with the treatment of alcoholism. There are, of course, many other forms of treatment.

There are some who say that no one can get sober without AA. Their response to someone who seems to get better without AA is that either he wasn't really addicted to alcohol in the first place, or he is not really sober but just on a "dry drunk."

Naturally, this whole line of reasoning is grandiose. It overstates the value of AA. Many people have stopped drinking and adopted a sober lifestyle without the use of AA or any other form of treatment. Some become sober through a religious experience, others for a variety of other reasons.

Nevertheless, participation in AA helps many people stop drinking, stay sober and build a rewarding life. Participation in AA makes a resumption of heavy drinking less likely.

AL-ANON AND ALATEEN

Al-Anon and Alateen are self-help organizations modeled on AA. Both serve "those who live with the problem of alcoholism" and welcome family members and friends of drinkers. Each organization uses AA's Twelve Steps as its cornerstone, but the two organizations are separate from AA. Each serves as the model for self-help groups for families and friends of other types of addicts.

Al-Anon and Alateen meetings generally follow the same form as AA meetings, though the details may differ. Both are designed to help family members and friends deal with the effects of the drinker's actions, both while he drinks and after he becomes sober. Many of the ideas of such programs have been incorporated into previous chapters. For example, Al-Anon emphasizes the need for support, self-care, limit-setting and living a full life.

We advise loved ones of addicts to become involved in these groups. They have been as helpful for families and friends of drinkers as AA has been for the drinkers themselves, especially in helping restore the self-esteem and equilibrium often lost in relationships with drinkers. Even if the addict chooses not to join in the recovery process, Al-Anon, Nar-Anon, FA, ACOA, and other support groups for loved ones are of immense value. Appendix 2 lists resources for finding out about family-oriented self-help groups in your area.

BECOMING INVOLVED IN SELF-HELP GROUPS

There are a number of steps one can take to become involved in self-help groups. The first step is just to approach them with curiosity and the desire to have a positive experience. It helps to remind yourself that there are many advantages to joining a self-help group.

For example, self-help groups are *well-established*. AA has been around for fifty years and has helped many hundreds of thousands of people in that time. Because many other self-help groups are based on AA's philosophy, when you choose one, you will not be dealing with some crackpot organization, the newest fad to come along.

Also, self-help groups are *free*. Addiction is an expensive hobby that taxes family finances. It becomes doubly expensive if it has led to unemployment, disability, alimony or attorney's fees. There are no charges for self-help groups. Any contributions they seek are voluntary.

Self-help group assistance is *immediate*. When you want help from a hospital, clinic or social service agency, sometimes you have to wait. You get help from self-help groups simply by going to a meeting.

And self-help group assistance is *widely available*. There are tens of thousands of self-help groups in the United States and around the world. In urban areas, people have a number of meetings available and can choose the ones best suited to them. In rural areas, meetings may not be as numerous, but they are often more accessible than treatment centers.

In addition, self-help group members are *supportive*. They are happy that others have come for help. Like those who stop smoking or lose weight, people who stop using drugs and their families report some disappointment when other people do not share their excitement at their accomplishment. "Is that all there is?" "Where's the parade?" In self-help groups, you will find people who are excited that you made a move to get help. In some groups, you are encouraged to celebrate "anniversaries" of your joining the group at three months, six months, one year and yearly thereafter. This kind of support is important, because not everyone will necessarily be happy that you got help. Addicted relatives may see your self-help group membership as a threat to their own well-being. Rather than be happy for your accomplishment, they may resume their addictive behaviors.

Another advantage is that self-help group meetings give you a chance to *socialize*. Many families report that they feel isolated by their reactions to an addicted relative. Often they have reduced their contacts with other people. Self-help group meetings can give a chance to start socializing again. It is not unusual for members to go out after meetings for dinner, coffee and other social activities. There are also group-sponsored social events like Christmas parties and New Year's Eve parties. So when you start attending meetings, you begin the process of rebuilding your social contacts outside the family.

Finally, self-help groups offer you *anonymity*. You need never even identify yourself by name if you do not want to. While the stigma of an addictive problem in your family may not be as severe as it once was, some people prefer to maintain their privacy as they seek help, and self-help groups respect that wish.

Beginning Attendance

The easiest way to start attending meetings, as with any other new activity, is to go with someone. It is often best to attend your first few meetings with someone who is familiar with the program. You may have a relative, neighbor or coworker who attends the group you select. He or she will probably be happy to accompany you to a meeting. You need not feel reluctant to ask for assistance, even if you have refused help in the past. There are very few members who took help when it was first made available to them.

If you are not aware of anyone who attends the group you choose, you can call the group's local number and arrange to have a member greet you at the meeting place and introduce you to other members.

Naturally, you are to free to attend meetings by yourself. However, sometimes unaccompanied new members isolate themselves and tend not to become very involved in the meetings.

People often ask, "How long should I attend meetings and how frequently should I go?" The answer is that you should go as often and as long as you think you need to. While there are no fixed rules regarding attendance, we have found that there are some minimum guidelines. One rule of thumb is that you should attend at least six meetings before you decide whether to continue. Make sure you include a mix of meetings.

In the early stages of self-help group participation, it is helpful to attend meetings of different groups of people to find the group in which you feel the most comfortable. Nevertheless, it is a good idea to pick one group that you will attend weekly and make it your "home group." With regular attendance you can form deeper relationships with the other members.

Family members and friends are welcome to attend open meetings of groups meant for addicts (for example, AA, Narcotics Anonymous, Cocaine Anonymous). In some cases it has been the first thing the addict and his family have done together in a long time. Joint attendance is particularly useful for the addict who becomes extremely active in a self-help group. Sometimes family and friends can feel left out. Some spouses say, "So what if he stopped the drugs? He used to spend all his time out on drugs. Now he spends all of it at meetings. I still never see him." Attending meetings together can be one way to mend these damaged relationships.

Two pieces of literature are especially helpful for the new member. The first is a schedule of the local meetings. It is easier to attend meetings if you have your own list of when and where they meet. The second we have mentioned before, *Alcoholics Anonymous* ("the Big Book"), which explains AA's principles and serves as a good introduction to other self-help groups. In case you do not have the funds to purchase a copy, there are usually copies available at the local library. Other members may lend you a copy if you ask them.

Millions of people have used self-help groups successfully over the years. We encourage you to try them.

OTHER SELF-HELP GROUPS

Having described Alcoholics Anonymous, we have given you an overview of how other self-help groups work. We can introduce you to the other relevant groups by briefly describing the focus of each. We tell how to contact each group in Appendix 2.

Narcotics Anonymous

Narcotics Anonymous (NA) was organized as a self-help group for men and women who have problems with their use of drugs. Members range in age from adolescents to the elderly, though the majority of its members are thirty-five or younger. People who choose NA have problems with a variety of drugs, including alcohol.

Cocaine Anonymous

Cocaine Anonymous (CA) is for those who have problems with cocaine. Because the widespread abuse of cocaine has come to public awareness only recently, CA is the newest of the self-help groups. Members include those from a variety of economic backgrounds and ages.

Families Anonymous

Families Anonymous (FA) is a self-help group for people whose friend or relative has a drug-abuse problem. Its focus is on helping members deal both with the abuser's problem with drugs and with the behaviors related to that abuse.

Gamblers Anonymous and Gam-Anon

We often think of addicts in terms of drug or alcohol abusers. But other addictive behaviors can have striking effects on families. Gamblers Anonymous (GA) is a self-help group that comes to the assistance of those whose gambling has reached destructive proportions. GA meetings have spread as addictive gambling has been more and more prominently publicized. Gam-Anon is to GA as Al-Anon is to AA or Nar-Anon is to Narcotics Anonymous. It is a program whose focus is on helping friends and families of addicted gamblers.

Overeaters Anonymous

Overeaters Anonymous (OA) focuses on the problems of food addicts. OA helps people who are recovering from compulsive overeating. Although at the surface overeating may not present as serious a problem in the addict's family as other addictions, it is often more destructive than it appears. The analyses we proposed in earlier chapters are surprisingly applicable.

Although self-help groups for alcohol and drug abusers and for gamblers have groups for families associated with them, so far OA does not have analogous groups. Support groups are provided to families by hospital eating-disorder programs, but typically they are run by professionals.

PROBLEMS PEOPLE HAVE WITH SELF-HELP GROUPS

People sometimes have problems getting involved in self-help groups. What follows are seven possible reasons for not doing so and also refutation of these beliefs.

A Similarity to Cults

For some, self-help groups seem to have the aura of cults. Their concern is that if they go to meetings or become members, the groups will require that they relinquish control of themselves, their beliefs and their lives, that they will be pressured to adopt fully the group's beliefs.

In truth, this is not the case. Groups do encourage sets of beliefs both about the problems their members share and about effective ways to solve those problems. But they are not coercive in their attempts to provide members with information and support. And contrary to some people's fears, the mission of the self-help groups is to help the member assume *more* responsibility for his life, not less.

Self-help groups are voluntary. Within each organization—AA, NA, FA, GA, OA and so on—are many, many individual groups, each with a somewhat different character. A person can shop around for one that fits his style.

Spirituality Versus Religiosity

Each of the self-help groups we discussed includes in its central tenets the concept of a "higher power." This is a difficult concept to grasp, and its meaning is often translated by prospective members as "God."

While a higher power for some *is* God, it need not be for all. The importance of the concept of the higher power is not a religious connotation but a spiritual one. Religiosity is just one of many forms of spirituality.

Spirituality differs from religiosity in its general application to humanity. It does not demand either belief in or allegiance to a particular God or set of religious beliefs. Spirituality is a quality one achieves by making commitments to values in concert with others. By working with a group of others to achieve common goals that are admired by the group, the individual gains strength, energy, self-esteem and a sense of purpose. The bond among group members is said to be spiritual. When the values chosen by the group stem from beliefs about God, then the commitments that flow from them are religious. Since self-help groups do not endorse any set of beliefs about God, most of their spiritual content is not religious. Spirituality is what you make of it.

If this issue is a stumbling block in your thoughts about self-help groups, try not to let it become an insurmountable obstacle. Try it out. Go to meetings and, if you feel a pressure toward a religious belief you do not like, discuss the matter with other group members. Many people have worked out a satisfactory compromise.

Shame

Popular lore through the ages has depicted addicts as weak-willed and purposefully evil. For some observers, it may appear that addicts' families are guilty because of their association with the addict. This guilt by association, in families' views, sometimes serves as an obstacle to involving themselves publicly in discussions—or even admissions—of their problems.

Although it is true that addictive behavior is shameful in some people's eyes, and although it is true that some people view addicts' families in the same scornful way, this is decidedly not the case among members of self-help groups. They have been there. To hold such contempt would be to hold themselves in contempt, and it just does not happen.

Feeling Different

Some prospective members shy away from groups because of a concern that they will be different from other members. This usually takes one or both of two forms.

First, people wonder if other group members will have experienced problems of the same severity in their families. "Will they have less severe problems and not understand mine fully, or will they have much more severe problems and make mine seem insignificant?'' In fact, there likely will be some with more, some with less and some with equally severe experiences. What is important is that you can learn from each group about alternate approaches to your own problems. If you feel belittled because of the extent of your problems, find another group. However, that is a rare experience. You are more likely to feel challenged by the insight others can give you about your problems.

Second, the question of possible ethnic differences with group members is sometimes of concern. Ethnic groups have different traditions, including about how openly and frankly to discuss personal or family problems. To the extent that ethnic diversity in a group may inhibit your ability to make best use of the group, try to find one in which you feel most comfortable. But be aware that the issue of its ethnic make-up may not be as important as you think.

Humiliation

Talking about family problems publicly is humiliating for some people. But stop for a moment and ask yourself whether *not* talking about problems means that others do not know about them or that they will get better. ''Out of sight, out of mind'' may only be trading short-term discomfort for long-term tragedy.

Even if you believe that public discussion of your family's problems will be humiliating, do not give up. Humiliation is often felt in anticipation of the reactions of others. Self-help groups are supportive, not destructive. While you may feel humiliated at first, the group's receptivity to your problem—and your effort to help yourself—usually makes short work of the feeling. There is no pressure to talk before you are ready.

If the feeling of humiliation is related to anticipation that your neighbors may attend the same groups, there is an easy solution to part of that problem: Try a meeting outside your neighborhood.

It's the Addict's Problem

So often we have heard families ask, ''Why should *we* go for help? *He* is the one with the problem.'' Well, partly true. The addict has a problem, no doubt about it. But, like it or not, his problem causes difficulties for you. And you probably have been sidetracked in your attempts to build a good life. That is why you are in the state of mind in which you find yourself. He needs help but may decline to accept it. You need help to get yourself back on track, even if he recovers fully. You are going for help, not to stop him from using drugs but to learn how you can flourish. Please do not let the addict's actions obscure your goal.

Inconvenience

Attending meetings *is* inconvenient. Definitely! And that is certainly part of what we meant before when we talked about short-term discomfort. In your busy life, scheduling time for a meeting or traveling to the meeting will be inconvenient initially. But, usually the inconvenience bows to a feeling of invigoration when you finally go to meetings. Talking about your problems with people who understand and getting new perspectives on going on with your life are valuable new parts of some members' lives, despite initial inconvenience.

We urge you to give self-help groups a fair trial. Find a group you like. Go for a while. Get to know fellow group members. Then decide if it is for you.

Epilogue

For many years, families of addicts have suffered in agonizing silence. Now there is hope. Although you cannot make the addict stop using drugs or go to and benefit from therapy, you can help yourself. Many families have undertaken their journeys successfully and now enjoy the rewards of life in Region III, a state of empowerment. You can get better, too, and this book can help you get started on the road to family growth and health.

By combining the elements we have discussed with you, you can define your family's problems clearly and in a manner that allows you to take effective action. By taking better care of yourself, living a full life and developing supportive relationships, you can strengthen yourself and set the stage for tackling the impact of the addiction on your family. Then, by using the benefits of family membership to support health and intervening to stop the chaos of addiction in your family, you can halt the downward spiral. Moving forward and getting better helps you to establish a healthier atmosphere in the household after the chaos has stopped and to establish new, more productive ways of relating to each other.

The view from Region I, exasperation, can seem bleak, but the visions of the possibilities in Region III, empowerment, can be enticing. We cannot stress enough the value of professional assistance along the way. Do not hesitate to go to self-help groups or to consult a qualified therapist when his or her help will direct you to productive paths or help you around obstacles. We have seen many families come to us in chaos and leave us with newfound purpose and meaning in their lives. It can be done, and it is worth doing. Good luck in your efforts, and good health!

Appendices

Drugs of Abuse

Following are listings of commonly abused addictive drugs, arranged in seven categories. We have given you some summary information for each category. The listings are not meant to be exhaustive and are not intended as guides for diagnosis of drug abuse or of the need for medical attention arising from such use. The effects of drugs depend on the physical and psychological condition of the user, the context of use, the dose and quality of the drug and the way it is administered. Please consult a trained health care professional for more information on specific questions you may have about the addict you know or about his treatment.

DRUG CATEGORY: OPIATES

The opiates include opium, heroin, codeine, morphine and related synthetic drugs such as Dilaudid, Darvon, Percodan and Methadone.

Background

Opiates have been around for a long time. They are derivatives or synthetic imitations of a part of the poppy plant *(Papaver somniferum)*. They have been used as analgesics (painkillers) and euphoriants for centuries. The poppy plant has been cultivated in the Mediterranean basin at least since 300 B.C. Opium seeds were brought to China by Arab traders in the eighth century, but seven centuries passed before opium itself was cultivated and used extensively by the Chinese. Opium was legalized in China only after that country lost two Opium Wars (1839–1843 and 1856–1860) to the British, who had exploited and fought to maintain a large Chinese market. Economically, opium provided a handsome return to the British in their trade with the Chinese for nearly half a century.

Opium reached India in the ninth century, again borne by Arab traders. Unlike its fate in China, opium was used in India primarily as a remedy for various medical ailments. Although recreational use in India was recorded, opium was not used as extensively as it was in China.

Opium use in England, continental Europe and the United States increased from the seventeenth until the mid-nineteenth century. Noted authors, poets and opinion makers lauded opium's helpful and healthful properties, and physicians prescribed opiate preparations quite extensively. They were the best drugs available at the time for the relief of pain and for sedation. Concern began to grow after the first third of the nineteenth century as reports appeared of growing addiction to opium, of opium's contribution to disability and death and of its potential for social disruption. The Pharmacy Act of 1868, passed by the British Parliament after a ten-year effort, was the first legislative attempt to regulate opium's use.

Opium was used rather frequently in the United States. Before the twentieth century, it was an ingredient of many patent medicines. Many farm women, for example, regularly used Lydia Pinkham's Vegetable Compound, an opium-based elixir designed to provide relief of menstrual cramps and other discomforts. Although it had long been unavailable, the compound's praises continued to be sung well into this century. One of our patients recalled hearing these two verses in 1938 at a roadhouse in Pymatuning, Pennsylvania.

Oh, Mrs. Brown had bladder trouble.
She tried so hard, but she couldn't pee.
She took two bottles of the compound.
Now they're piping her to the sea.

Chorus
*So we will sing, sing for Lydia Pinkham
And her love for the human race.*

She made the famous compound.
Now the papers publish her face.

Now Mrs. Green, she had no children.
But she wanted some children dear.
She drank three bottles of the compound.
Now she has them twice a year.

Chorus

Morphine, a concentrated and more powerful form of opiate, was developed shortly before the Civil War in the United States. Morphine addiction came to be known as "the soldier's disease," after many treated for war wounds with it became addicts. In 1874, a German company synthesized heroin from morphine and developed it as a safe cure for morphine addiction, diarrhea and stomach cramps. It was given out in free samples at first and then available on the market until the early 1900's, when the world noticed that heroin had great addiction potential. In 1914, the Harrison Narcotic Act was passed by the U.S. Congress in an attempt to control heroin's use. Addiction to heroin became more and more of a social problem as it was introduced to the lower classes and was associated almost exclusively with social blight. In the 1970's, heroin became a problem for the middle class as well.

Today heroin and opium byproducts are produced in laboratories and factories around the world. The Golden Triangle in Southeast Asia and the Golden Crescent in the Middle East account for most of the opiates that find their way to the United States. Synthetic opiates were developed as alternatives to opium, morphine and heroin. Among the more commonly used synthetic opiates are Dilaudid, Percodan, Darvon and Darvocet. Synthetics are frequently prescribed for pain by physicians and dentists.

Varieties and Form

Heroin: powder (typically brown or white), dissolvable in water
Morphine: clear liquid, tablets and capsules
Opium: paste, tablets or capsules
Codeine and synthetics: tablets and capsules

Routes of Administration

Heroin: by injection, by inhalation ("snorting") or by mouth
Morphine: by injection or by mouth
Opium: smoked or by mouth
Codeine and synthetics: by mouth or by injection

Short-term Effects

Physiological: initial "rush," relief of pain, sweating and constricted pupils immediately after injection; drowsiness or sleepiness, feeling of warmth thereafter; extreme lethargy, difficulty with arousal, comalike symptoms with high initial doses.

Psychological: feeling of well-being, detachment from worldly problems and concerns, general oblivion.

Long-term Effects

Physiological: various heart, liver, lung and other organ damage from use of contaminated injection needles and from contaminants in drugs; tolerance of and demand for increasingly higher dosage of drugs; complications during pregnancy and birth; addicted newborn babies of addicted mothers.

Psychological: chronic deterioration of relationships with family and friends; focus of life on drugs; social isolation and psychological regression; development of antisocial trends in some addicts; reduced tolerance to pain or emotional discomfort; irresponsibility and manipulativeness.

Abstinence Syndromes

Discomfort, runny nose, diarrhea, cramping (especially in abdomen), headache, goosepimples, tearfulness, flushing; onset depends on type of drug. For heroin, symptoms typically begin four to six hours after last use of drug, peak in two to three days and pass within seven days. Some lingering effects last up to six months. For other opiates, abstinence symptoms can begin as long as thirty-six hours after last dose and last up to ten days.

Other Information

Withdrawal from alcohol can be life-threatening more frequently than withdrawal from opiates.

"T's and Blues," a combination of a prescription painkiller (pentazocine hydrochloride, or Talwin) and an antihistamine (Pyribenzamine) produce an effect when used together that simulates that of heroin for many users.

Opiates are commonly used in connection with other drugs, particularly stimulants and alcohol. The best-known combination is cocaine and heroin, or a "speedball," which resulted in the well-publicized deaths of John Belushi and David Kennedy.

Users run a potential risk of overdosing, particularly with street preparations, because they vary greatly in potency.

DRUG CATEGORY: SEDATIVE-HYPNOTICS

The sedative-hypnotics include alcohol, barbiturates and synthetics, and minor tranquilizers.

Background

Beverage alcohol, or ethanol, has a long history. Wine, for example, is mentioned more than five hundred times in the Bible. Beer was well known in ancient Sumeria as early as 6000 B.C. In fact, alcohol probably was known before written historical records appeared.

The passage of time expanded the variety of available alcohol. Distilled spirits, with their higher alcohol content, were introduced to Europeans in the eleventh century, two centuries or so after the process of distillation was discovered in the Middle East. One distilled beverage, gin, plays a very important role in the history of alcohol abuse and its prevention. Distilled first in Holland, gin led to a major social upheaval as it was consumed in excess by England's poor as a way to help them forget their poverty. As a result, it was the focus of one of the first organized efforts by a society to control the use of alcohol by its citizens.

Attempts to control drunkenness in England began in the sixteenth century, when it first became a crime. Gin was the target of two Gin Acts in the eighteenth century and the focus of riots and continuing social unrest as its production and consumption rose for a century.

As was to be the experience in the United States two hundred years later, each attempt at prohibition was met by the production of bootleg gin, much of it of inferior quality and some of it deadly poison.

In early seventeenth-century colonial America, drinking and drunkenness were already recognized problems. Over the next hundred years, a series of legislative moves in several colonies sought to restrict, regulate and define the legitimate sale and use of beer, wine and spirits, even in the home. As early as 1671, the symptoms of what we now call alcoholism already had been spelled out in colonial laws.

The use and abuse of alcohol was the subject of debate and legislation all over colonial America for the next century. As the abuse of alcohol rose, so did efforts to control it. Official actions included the establishment of laws and assessment of fines and punishments for public inebriates and those who permitted and aided their intoxication.

At the same time, a series of temperance societies sprang up. These groups were organized for a single purpose: to discourage the consumption of alcohol in any form and to promote sobriety. While the societies were weak at first, they gained strength from the work of Benjamin Rush, known as the father of both American medicine and American psychiatry. His 1785 book, *Inquiry into the Effects of Ardent Spirits on the Human Body and Mind,* served as the rallying point for the fledgling temperance movement. Fifty years later, these societies were to reach their greatest prominence as society attempted to control what had become a traditional acceptance of excessive drinking.

Barbiturates are synthetic derivatives of barbituric acid. Their effects range from extremely rapid onset but brief duration to less rapid onset but more prolonged duration. Commonly abused barbiturates fall into the middle-range categories. Drugs which produce only brief effects and those whose effects can be felt only after an hour or so are of little interest to the abuser.

Minor tranquilizers have been marketed for about thirty-five years and are widely used for the relief of tension, anxiety and muscle spasms. Originally considered to have little abuse potential, they quickly became among the most frequently prescribed drugs in the country. But soon minor tranquilizer abuse took its place with other drug problems, and the minor tranquilizers came under greater scrutiny and control.

Varieties and Form

Alcohol: liquid
Minor tranquilizers: tablets and capsules; injectable liquid
Barbiturates: most commonly a white powder in tablet or capsule form;
   sometimes available as a liquid or in suppository form
Methaqualone (Quaaludes): tablets

Routes of Administration

Alcohol: by mouth
Minor tranquilizers: by mouth or by injection
Barbiturates: by mouth, by injection or as a suppository
Methaqualone (Quaaludes): by mouth

Short-term Effects

Physiological: Dilation of blood vessels; slowing of reaction time; impairment of judgment, memory, coordination (slurred speech and altered gait) and sense of time; in larger doses, death from heart or lung failure.
   Psychological: Feelings of relaxation, well-being and reduction of severity of problems and worries; decreased inhibitions; both sedation and stimulaton.

Long-term Effects

Physiological: Damage to central nervous system (brain, spinal cord and peripheral nerves), major organ systems (liver and pancreas, especially) and other body systems (gastrointestinal tract, skin and circulatory systems, for example); danger to fetus of pregnant user.
   Psychological: Loss of family, friends and employment; in extreme, detachment from the world as a result of severe and irreversible damage to the brain.

Abstinence Syndromes

Shaking, headaches, nausea, vomiting, feverishness, sweating, muscle aches; more severe withdrawal may include delerium, hallucinations (seeing, feeling or hearing things that are not really there), delusions (irrational beliefs that "people are out to get me" or the like) or seizures. Death may result in as many as 15 percent of unsupervised withdrawals in which patients enter the "DT's" (delerium tremens).

Other Information

The generic and brand names of the common minor tranquilizers are diazepam (Valium), chlordiazepoxide hydrochloride (Librium), chlordiazepoxide hydrochloride with clidinium hydrochloride (Librax), flurazepam hydrochloride (Dalmane), oxazepam (Serax), chlorazepate dipotassium (Tranxene), alprazolam (Xanax) and lorazepam (Ativan).

The generic and brand names of the common barbiturates are amobarbital (Amytal), secobarbital (Seconal), pentobarbital (Nembutal), phenobarbital (Leminal), butabarbital (Butisol). Some street names of barbiturates are barbs, downers, reds, yellow jackets and amies.

The brand names of methaqualone are Quaalude, Mandrax, Sopor and Optimil. Its common street name is ludes.

Look-alikes are commonly available.

DRUG CATEGORY: STIMULANTS

The stimulants include amphetamines, caffeine and cocaine.

Background

Amphetamines were developed in the United States in the 1930's. They quickly became popular for the treatment of depression and obesity and for pain control, attention control and many other problems. In the early 1950's, it was noted at Bellevue Hospital in New York City that 30 percent of patients coming in with symptoms of depression, mania and psychosis had been taking prescribed amphetamines. When their amphetamines were discontinued, the toxic psychoses and other side effects lifted, and patients were able to go home. Slowly, the apparent beneficial effects of amphetamines were questioned, and today there are very few recognized uses for them. Amphetamines include methamphetamine, dextroamphetamines, phenmetrazine and diethylpropion.

Methylphenadate hydrochloride (Ritalin) is a related compound. It has a paradoxical effect in children and is used to treat attention disorders and hyperactivity.

Perhaps the most common time of introduction to amphetamines is during college. Amphetamines have been commonly used as aids to studying. A representative story of amphetamines' effects is that of a graduate student who, fearing that he would not do well in an exam, kept himself up for seven days with amphetamines. He was able to absorb an immense amount of material during that time. He arrived at the exam in a confident mood. He wrote fourteen pages of what he thought were brilliant answers to exam questions. However, he wrote it all on one side of one sheet of paper. Amphetamines had impaired his judgment. Many of those who use amphetamines to increase learning power discover that they can use what they have learned only in a similar state—that is, if they are intoxicated with amphetamines at exam time.

Cocaine has been known for quite some time. It is derived from coca plants (*erythroxylon coca*), the leaves of which have been chewed for centuries by Inca Indians. The first report of medicinal use of coca leaves was made by Nicholas Monardeth, a Spanish physician in 1596. However, it was not until the mid-1800's that cocaine was isolated from coca leaves. It has often been thought that the Incas use coca leaves without ill effect, but more recent investigators have discovered it has harmed the Indians' health when used regularly. It is used frequently to alleviate intolerable work conditions at high altitudes, and the effects of the coca leaves and the low oxygen combine to cause injury.

Cocaine's use in medicine was given its greatest exposure by Sigmund Freud. His first major paper on the subject, *Über Coca*, appeared in 1884, and in it he reported that cocaine was helpful in the treatment of depression, digestive disorders and asthma. Freud himself used cocaine for twelve years and was addicted to it for part of that time. He described his own use of cocaine in letters to his fiancée and to his close friend Wilhelm Fliess in which he lauded the drug's effect, and he prescribed it for friends and relatives. The other use for cocaine on which Freud reported was as a local anesthetic in the treatment of eye, ear, nose and throat disorders.

In the early 1900's, cocaine was used in the preparation of Coca Cola. Once its addictive potential was recognized, however, it was removed from Coca Cola (in 1903), and ultimately declared illegal. Cocaine was lumped together with opium and classified (incorrectly) as a narcotic by the Harrison Narcotic Act of 1914. It had been the focus of increasing concern in the United States for many years, primarily for political reasons. Concern rose in the South after the Civil War that blacks, under the influence of cocaine-induced altered states of consciousness, would rebel against the newly reconstructed South. Although little evidence was presented to substantiate these claims, they seemed to gain audiences. Cocaine restrictions and penalties eventually became more severe than those for the use and sale of opium.

Currently, cocaine enjoys its greatest popularity, aided in large part by the recent introduction of "crack" to the American market. Crack, a relatively cheaply produced form of processed cocaine, is sold in "rocks" and smoked. Initially, cocaine's high price restricted its popularity to middle- and upper-class users. More recently, however, an abundance of cocaine and crack in U.S. markets has driven down its price and brought it into reach of many more addicts.

Varieties and Form

Amphetamines: tablets, liquids and sprays
Caffeine: liquid (coffees, teas, colas, cocoa) and tablets
Cocaine: white powder, paste or small "rocks"

Routes of Administration

Amphetamines: by mouth, by injection and by inhalation
Caffeine: by mouth
Cocaine: through the nose ("snorted") and other mucous membranes, sometimes by injection or smoked in "freebase" form

Short-term Effects

Physiological: Decreased appetite, increased heart and breathing rates, dilated pupils; insomnia, dry mouth, increased interest in sex with decreased sexual performance; in higher doses, irregular heart rate, fluctuating blood pressure, confusion, lack of coordination, possible loss of consciousness and death.

Psychological: Sense of increased energy and well-being ("speeding"); sometimes increased anxiety; grandiosity, euphoria; reduced perception, judgment and logical abilities; rapid speech rate, agitation, increased susceptibility to startle and panic, hyperventilation, fear of heart attack.

Long-term Effects

Physiological: Cardiovascular damage; for cocaine, dependence to avoid physical discomfort, irritability, chronic sinus problems (runny noses are common), perforated septum, lung damage, seizures, nerve and muscle damage; itching all over the body, sometimes with open sores.

Psychological: Hallucinations (seeing, hearing, feeling, or smelling things that are not there); decreased social relationships as life revolves around obtaining and using the drug.

Abstinence Syndromes

Irritability and appetite disturbance, possible depression when person "crashes" from the high. Amphetamine psychosis is sometimes associated with violent or bizarre behavior during both use of the drug and withdrawal.

Other Information

Common street names of amphetamines are uppers, speed, white crosses, bennies, crystal, crank, black beauties, meth, copilots, truck drivers, pep pills.

Common street names for cocaine are girl, coke, blow, snow, base, lady, white, flake.

Look-alikes have given way to act-alikes to circumvent state laws prohibiting manufacture and sale of drugs that resemble amphetamines in appearance.

Death sometimes results from overdose.

DRUG CATEGORY: INHALANTS

The inhalants include industrial and household chemicals, and glue.

Background

Inhalants have been rumored to produce brain, kidney and liver damage, but the consequences of their use are not well substantiated. There are several main groups of inhalants used by different populations. The most popularly abused (though not the most heavily abused) substance is glue. Glue is abused primarily by eight-to-fourteen-year-old children who typically gather together for glue-sniffing parties.

Related to glue chemically are the organic solvents. Most include acetone. Their effects are similar to those of ether or halathane; they are synthetic general anesthetics. The effect is usually a ten-to-fifteen-minute high with hallucinations and blood pressure changes. There are also some side effects for the heart. Peripheral neuropathy—or loss of sensation in the limbs—is also a side effect. Organic solvents are abused mostly by young adults who are exposed to them at work and may bring some home for inhalation.

Another major grouping of inhalants are the nitrates. Amyl nitrate and butyl nitrates (commonly called poppers) cause rapid dilation of, and possible damage to, blood vessels, with a consequent rapid drop in blood pressure. Butyl nitrate affects the oxygen-carrying capacity of the blood and can sometimes lead to ruptured arteries or unconsciousness as a result of a precipitous drop in blood pressure.

Nitrous oxide is another inhalant that is sometimes abused. Nitrous oxide (or laughing gas, as it is sometimes called) is a short-term anesthetic used by dentists, among others.

Freon, a gas used in spray cans and in refrigeration and air-conditioning systems, is also abused as an inhalant. Freon's rapid cooling as it expands when released from pressure can seriously damage and even freeze lung tissue. Its effect is similar to that of other inhalants, including its effect on the heart. A dangerous side effect of inhaling spray-can gases is that they often carry substances with them that can coat the lungs and result in death. Sprayable lubricants, including those used in cooking, fall into this category.

Gasoline fumes are also inhaled by some people. They, too, have serious health consequences.

Varieties and Form

Liquid sprays.

Routes of Administration

Inhaled, sniffed.

Short-term Effects

Physiological: Typically, profound changes in pressure and pulse, possible loss of consciousness and/or vomiting, possible death.

Psychological: Loss of self-control; loss of touch with reality; violent, uncontrolled behavior.

Long-term Effects

Physiological: Possible permanent damage to brain and nervous system; body chemistry imbalances; damage to organ systems; chronically lower energy level.

Psychological: Reduced mental ability; brain damage that impairs mental functioning.

Abstinence Syndromes

Vary according to chemical inhaled.

Other Information

Most inhalants are not actually drugs. They are usually household or industrial chemicals (glue, paint thinner, spray-can gases, etc.), which were never developed to be ingested in any form. Since one drug in this category (amyl nitrate) was removed form over-the-counter to prescription status, another (butyl nitrate) has taken its place in illicit drug circles.

DRUG CATEGORY: HALLUCINOGENS

The hallucinogens include LSD, peyote (from which mescaline is derived), psilocybin, DMT, MDA, MMDA, DOM and DOB.

The majority of hallucinogens are derived from plants. LSD is drawn from a fungus that grows on the rye plant, mescaline from the peyote cactus and psilocybin from Psilocybe mushrooms. Hallucinogens have been used in rituals in a number of ethnic communities. Some Native American groups currently use peyote in religious ceremonies and have been granted governmental permission to do so. All of these drugs distort perceptions, but they also have stimulant properties.

One of the most intriguing questions about hallucinogens is how their induced hallucinations differ from those of schizophrenia. A number of differences exist. One is that hallucinations from drugs tend to be visual rather than auditory. Users of these drugs can differentiate drug-induced hallucinations from reality. They know they are not real. Also, the user can sense the drug effect when alerted to it. Even during a bad trip, drug counselors can usually talk to users and effectively explain that the hallucinations result from the drug. Finally, users typically can remember what the experience was like after it is over. Psychotic experiences are not as easily recalled by a disturbed person during a lucid period.

The average dose of LSD is between 50 and 150 micrograms. The effects last between eight and twelve hours. It takes about forty-five minutes for the effects to come on, and then they come in waves, which increase in frequency and intensity for the first four to five hours, then decrease.

Varieties and Form

Tablets, capsules, liquids.

Routes of Administration

By mouth, smoked or injected.

Short-term Effects

Physiological: Increased heart rate, blood pressure, body temperature.

Psychological: Loss of orientation, illusions, hallucinations (seeing, hearing or feeling things that are not there); rapidly changing emotional reactions to surroundings; increased, sometimes extreme anxieties; bizarre behavior.

Long-term Effects

Physiological: Damage to brain functions, including memory, concentration, attention and thinking difficulties; hallucinogen use is believed to have serious consequences for the fetus of the pregnant user.

Psychological: Impaired social relationships; depression, confusion, sometimes resulting from physiological damage. Flashbacks are possible after use has continued for some time.

Abstinence Syndromes

No recorded abstinence syndrome exists.

Other Information

Although hallucinogen use may not cause death directly, the altered sense of reality and the bizarre behavior that sometimes result from their use have in very rare instances been reported to lead the user to do things that resulted in serious injury or death.

DRUG CATEGORY: PCP (PHENCYCLIDINE)

Background

Phencyclidine, or PCP, has been known for about thirty years. Originally tested as an anesthetic, its potential for human use quickly diminished because of unpredictable, unpleasant and severe side effects. Experimental subjects became disoriented, confused and delerious, and testing of the drug ceased.

Phencyclidine was introduced in the mid-1960's for use in veterinary medicine but was removed from the market a decade later. PCP in use today comes from illicit producers.

Varieties and Form

Tablets, capsules, liquid.

Routes of Administration

By mouth, by injection or smoked.

Short-term Effects

Physiological: PCP has unpredictable results that can include those of stimulants, tranquilizers and hallucinogens.

Psychological: Difficulty thinking logically; racing, bizarre thoughts; loss of touch with one's surroundings; violent behavior; relaxation; profound sedation and psychomotor retardation.

Long-term Effects

Physiological: Damage to the brain, perhaps including coma and death; convulsions; stroke; damage to heart, lungs, and blood vessels. PCP use is believed to have serious consequences for the fetus of the pregnant user.

Psychological: Deterioration of memory, perception and concentration; diminished capacity for judgment; hallucinations.

Abstinence Syndromes

Prolonged period of recovery following last use of drug is typical. Common symptoms include speech, memory, perceptual and thought-process problems; confusion; increased suspiciousness and depression, sometimes accompanied by thoughts of suicide. Newly abstinent addicts sometimes become assaultive.

Other Information

Other effects are similar to those of hallucinogens.

Although PCP use may not cause death directly, the altered sense of reality and the bizarre and violent behavior that sometimes result from its use may lead the user to do things that result in serious injury or death.

PCP is known by a variety of slang names, including angel dust, animal tranquilizer (which, by the way, it was), hog, rocket fuel, PeaCe Pill, crystal, cyclones, and tic tac. People who think they are buying amphet-amines, pure THC (marijuana's active ingredient), a hallucinogen (LSD or mescaline, for example) or cocaine often are really being sold PCP.

DRUG CATEGORY: MARIJUANA (HASHISH)

Background

Marijuana was brought to Jamaica in the nineteenth century by people traveling from India. It soon became quite popular and by the latter part of the century was described as a cause of "lunacy." By the early twentieth century, marijuana was a matter of great concern because of its alleged impact on crime and general malaise among native and immigrant Jamaicans. Increasing penalties for its use were imposed. As time passed, laws distinguished use from selling of marijuana, and harsher penalties were imposed for the latter.

Marijuana use spread to the U.S. from Mexico around the turn of the century. It was not long before regulations appeared concerning its nonmedical use. Although the trend to prohibition was slow and irregular, by 1931 many states had banned marijuana. Interestingly, at one time (in a 1920 pamphlet) the U.S. Department of Agriculture actually encouraged Americans to grow marijuana.

Debate during the latter two-thirds of the nineteenth and first third of the twentieth centuries frequently focused on marijuana's medicinal uses. What seemed like a wide range of therapeutic applications dwindled as new medications were synthesized and drug research became more sophisticated. In 1941, its few remaining medical uses were obliterated when marijuana was removed from official listings of approved drugs.

Debate continued for the next few decades about the harmful effects of marijuana on users' health and on the national social fabric. As debate continued, social policies to control marijuana fluctuated. Today, the debate and efforts to control marijuana's production, importation and use continue.

Recently, physicians have advocated the use of marijuana to treat glaucoma and to alleviate the side effects of chemotherapy in cancer treatment.

Varieties and Form

Dried leaves of the plant *Cannabis sativa*, usually brown. Hashish, the resin from the plant's leaves and flowers, contains a greater concentration of the main ingredient, THC (Delta-9-Tetrahydrocannabinol), than does marijuana.

Routes of Administration

Smoking or eating.

Short-term Effects

Physiological: Dry mouth or throat, increased pulse; decreased coordination and reaction time.

Psychological: Subjective feeling of well-being; impaired judgment and concentration; tendency to talk, giggle or laugh more than usual. Distorted sense of time.

Long-term Effects

Physiological: Respiratory diseases (as with tobacco smokers); diseases of the gastrointestinal system (digestive diseases, diarrhea, abdominal pain); altered levels of sex hormones.

Psychological: Dependence on marijuana and its acquisition, resulting in a narrowing of interest in other activities or people, lethargy and general slowing of functioning; confusion.

Abstinence Syndromes

Abstinence syndromes result from chronic heavy use. They include headaches, agitation and racing thoughts, insomnia, appetite disturbance, confusion lasting eight to ten days after last use, with less severe effects lasting from one to eight months.

Other Information

Common street names of marijuana are pot, weed, joints (cigarettes), smoke, shit, dope, grass, reefer, stick, tea, and ganja.

Common street names of hashish are hash and soles.

THE SOURCES OF DRUGS

Drugs can be obtained in any number of ways, and the sources of drugs a user develops have an important impact on several facets of his problem.

First, *source affects quality*. Drugs come to the user by different routes and in different forms. By the time they reach the user on the street, they are usually diluted ("cut" or "stepped on" in common parlance) with a number of inactive substances. Sometimes street drugs are simply substitutions of other drugs (PCP for amphetamines, for example). Street drugs vary in quality based on their origins and the number of middlemen through which they have passed.

If the source of a user's drugs is prescription pharmaceuticals (as when a physician prescribes them for the user or for himself) or commonly marketed alcoholic beverages, the quality of the drug is likely to be consistent and high.

Second, *source affects risk*. The greater the uncertainty as to a drug's purity or nature, the greater the risk to the user that the drug will injure or even kill him. Especially when street drugs are substitutes for other drugs, the user may not even be sure what or how much he is taking.

Third, *source affects behavior*. The user who must obtain drugs illicitly often faces the disruptive tasks of obtaining large (and often increasing) amounts of money and spending inordinate amounts of time to support his addiction. The more time the addiction requires, the more he is drawn to the single pursuit of drugs, and the less time and energy he has to devote to other areas of his life. The user with the semilegitimate source of drugs faces a less complicated, cheaper and less disruptive task to support his habit.

Fourth, *source affects susceptibility* of the user to intervention in his drug use. The user who clearly is consumed by obtaining and using his largely illicit drug(s) of choice may be more susceptible to others' efforts to reach him than the user who obtains his drugs semilegitimately. The user whose physician prescribes his drugs for him or the physician who prescribes required quantities of drugs for himself, for example, may seem to be functioning fairly well in day-to-day matters. This guise of normalcy may allow the user to deny the extent of his problem and shield himself from efforts to help him.

Fifth, *source affects the family*. Depending on the source of an addict's drugs and the lengths to which he must go to obtain them, the family's feelings of helplessness and hopelessness may fluctuate. The user whose source is abhorrent to the family (the user of street drugs, for example) may leave his family feeling quite helpless and frightened and, therefore, hopeless about the future. The abuser of semilegitimately obtained drugs, however, may allow the family to maintain a shred of hope when they see what appears, on the surface at least, to be an addict whose life remains fairly respectable.

Useful Organizations

This appendix lists a number of organizations that offer information and self-help experiences for addicts and their families.

NATIONAL ORGANIZATIONS

1. Al-Anon Family Group Headquarters
   P.O. Box 862
   Midtown Station
   New York, NY 10018-0862
   Phone: 212-302-7240
   See comments under item 2, Alcoholics Anonymous.

2. Alcoholics Anonymous (AA)
   P.O. Box 459
   Grand Central Station
   New York, NY 10163
   Phone: 212-686-1100
   You can write to AA's national office for information on AA publications, on AA chapters nationwide and on Al-Anon, Alateen and Alatot chapters around the country. But before you do, check the white pages of your local phone book under "Alcoholics Anonymous." You will probably find a local phone number to call, and you will save yourself

some time. Your local chapter can refer you to local AA, Al-Anon, Alateen and Alatot resources.

3. American Council for Drug Education (ACDE)
    204 Monroe St.
    Rockville, MD 20850
    Phone: 301-294-0600
    Write to ACDE for information on the uses of drugs.

4. Cocaine Anonymous (CA)
    P.O. Box 1367
    Culver City, CA 90232
    Phone: 213-559-5833

Cocaine Anonymous (CA) is a self-help group for cocaine users which is similar in structure and philosophy to Alcoholics Anonymous (AA). In addition to CA, there are other resources to which cocaine users can turn. 1-800-COCAINE (1-800-262-2463) is a 24-hour national hotline whose counselors can help cocaine users over the phone and provide referrals to local treatment resources. 1-800-662-HELP (1-800-662-4357), a confidential referral service of the National Institute on Drug Abuse, can help as well with referrals to local treatment services.

Cocanon is the newly established self-help group for families of cocaine users and is to CA what Al-Anon is to AA. Currently, Cocanon has two offices, in Los Angeles (213-859-2206) and New York (212-713-5133). These offices and 1-800-COCAINE and 1-800-662-HELP will be able to direct interested family members to additional Cocanon chapters around the country as they are formed.

5. Families Anonymous (FA)
    P.O. Box 528
    Van Nuys, CA 91408
    Phone: 818-989-7841

FA chapters have been organized in many areas. Look in the white pages of your phone directory or in your local newspaper for a local FA chapter. You can also call a crisis service in your area, a community mental health center, the community relations department of your hospital or your local drug and alcoholism treatment center. If you are unable to find a convenient FA chapter, contact FA at the address or phone number above.

6. Gam-Anon (and Gam-Ateen)
   International Service Office
   P.O. Box 157
   Whitestone, NY 11357
   Phone: 718-352-1671
   See comments under item 7, Gamblers Anonymous.

7. Gamblers Anonymous (GA)
   National Service Office
   P.O. Box 17173
   Los Angeles, CA 90017
   Phone: 213-386-8789

   Contact your local GA chapter by consulting the white pages of your local phone book. In the event none is listed, contact GA at the address and phone number above. Gam-Anon is GA's companion program for families and friends of compulsive gamblers.

8. Hazelden Educational Services
   Box 176
   Center City, Minnesota 55012
   Phones: 800-328-9000 (Continental United States)
            800-257-0070 (Minnesota only)
            612-464-8844 or 464-3100 (Twin Cities Minnesota area)

   Contact Hazelden for information on alcohol abuse and other drug abuse publications. Hazelden's catalog contains many of AA's publications, as well as a variety of other publications and audiovisual aids dealing with addictive problems.

9. Nar-Anon
   P.O. Box 2562
   Palos Verdes Estates, CA 90274
   Phone: 213-547-5800
   See comments under item 10, Narcotics Anonymous.

10. Narcotics Anonymous (NA)
    Narcotics Anonymous World Service Office
    Box 9999
    Van Nuys, CA 94109
    Phone: 818-780-3951

Contact NA locally through the white pages of your telephone directory. If there is no listing, you can contact a local drug abuse program, hospital or community mental health center for information on NA. Failing these local avenues, contact NA's national office at the address above. Nar-Anon, the related organization for families of addicts, has recently begun organizing local chapters nationwide. For information, contact your local NA office or write to Nar-Anon at the address in item 9 above.

11. National Association for Children of Alcoholics (NACA)
    31706 Coast Highway
    Suite 201
    South Laguna, CA 92677
    Phone: 714-499-3889

NACA is a nonprofit group established recently to deal with the problems of young and adult children of drinkers. NACA will send a list of resources, and membership privileges include a newsletter.

12. National Center for Pathological Gambling, Inc.
    651 Washington Blvd.
    Baltimore, MD 21230
    Phone: 301-332-1111

This organization provides information on and treatment of compulsive gambling.

13. National Clearinghouse for Alcohol and Drug Information (NCADI)
    P.O. Box 2345
    Rockville, MD 20850
    Phone: 301-468-2600

NCADI is a branch of the United States government's Department of Health and Human Services (DHHS). It has a large and very useful collection of books, pamphlets and references that it can either provide or direct you to. Write to NCADI for a listing of their publications and services. 1-800-662-HELP is a confidential referral service of the National Institute on Drug Abuse whose counselors can help callers find local treatment service.

14. National Council on Alcoholism, Inc. (NCA)
    12 West 21st Street
    7th floor
    New York, NY 10010
    Phone: 212-206-6770

Write to NCA for information on alcoholism and its effects on health, family life and society. NCA can also refer you to the council on alcoholism in your area.

15. National Council on Compulsive Gambling, Inc. (NCCG)
    Room 3207S
    John Jay College
    444 West 56th Street
    New York, NY 10019
    Phone: 212-765-3834
                800-522-4700 (New York State, outside New York City)

NCCG provides information on compulsive gambling. This organization can also refer interested gamblers to treatment programs. NCCG's newsletter is published quarterly.

LOCAL RESOURCES

Hospitals

Hospitals in your area are likely to deal with large numbers of alcohol and drug addicts. Sometimes addicts are treated only for the medical consequences of their abuse, but others enter specialized programs for treatment for their addictions. Hospitals generally—and specialized treatment programs in particular—are good resources for information about addictions and their effects on families.

Self-help Group Literature

Self-help groups publish their own pamphlets and books that deal with the problems their members experience as a result of their own or someone else's addictive behavior. These publications are excellent sources of information. They are easily obtained through the self-help groups' local

261

or national offices, and the literature is frequently available at local meetings of the group. You may want to combine a review of a group's literature with attending its meetings to get a well-rounded impression of how the group may be helpful to you and your family.

Health Departments

State, county and local health departments frequently sponsor health care and health education programs for constituents of the areas they serve. Those programs frequently consist of lectures and discussion groups for people who want information on addictions for themselves or for somebody else.

State Departments of Alcoholism and Drug Abuse

Your state government supports an office of alcoholism and drug abuse. Such offices typically are involved in coordinating and cataloguing addictions services and educational resources. Frequently, they are excellent sources for educational material about addictions and for information about treatment for addicts. Appendix 3 lists the offices for each of the fifty states and Washington, D.C.

State Programs

This directory of state alcoholism and drug abuse programs is based on one compiled by the National Clearinghouse for Alcohol Information. Because addresses and telephone numbers may change, you may want to contact:

National Clearinghouse for Alcohol and Drug Information
  PO Box 2345
  Rockville, MD 20852
  301-468-2600

ALABAMA
Alcoholism Program
Department of Mental Health
200 Interstate Pk Dr-Box 3710
Montgomery, AL 36193
205-271-9253

ALASKA
Office of Alcoholism and
Drug Abuse
Pouch H-05F
Juneau, AK 99811
907-586-6201

ARIZONA
Alcohol Abuse Section Division
of Behavioral Health Svcs
2500 E Van Buren St
Phoenix, AZ 85008
602-255-1238

ARKANSAS
Office of Alcohol and
Drug Abuse Prevention
1515 West 7th Ave Ste 310
Little Rock, AR 72201
501-371-2603

CALIFORNIA
Department of Alcohol
and Drug Programs
111 Capitol Mall
Sacramento, CA 95814
916-445-1940

COLORADO
Colorado Department of Health
Alcohol & Drug Abuse Division
4210 East 11th Ave
Denver, CO 80220
303-320-6137

CONNECTICUT
Connecticut Alcohol and Drug
Abuse Commission
999 Asylum Ave 3rd Fl
Hartford, CT 06105
203-566-2089

DELAWARE
Alcoholism Services
Lower Kensington
Environmental Ctr
1910 N Dupont Highway
New Castle, DE 19720
302-421-6111

DISTRICT OF COLUMBIA
Alcoholism and Drug Abuse
Administration, Central Office
1875 Connecticut Ave Ste 837
Washington, DC 20009

FLORIDA
Alcohol & Drug Abuse Program
Department of Health & Rehab
1317 Winewood Blvd
Tallahassee, FL 32301
904-488-0900

GEORGIA
Alcohol and Drug Abuse
Service Station
878 Peachtree St Ste 319
Atlanta, GA 30309
404-894-4785

HAWAII
Alcohol and Drug Abuse Branch
PO Box 3378
Honolulu, HI 96801
808-548-4280

IDAHO
Substance Abuse Section
Health & Welfare Department
450 W State St
Boise, ID 83720
208-334-4368

ILLINOIS
Department of Mental Health &
Developmental Disabilities
902 S Wind Rd
Springfield, IL 62703
217-786-6314

INDIANA
Division of Addiction Services
429 N Pennsylvania St
Indianapolis, IN 46204
317-232-7816

IOWA
Iowa Dept of Substance Abuse
507 10th St Ste 500
Des Moines, IA 50319
515-281-3641

KANSAS
Kansas Alcohol & Drug Abuse
Svcs, Dept of Social & Rehab
Biddle Bldg-2700 W 6th St
Topeka, KS 66606
913-296-3925

KENTUCKY
Division of Substance Abuse
Dept for MHMR Services
275 E Main St
Frankfort, KY 40621
502-564-2880

LOUISIANA
Office of Prevention
& Recovery
from Alcohol & Drug Abuse
2744B Wooddale Blvd.
Baton Rouge, LA 70805
504-922-0728

MAINE
Office of Alcoholism
and Drug Abuse Prevention
State House Stn 11
Augusta, ME 04333
207-289-2781

MARYLAND
Alcoholism Control
Administration
201 SW Preston St 4th Fl
Baltimore, MD 21202
301-383-2781

MASSACHUSETTS
Division of Alcoholism
150 Tremont St
Boston, MA 02111
617-727-1960

MICHIGAN
Office of Substance Abuse Svcs
Dept of Public Health
3500 N Logan
Lansing, MI 48914
517-373-8600

MINNESOTA
Chemical Dependency Prog Div
Dept of Human Services
444 Lafayette Rd
St Paul, MN 55101
612-296-3991

MISSISSIPPI
Division of Alcohol
& Drug Abuse
1102 Robert E Lee Bldg
Jackson, MS 39201
601-359-1297

MISSOURI
Division of Alcohol
& Drug Abuse
Dept of Mental Health
2002 Missouri Blvd
Jefferson City, MO 65101
314-751-4942

MONTANA
Department of Institutions
Alcohol & Drug Abuse Division
1539 11th Ave
Helena, MT 59620
406-444-2827

NEBRASKA
Division of Alcoholism
and Drug Abuse
Box 94728
Lincoln, NE 68509
402-471-2851

NEVADA
Bureau of Alcohol & Drug Abuse
505 King St Kinkead Bldg 500
Carson City, NV 89701
702-885-4790

NEW HAMPSHIRE
New Hampshire Office of
A & D Abuse Prevention
H & W Bldg Hazen Dr
Concord, NH 03301
603-271-4627

NEW JERSEY
Division of Alcoholism
CN 362
Trenton, NJ 08625
609-292-8947

NEW MEXICO
Alcoholism Bureau Behavioral
Health Services Division
PO Box 968
Santa Fe, NM 87504
505-984-0020

NEW YORK
NYS Division of Alcoholism &
Alcohol Abuse
194 Washington Ave
Albany, NY 12210
518-474-3377

NORTH CAROLINA
Alcohol and Drug Abuse Svcs
Division of Human Resources
325 N Salisbury St
Raleigh, NC 27611
919-829-4670

NORTH DAKOTA
Division of Alcoholism & Drug
Abuse, Dept of Human Services
Judicial Wing 3rd Fl Capitol
Bismarck, ND 58505
701-224-2769

OHIO
Bureau on Alcohol Abuse
and Alcoholism Recovery
170 N High St 3rd Fl
Columbus, OH 43215
614-466-3445

OKLAHOMA
Department of Mental Health
Programs Division
PO Box 53277 Capitol Station
Oklahoma City, OK 73105
405-521-0044

OREGON
Programs for Alcohol and Drug
Problems
301 Public Service Bldg
Salem, OR 97310
503-378-2163

PENNSYLVANIA
PA Dept of Health
Office of D&A Programs
PO Box 90
Harrisburg, PA 17108
717-787-9857

RHODE ISLAND
Division of Substance Abuse
Detoxification Unit
412 Howard Ave Ben Rush Bldg
Cranston, RI 02920
401-464-2531

SOUTH CAROLINA
South Carolina Commission
on Alcohol and Drug Abuse
3700 Forest Dr Ste 300
Columbia, SC 29204
803-758-2521

SOUTH DAKOTA
State Department of Health
Div of Alcohol & Drug Abuse
Joe Foss Bldg 523 E Capitol
Pierre, SD 57501-3182
605-773-3123

TENNESSEE
Tennessee Dept of Mental Hlth
Div of A&D Abuse Svcs
505 Deaderick St 4th Fl
Nashville, TN 37219
615-741-1921

TEXAS
Commission on Alcoholism
1705 Guadalupe
Austin, TX 78701
512-475-2577

UTAH
Division of Alcoholism & Drugs
PO Box 45500
150 SW N Temple 350
Salt Lake City, UT 84145-0500
801-533-6532

VERMONT
Office of Alcohol and Drug
Abuse Programs
103 S Main St
Waterbury, VT 05676
802-241-2170

VIRGINIA
Office of Substance Abuse
Department of Mental Health
PO Box 1797
Richmond, VA 23214
804-786-1524

WASHINGTON
Office on Alcoholism, Dept of
Social and Health Services
Mail Stop OB-44W
Olympia, WA 98504
206-753-5866

WEST VIRGINIA
Div on Alcoholism & Drug
Abuse
West Virginia Dept of Health
1800 Washington St E
Charleston, WV 25305
304-348-2276

WISCONSIN
Office of Alcohol & Other Drug
Abuse
1 W Wilson St-PO Box 7851
Madison, WI 53707
608-266-2717

WYOMING
Substance Abuse Division
of Community Programs
State Office Bldg
Cheyenne, WY 82002
307-777-7115

Appendix 4

Recognizing and Increasing the Self-care Skills of the Family

A. General health and hygiene
   1. Current habits, standards and strengths

   2. Valuable old habits currently neglected

   3. New habits to be developed

B. Rules and habits to protect the safety and well-being of the family
   1. Current habits, standards and strengths

   2. Valuable old habits currently neglected

3. New habits to be developed

C. Stress Management
   1. Direct active
      a. Current habits, standards and strengths

      b. Valuable old habits currently neglected

      c. New habits to be developed

   2. Direct inactive
      a. Current habits, standards and strengths

      b. Valuable old habits currently neglected

      c. New habits to be developed

   3. Indirect active
      a. Current habits, standards and strengths

        b. Valuable old habits currently neglected

        c. New habits to be developed

4. Indirect inactive
        a. Current habits, standards and strengths

        b. Valuable old habits currently neglected

        c. New habits to be developed

Improving Stress Management

Objective	Possible Methods	Getting Started
Improve my ability to cope with stress.	Pick up a neglected hobby, escape or support that has been dropped. Choose one that was truly effective or one that sounds appealing.	Review the stress checklist and select a promising item; commit yourself to do it. Take immediate action (e.g., call a friend to join you, put it on the calendar, get more information).
Learn to relax.	Become more aware of your tension level. Practice yoga. Take an aerobics class. Learn relaxation techniques. Set aside time for massage, steam or whirlpool.	Select a convenient YMCA, Jewish Community Center or health club; join and set aside regular times to go. Call for information.

Objective	*Possible Methods*	*Getting Started*
Improve problem-solving ability.	Fix the weak links in the problem-solving chain (e.g., defining the problem, talking with others, generating alternate solutions, etc.). Take a class or workshop in problem-solving.	Review the items under "Active, Direct Methods of Reducing Stress," pages 75–76, to identify the weak links. Call your state psychological association or local college to get information.

Living a Full Life: Clarifying Wants, Standards, Strengths and Feelings

List one example in each of the following categories:

1. Important wants
   Current

   Neglected

   Potential future wants

2. Important standards
   Current

   Neglected

   Potential future standards

3. Important strengths
   Current

   Neglected

   Potential strengths to be developed

4. Important Feelings
   Current

   Neglected

   Possible feelings to be experienced

Living a Full Life: Examples

Objective	Possible Methods	Getting Started
Regularly spend more time with friends.	List your friends and acquaintances along with the things you might enjoy together.	Plan an activity for next weekend and invite a friend.
	Stop declining invitations so automatically; examine reasons carefully before declining.	
	Join a group, club or class to meet new people or join with a current friend.	
Increase the quality of time spent with the kids.	Brainstorm with each child to get a long and practical list of activities or ways of being together.	Pick an activity that sounds attractive both to you and the children; discuss ways of making it practical and put it on the calendar.

Objective	Possible Methods	Getting Started
Learn to use a computer.	Take a class.	Phone the local library or community college.
Take better care of the apartment.	Spell out routine maintenance tasks and schedules.	Get organized by listing the changes in the care of the house that would most improve family life.
	Assign regular jobs to the members of the household.	
	Provide the kids with rules, encouragement, rewards and consistent monitoring while setting an example of regard.	

Developing Support

1. Involvement that supports identity. (List examples of roles that strengthen your identity—e.g., father, daughter, colleague—in the appropriate section below.)

   a. Current roles in which I am successful

   b. Neglected roles

   c. Potential future strengths: roles I'd like to strengthen

2. Involvement that enriches life. (Draw examples from Exercise 4 on pages 97–98 in parts I, II and III, respectively.)

   a. Recent valuable experiences

   b. Neglected social needs: experiences I used to arrange for myself that no longer are as much a part of my life

      c. Potential future experiences with other people

3. Relationships that provide emotional support and/or challenge
    a. Current

    b. Neglected

    c. Potential sources of social support and challenge

4. Relationships that provide informational support and/or challenge
    a. Current

    b. Neglected

    c. Potential sources of informational support and challenge

After filling in this appendix, take a moment to review Appendix 9.

Developing Support: Examples

Objective	Possible Methods	Getting Started
Find a forum in which to talk about and get more understanding of family problems.	Talk with a very close friend. Begin therapy. Join Al-Anon. Talk with sober family members.	Select a friend or family member to talk with. Phone him or her today to set up a time for a private serious talk. Call a local teaching hospital to get the name of a therapist who works with families who are concerned about addiction. Call the therapist to arrange an appointment. Call the Al-Anon central number to find out the time and place of a meeting that suits your family's needs.

Objective	Possible Methods	Getting Started
Become closer with a friend.	Add to the things you have in common by doing or saying something new: • Activities, invitations • New topics of conversation • Information about self • Understanding of personal feelings Identify and resolve conflicts that bog down a friendship. Tell your friend how you feel about him.	Recognizing that closeness develops over time, do not try everything at once. At a time that feels right, take one step to become closer. See how your friend responds. Is there similar effort on his part?
Increase opportunities for meeting new people.	Join a religious, social, or community group that meets regularly.	Review Part III of Exercise 4 on page 98 to find the type of social support or contact you'd most like to add to your life. Find a group that is likely to offer that kind of contact.

Objective	*Possible Methods*	*Getting Started*
		Listings of groups appear in local magazines, newspapers, and the yellow pages. Phone the group, get the date of a meeting open to prospective members, and plan to go to the meeting (or service or orientation, etc.).

About the Authors

Stephen E. Schlesinger, Ph.D., is an Illinois-licensed psychologist and a Certified Senior Addictions Counselor in independent practice with offices in Chicago and Oak Park, Illinois. He is on the staffs of Chicago Lakeshore Hospital and Hines Veterans Administration Hospital, and is an Assistant Professor in the Department of Psychiatry at Loyola University's Stitch School of Medicine.

Lawrence K. Horberg, Ph.D., is an Illinois-registered psychologist in independent practice, with offices in Chicago and Skokie, and with appointments on the staffs of Northwestern Memorial, Illinois Masonic and Chicago Lakeshore hospitals. He is Assistant Professor of Clinical Psychiatry and Behavioral Science at Northwestern University Medical School. Dr. Horberg directed the Outpatient Chemical Dependence Program at Northwestern Memorial Hospital for six years.